BEST ROAD TRIPS
PACIFIC NORTHWEST
ESCAPES ON THE OPEN ROAD

BECKY OHLSEN, ROBERT BALKOVICH, CELESTE BRASH,
JOHN LEE, CRAIG MCLACHLAN, MASOVAIDA MORGAN,
BRENDAN SAINSBURY

Contents

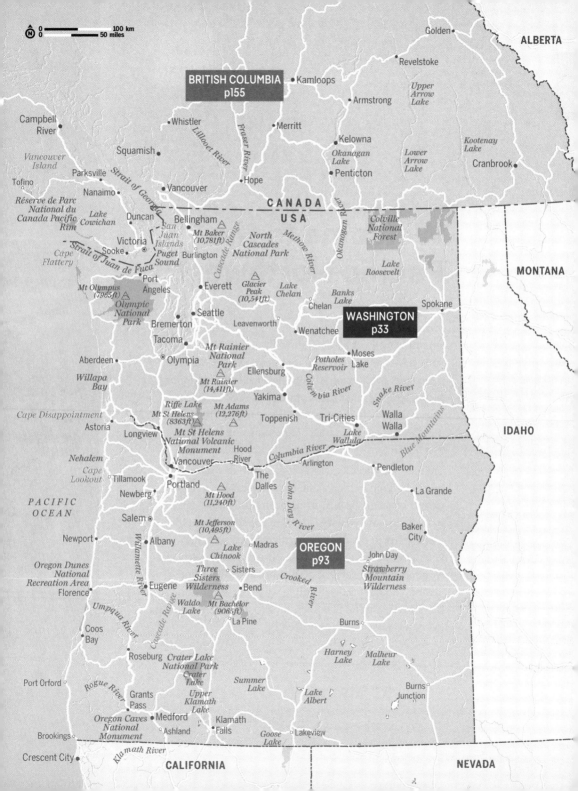

Welcome to the Pacific Northwest

Picture yourself rounding a sun-dappled corner of smooth pavement alongside a winding river, making your way through a coastal mountain range toward steep cliffs overlooking the Pacific Ocean. Or whipping through high-desert fields of fragrant sage and pine trees, stopping to identify fossils and admire the otherworldly painted hills before finishing the day's journey in a city full of restaurants and brewpubs.

These experiences are closer together than you might think. Driving in the Pacific Northwest offers a huge variety of scenic beauty, from rainforests and waterfalls to badlands and wheat fields. And the stops along the way are worth the drive all by themselves, whether you're into regional wines, historical sights, geological wonders, local dishes, or bookstores and coffeeshops. The only tough part is deciding where to begin – and that's where this book comes in, with itineraries ranging from the classics to the backroads.

Mt Shuksan and Picture Lake (p86), Washington
TIM MATURO/SHUTTERSTOCK ©

Our Picks

BEST COASTAL DRIVES

Cruising along the stunning Pacific Coast is an unforgettable experience, with crashing waves, lighthouses and rolling fog around every bend. Lofty headlands reach out to the ocean, offering spectacular views, while steep mountains of rock jut offshore like giant sentinels. Small coastal museums offer peeks at local history. Stroll beaches, explore tide pools, watch for whales and eat your fill of fresh seafood on these drives.

PACIFIC OCEAN

The Pacific Ocean spans 60 million sq miles – larger than all of earth's land masses combined.

Graveyard of the Pacific Tour

Lighthouses, nautical museums and shipwrecks illuminate maritime history at the mouth of the Columbia River.

P48

San Juan Islands Scenic Byway

Whale-watching, kayaking and biking are the main attractions in these mostly rural islands off Washington's coast.

P52

Highway 101 Oregon Coast

It's all coast all the time on this drive full of tide pools, ocean surf and small-town stops for seafood and trinkets.

P96

Three Capes Loop

This delightfully slow, winding alternative to Hwy 101 hugs the shoreline traversing three headlands you'd otherwise miss.

P104

Sea to Sky Highway

Go from coastal towns to snowy peaks with classic BC sights and views en route.

P164

OREGON

Founded in 1811, Astoria, Oregon, claims the title of oldest US-founded settlement west of the Mississippi.

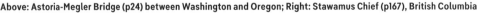

Above: Astoria-Megler Bridge (p24) between Washington and Oregon; Right: Stawamus Chief (p167), British Columbia

THE CHIEF

Towering 2297ft (700m) above the waters of Howe Sound, the Stawamus Chief is the world's second-largest freestanding granite monolith.

MT MAZAMA

Before it erupted 7500 years ago to form Crater Lake, Mt Mazama was 12,000ft tall.

Our Picks

BEST VOLCANO & MOUNTAIN DRIVES

One of the benefits of being in a geological area known for earthquakes and volcanoes is the landscape they leave behind. Snowcapped ranges dominate the terrain, providing scenic backdrops and abundant recreational opportunities – from skiing to hiking to searching for Bigfoot. Mountain drives in this region can be treacherous in bad weather, but the stunning vistas in every direction make it well worth the effort to get here whenever possible.

HILLY BC

Around 75% of the territory of British Columbia is covered with mountains.

Columbia River Gorge & Mt Hood

This area reveals some of nature's most dramatic earth-shaping work, from steep gorge to snowy peak.

P26

Cascade Drive

This altitudinous route through the northern Cascades is alive with rugged beauty.

P60

TAHOMA

The Puyallup name for Mt Rainier is Tahoma, meaning 'the source of nourishment from the many streams coming from the slopes.'

Mt Rainier (p66), Washington

Mt Rainier Scenic Byways

At 14,411ft, volcanic Mt Rainier is the highest peak in the Cascades and deservedly regarded with awe by locals.

P66

Mt St Helens Volcano Trail

Marvel at the destruction left behind after Mt St Helens' 1980 eruption and the impressive recovery taking place.

P74

Oregon Cascades Scenic Byways

Waterfalls, hot springs and lakes break up the almost nonstop greenery on this unmissable central Oregon route.

P134

Left: Crater Lake (p145), Oregon

Our Picks

BEST DRIVES THROUGH HISTORY

History buffs can follow in the footsteps of Native Americans, explorers, pioneers and Gold Rush prospectors on these drives, which take in some of the key sites in the region's cultural history. The area's maritime past is reflected in small towns along the Pacific Coast, including some photogenic shipwrecks and heroic tales of adventure. Too recent for you? Explore fossil beds in Eastern Oregon that date back millions of years.

GHOST TOWNS

By some counts, Oregon has more than 200 ghost towns, more than any other state in the US.

On the Trail of Lewis & Clark

Follow along with the famous explorers on the final segment of their 1804–06 journey.

P20

Graveyard of the Pacific Tour

Lighthouses, nautical museums and shipwrecks illuminate maritime history.

P48

International Selkirk Loop

Find the forgotten corners of Washington, Idaho and British Columbia in a border-crossing adventure.

P88

Journey Through Time Scenic Byway

If ghost towns and a wide horizon are what you're after, this is the place.

P116

Vancouver & the Fraser Valley

East of Vancouver, learn more about British Columbia's pioneer past and explore a fertile river valley.

P158

LEWIS & CLARK

Lewis and Clark's expedition traveled more than 8000 miles on its way to the Pacific Ocean.

Above: Lewis & Clark National Historical Park (p25), Oregon; Right: Kootenay Lake Ferry (p202), British Columbia

FERRY TRIP

The ferry across Kootenay Lake in British Columbia is the longest free, scenic, vehicle-carrying ferry in the world.

Our Picks

BEST FOODIE DRIVES

The Pacific Northwest leads the continent in locally grown, sustainable and organic produce, and it's known for the creative use of regional ingredients in its signature cuisine. Great food demands great wine, and you can get your fill of both in the wine regions of Oregon, Washington and British Columbia. And hopheads know there's no better place to visit for good beer.

WINES

Oregon is pinot country, while Washington's offerings include syrah and riesling. BC's more diverse soil allows a wider variety of grapes.

 Mountains to Sound Greenway

Plenty of places to eat and drink from the *Twin Peaks* diner to Seattle's Pike Place Market.

P36

 Chuckanut Drive & Whidbey Island

Nosh your way from cheese shops to oyster farms and farm-to-plate restaurants.

P56

 Washington Wine Tour

Columbia Valley's laid-back wine country is emerging as a major wine-making destination.

P78

 Willamette Valley Wine Tour

Oregon's wine country showcases some of the area's best food and wine.

P110

 Okanagan Valley Wine Tour

Explore Canada's hill-lined, lakeside wine region.

P190

GARYSFRP/GETTY IMAGES ©

CRAB SEASON

Dungeness crab, a meaty Pacific Northwest specialty, is in season December through April and worth seeking out.

Dungeness crab roll

Our Picks

BEST WATERFALL DRIVES

Tiered falls, plunging falls, curtain falls, ribbon falls – hundreds of waterfalls in the Pacific Northwest give you ample opportunity to witness firsthand all the variations in the waterfall vernacular. Take your pick from more than 70 falls in the Columbia River Gorge alone, or mix-and-match falls with hot springs in the Cascades. Springtime is best if you're chasing waterfalls at their fastest and most thunderous.

DELLA FALLS
Della Falls on Vancouver Island are the highest falls in Canada, with a vertical drop of 1445ft.

EDDY SAVAGE/SHUTTERSTOCK ©

Della Falls, British Columbia

Columbia River Gorge & Mt Hood

Splitting Washington and Oregon apart, the gorge provides both with dramatic views, countless waterfalls and great hikes.

P26

2

Mountains to Sound Greenway

Waterfalls, aquariums and interesting museums make this trip fun for everyone.

P36

To Bend & Back

This trip lets you hit 10 waterfalls in one single state park.

P130

4

Oregon Cascades Scenic Byways

Get lost in a maze of forests, lakes, hot springs and waterfalls in the Oregon Cascade mountains.

P134

5

Crater Lake Circuit

The best route to this must-see lake takes you through forest studded with waterfalls.

P144

When to Go

The Pacific Northwest shines in summer and peaks in the fall, with long warm days and gorgeous autumn colors.

Cold and rainy weather make this a challenging place to drive in winter and early spring – in fact, many of the most beautiful scenic drives on mountain roads are closed due to snowfall, often until mid-May or early June. Spring hits different parts of the region at different times. At the lower elevations, April and May are often rainy but also iridescently green and alive. Rhododendrons and magnolias explode with hot-pink and purple flowers all over city parks and front yards in Portland and Seattle. On the east side of the Cascade mountains, the high desert spring is subtler but equally beautiful, as flora and fauna soak up moisture in the wake of frequent and sudden storms.

Summers have become increasingly humid in the major cities; head for the coast or the drier eastern climes in July and

GARY GILARDI/SHUTTERSTOCK ©

Spring flowers, Columbia River Gorge (p26), Washington

Weather Watch (Seattle)

JANUARY	FEBRUARY	MARCH	APRIL	MAY	JUNE
Avg daytime max: **47°F**	Avg daytime max: **50°F**	Avg daytime max: **54°F**	Avg daytime max: **58°F**	Avg daytime max: **65°F**	Avg daytime max: **70°F**
Days of rainfall: **18**	Days of rainfall: **14**	Days of rainfall: **16**	Days of rainfall: **14**	Days of rainfall: **12**	Days of rainfall: **9**

JUDEAND/SHUTTERSTOCK ©

Hikers, Hoh Rainforest (p46), Washington

RAIN SHADOW

On the west side of the Cascade Mountains, a typical year sees 40–80in of rain. But the mountains trap and block the rain from reaching the eastern parts of the region, which get as little as 15in of annual rainfall.

BIG EVENTS

The century-old **Rose Festival** takes over downtown Portland each summer, with races, treasure hunts, fireworks, visiting sailors, a festival queen and lots of parades. **June**

An air show, parade, classic cars, fireworks and a high-speed hydroplane boat race mark the culmination of Seattle's month-long **Seafair Festival** on Puget Sound. **August**

Legendary Northwest music festival **Bumbershoot** brings performance art, film, dance, visual arts and more to Seattle Center, along with an amazing lineup of musicians and surprisingly reasonable ticket prices. **September**

Vancouver International Jazz Festival brings 1800 artists, from big names to up-and-comers, performing over 12 days in venues around the city. **June–July**

August. This is also a great time to explore higher elevations, such as scenic drives around Mt Rainier.

The best time for a road trip is the fall, when the temperatures are cooler but the rain hasn't fully returned, the trees are changing color, the afternoon light is magical, and autumnal produce turns up on market shelves and restaurant menus.

Accommodation

Hotel prices increase during peak season (June to August), especially in cities, but you can usually save by booking ahead. Reservations are especially important in places like the coast and many campgrounds, as these book up months in advance.

TEMPERATE RAINFOREST

The Olympic Peninsula and the mossy coastal forests of the Pacific Northwest contain some of the few remaining examples of temperate rainforest in the continental United States. Their existence depends on the 12ft to 14ft of rainfall they get each year.

JULY	AUGUST	SEPTEMBER	OCTOBER	NOVEMBER	DECEMBER
Avg daytime max: **76°F**	Avg daytime max: **76°F**	Avg daytime max: **71°F**	Avg daytime max: **60°F**	Avg daytime max: **51°F**	Avg daytime max: **46°F**
Days of rainfall: **5**	Days of rainfall: **4**	Days of rainfall: **7**	Days of rainfall: **13**	Days of rainfall: **18**	Days of rainfall: **17**

Get Prepared for the Pacific Northwest

Useful things to load in your bag, your ears and your brain

WATCH

Wild
(Jean-Marc Vallée; 2014) Reese Witherspoon adaptation of Cheryl Strayed's memoir about hiking the Pacific Crest Trail after losing her mother.

Sometimes a Great Notion
(Paul Newman; 1971) A small-town lumber strike on the Oregon coast; based on Ken Kesey's 1964 novel.

Sleepless in Seattle
(Nora Ephron; 1993) Meg Ryan and Tom Hanks rom-com featuring iconic Seattle locations like Pike Place Market.

Leave No Trace
(Debra Granik; 2018) A father and daughter live off-grid until they're forced to adjust to city life.

Pig
(Michael Sarnoski; 2021) Nicolas Cage is a truffle hunter searching for his stolen foraging pig around Portland.

Clothing

Raingear, raingear and more raingear The eastern part of the region is prone to surprise thunderstorms, while the west side of the Cascade mountain range gets above-average rainfall most of the year.

Hat and sunglasses For those glorious days when you luck out and don't need the raingear. Throw in some sunscreen, too – you can get sun damage even when there's cloud cover.

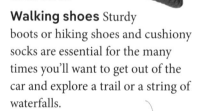

Walking shoes Sturdy boots or hiking shoes and cushiony socks are essential for the many times you'll want to get out of the car and explore a trail or a string of waterfalls.

Swimwear The Pacific coast is not your average beach – the water is really cold year-round – but it's hard to resist a quick dip anyway. Just remember to keep a towel and a warm hoodie in the car for after your swim.

Layers Winters can be cold and damp, so warm clothes are key – but even in summer, expect the temperatures to change abruptly from sweltering afternoons to cool evenings.

Stretchy pants Denim is over. Bring leggings or pants that are comfortable to drive in and, most importantly, won't restrict your ability to fully enjoy the food and beverage bounty this region provides.

Mt Rainier (p66), Washington

Words

Cascadia A movement to create an independent nation-state by merging British Columbia, Oregon and Washington (the Cascadia bioregion); the movement has its own flag, the Doug, featuring a Douglas fir tree.

Chinook A group of indigenous people and their languages; also the largest type of Pacific salmon, important in many indigenous cultures.

Fish Ladder Provides a detour for migrating fish to go around a dam or other artificial obstacle; a great place to see salmon in action July to September at Seattle's Hiram M Chittenden Locks.

Skookum A word from the Chinook Jargon language still in use, meaning strong, tough, big and capable.

The Mountain The name people in Seattle affectionately give to Mt Rainier.

Tillicum A Chinook jargon word meaning 'the people,' used in many place names around the region.

ROAD TRIPS

CAPTION
CHRIS AMSON/SHUTTERSTOCK ©

Contents

01

BEST FOR HISTORY

Lewis & Clark Interpretive Center in Cape Disappointment State Park

On the Trail of Lewis & Clark

DURATION	DISTANCE	GREAT FOR
3-4 days	620km / 385 miles	History, Families

BEST TIME TO GO	Year-round, if you don't mind frequent rain.

Cape Disappointment State Park (p24)

It would take most people their combined annual leave to follow the Lewis and Clark trek in its entirety from St Louis, MO, to Cape Disappointment. Focusing on the final segment, this trip documents the mix of crippling exhaustion and building excitement that the two explorers felt as they struggled, worn out and weather-beaten, along the Columbia River on their way to completing the greatest overland trek in American history.

Link Your Trip

5 Graveyard of the Pacific Tour

Lewis and Clark survived, but others didn't. Find out about the tumultuous maritime history of southwest Washington's coast.

11 Washington Wine Tour

After all that Lewis and Clark history, you'll need a glass of wine. Break off in the Tri-Cities for some relaxed quaffing opportunities.

01 TRI-CITIES

This trip's starting point has a weighty historical significance. The arrival of Lewis and Clark and the Corps of Discovery at the confluence of the Snake and Columbia Rivers on October 16, 1805, marked a milestone achievement on their quest to map a river route to the Pacific. After a greeting by 200 Native Americans singing and drumming, the band camped at this spot for two days, trading clothing for dried salmon. The **Sacajawea State Park Interpretive Center** (parks.state.wa.us/250), situated at the river confluence 5 miles southeast

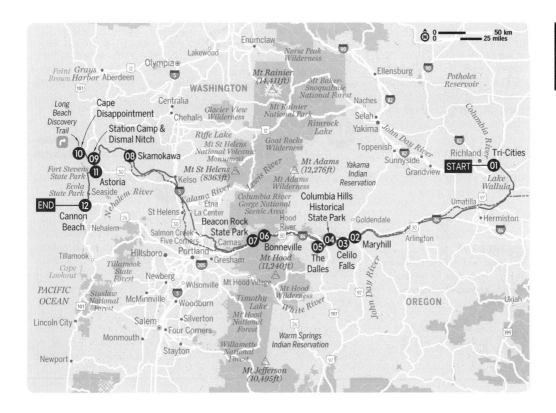

of present-day Pasco, relates the story of the expedition through the eyes of Sacajawea, the Shoshone Native American guide and interpreter the Corps recruited in North Dakota.

 THE DRIVE
Head south on I-82 before switching west at the Columbia River on SR 14, aka the Lewis & Clark Hwy. Here, in dusty sagebrush country, you'll pass a couple of minor sites – Wallula Gap, where the Corps first spotted Mt Hood, and the volcanic bluff of Hat Rock, first named by William Clark. Maryhill is 107 miles from Tri-Cities.

02 MARYHILL
Conceived by great Northwest entrepreneur and road builder Sam Hill, the **Maryhill Museum of Art** (maryhillmuseum.org) occupies a mansion atop a bluff overlooking the Columbia River. Its eclectic art collection is enhanced by a small Lewis and Clark display, while its peaceful gardens are perfect for a classy picnic punctuated by exotic peacock cries. Interpretive signs point you to fine views down the Columbia Gorge to the riverside spot (now a state park) where Meriwether Lewis and William Clark camped on October 21, 1805. The park is

just one of several along this trip where you can pitch a tent within a few hundred yards of the Corps' original camp. Another of Hill's creations – a life-size, unruined replica of **Stonehenge** (Hwy 97) – lies 2 miles to the east.

THE DRIVE
Continue west from Maryhill on SR 14 for 5 miles to the site of the now submerged Celilo Falls.

03 CELILO FALLS
A vivid imagination can be as important as sunscreen when following the trail. One example of this is the turnout 5 miles west of Maryhill

that overlooks what was once the Native American salmon fishing center of Celilo Falls. The explorers spent two days here in late October 1805, lowering their canoes down the crashing falls on elk-skin ropes. A century and a half later, the rising waters of the dammed Columbia drowned the falls – which were the sixth-most voluminous in the world – destroying a centuries-old fishing site and rendering much of Clark's description of the region unrecognizable.

 THE DRIVE
Head west on SR 14, paralleling the mighty Columbia, for another 15 miles to Columbia Hills Historical State Park.

04 COLUMBIA HILLS HISTORICAL STATE PARK

Native American tribes like the Nez Percé, Clatsop and Walla Walla were essential to the success of the Lewis and Clark expedition, supplying them with food, horses and guides. One of the best places to view tangible traces of the region's Native American heritage is the Temani Pesh-wa (Written on Rocks) Trail at Columbia Hills Historical State Park, which highlights the region's best petroglyphs. Reserve a spot in advance on the free guided tours on Friday and Saturday at 10am to view the famous but fragile pictograph of the god Tsagaglalal (She Who Watches). The park is also a popular site for rock climbers and windsurfers.

THE DRIVE
Two miles west of Horsethief Lake, turn south onto US 197, which

takes you across the Columbia River into The Dalles in Oregon. Two miles upriver sits The Dalles Dam, which completely submerged the once magnificent Celilo Falls and rapids on its completion in 1957.

05 THE DALLES

Once the urban neighbor of the formidable Celilo Falls, The Dalles has a more mundane image these days. The local economy focuses on cherry-growing, computer technology and outdoor recreation. Notwithstanding, the city hosts one of the best Lewis and Clark–related museums along this stretch of the Columbia, sited in the **Columbia Gorge Discovery Center** on the western edge of town. Displays detail the 30 tons of equipment the Corps dragged across the continent and the animals they had to kill to survive (including 190 dogs and a ferret). Kids will get a kick out of dressing up in Lewis and Clark period costume.

 THE DRIVE
You can continue west from The Dalles on either side of the Columbia (the expedition traveled straight down the middle by canoe) via SR 14 (Washington), or the slower, more scenic SR 30 (Oregon). En route to Bonneville, 46 miles away, look for views down to macabre Memaloose Island, where Native Americans would leave their dead in cedar canoes.

06 BONNEVILLE

There are two Bonne-villes: Bonneville, Oregon, and North Bonneville, Washington. At this stage in their trip, Lewis and Clark were flea-infested and half-starved from a diet of dog meat and

starchy, potatolike wapato roots. Fortunately, 21st-century Bonneville – which is famous for its Depression-era dam, completed in 1938 – has some tastier culinary offerings to contemplate.

 THE DRIVE
Just west of North Bonneville on SR 14 lies Beacon Rock State Park.

07 BEACON ROCK STATE PARK

On November 2, 1805, a day after passing modern Bonneville, Clark wrote about a remarkable 848ft-tall monolith he called Beaten Rock, changing the name to Beacon Rock on his return. Just over a century later, Henry Biddle bought the rock for the bargain price of $1 (!) and you can still hike his snaking 1-mile trail to the top of the former lava plug in **Beacon Rock State Park** (parks.state.wa.us/474). As you enjoy the wonderful views, ponder the fact that you have effectively climbed up the *inside* of an ancient volcano. For the Corps, the rock brought a momentous discovery, for it was here that the excited duo first noticed the tide, proving at last that they were finally nearing their goal of crossing the American continent.

THE DRIVE
Your next stop along SR 14 should be the Cape Horn overview, with its fantastic views of the flood-carved gorge and its impressive cascades. From here, it's a straight shot on I-5 to Kelso and then over the Lewis and Clark Bridge to parallel the Columbia River westward on SR 4. Skamokawa is 103 miles from the state park.

08 SKAMOKAWA

For most of their trip down the Columbia River, Lewis and Clark traveled not on foot but by canoe. There's nowhere better to paddle in the Corps' canoe wake than at **Pillar Rock**, where Clark wrote of his joy at finally being able to camp in view of the ocean. **Columbia River Kayaking** (columbiariverkayaking.com) in the town of Skamokawa offers one- and two-day kayak tours to this site, as well as to Grays Bay.

THE DRIVE
Continue on SR 4 northwest out of Skamokawa. In Naselle, go southwest on SR 401. Skamokawa to Dismal Nitch is 35 miles, along the north bank of the Columbia River.

09 STATION CAMP & DISMAL NITCH

Just east of the Astoria–Megler Bridge on the north bank of the Columbia River, a turnout marks Dismal Nitch, where the

---

WHY I LOVE THIS TRIP

Becky Ohlsen, writer

This is about as classic as an American road trip gets: retracing the steps of Lewis and Clark, the great explorers who, with their Corps of Discovery, plunged into the wilderness of the 'New World' in a spirit of curiosity more than conquest. To get the most out of the trip, bring a copy of the journals they kept during the expedition to read along the way.

Photo opportunity

Indian Beach, Ecola State Park – the Oregon coast epitomized.

---

drenched duo were stuck in a pounding weeklong storm that Clark described as the most disagreeable time he had ever experienced. The Corps finally managed to make camp at Station Camp, 3 miles further west, now an innocuous highway pullout, where they stayed for 10 days while the two leaders, no doubt sick of each other by now, separately explored the headlands around Cape Disappointment.

THE DRIVE
You're nearly there! Contain your excitement as you breeze the last few miles west along US 101 to Ilwaco and the inappropriately named Cape Disappointment.

10 CAPE DISAPPOINTMENT

Disappointment is probably the last thing you're likely to be feeling as you pull into blustery cliff-top **Cape Disappointment State Park** (parks.state.wa.us/486). Find time to make the short ascent of Mackenzie Hill in Clark's footsteps and catch your first true sight of the Pacific. You can almost hear his protracted sigh of relief more than two centuries later. Located on a high bluff inside the park not far from the Washington town of Ilwaco, the sequentially laid-out **Lewis & Clark Interpretive Center** (capedisappointment.

---

org) faithfully recounts the Corps of Discovery's cross-continental journey using a level of detail the journal-writing explorers would have been proud of. Information includes everything from how to use an octant to what kind of underpants Lewis wore! A succinct 20-minute film backs up the permanent exhibits. Phone ahead and you can also tour the impressive end-of-continent North Head Lighthouse (northheadlighthouse.com) nearby.

THE DRIVE
From Ilwaco, take US 101 back east to the 4.1-mile-long Astoria–Megler Bridge, the longest continuous truss bridge in the US. On the other side, 18 miles from Cape Disappointment, lies Astoria in Oregon, the oldest US-founded settlement west of the Mississippi.

DETOUR
Long Beach Discovery Trail
Start: 10 Cape Disappointment
Soon after arriving in Station Camp, the indefatigable Clark, determined to find a better winter bivouac, set out with several companions to continue the hike west along a broad sandy peninsula. They came to a halt near present-day 26th St in Long Beach, where Clark dipped his toe in the Pacific and carved his name on a cedar tree for posterity. The route of this historic three-day trudge has been re-created in the Long Beach Discovery Trail, a footpath that runs from the small town of Ilwaco, adjacent to Cape Disappointment, to Clark's 26th St turnaround. Officially inaugurated in September 2009, the trail has incorporated some dramatic life-size sculptures along its 8.2-mile length. One depicts a giant gray whale skeleton, another recalls Clark's recorded sighting of a washed-up sea

sturgeon, while a third re-creates the original cedar tree (long since uprooted by a Pacific storm) in bronze.

 ASTORIA

After voting on what to do next – a decision often described as the first truly democratic ballot in US history, since everyone in the party had a say – the Corps elected to make their winter bivouac across the Columbia River in present-day Oregon. A replica of the original **Fort Clatsop**, where the Corps spent a miserable winter in 1805–06, lies 5 miles south of Astoria. Also on site are trails, a visitor center and buckskin-clad rangers who wander the camp between mid-June and Labor Day sewing moccasins (the Corps stockpiled an impressive 340 pairs for their return trip), tanning leather and firing their muskets.

THE DRIVE
From Fort Clatsop, take US 101, aka the Oregon Coast Hwy, south through the town of Seaside to Cannon Beach, 25 miles from Astoria.

12 CANON BEACH

Mission accomplished – or was it? Curiosity (and hunger) got the better of the Corps in early 1806 when news of a huge beached whale lured Clark and Sacajawea from a salt factory they had set up near the present-day town of Seaside down through what is now Ecola State Park to Cannon Beach. **Ecola State State Park** (oregonstateparks.org) is the Oregon you may have already visited in your

NAGEL PHOTOGRAPHY/SHUTTERSTOCK ©

Fort Clatsop

LEWIS & CLARK NATIONAL HISTORICAL PARK

The **Lewis & Clark National Historical Park** (www.nps.gov/lewi) combines 10 different historical sites clustered around the mouth of the Columbia River, each of which relates to important facts about the Corps of Discovery and its historic mission to map the American West. It was formed through the amalgamation of various state parks and historic sites in 2004, and is run jointly by the National Park Service (NPS) and the states of Washington and Oregon. Highlights include Cape Disappointment, Fort Clatsop and the 6.5-mile **Fort to Sea trail** linking Clatsop and the ocean at Sunset Beach.

dreams: sea stacks, crashing surf, hidden beaches and gorgeous pristine forest. Crisscrossed by paths, it lies 1.5 miles north of Cannon Beach, the high-end 'antiresort' resort so beloved by Portlanders. Clark found the whale near **Haystack Rock**, a

295ft sea stack that's the most spectacular landmark on the Oregon coast and accessible from the beach. After bartering with the Tillamook tribe, he staggered away with 300lb of whale blubber – a feast for the half-starved Corps of Discovery.

02

BEST FOR VIEWS

A panorama of the gorge's lushest part from Vista House

Vista House

Columbia River Gorge & Mt Hood

DURATION	DISTANCE	GREAT FOR
3 days	346km / 215 miles	Food & drink, Outdoors

BEST TIME TO GO	May to October: fruit is in season and all roads are open.

Few places symbolize the grandeur of the Pacific Northwest like the Columbia River Gorge and Mt Hood. Start along this massive cleft in the Cascade Range that measures up to 4000ft deep and is graced by 77 waterfalls. Meanwhile, Mt Hood peeks out from behind it all in its 11,240ft glory. As you drive up the mountain from the gorge, you'll be treated to a heaven of fruit farms and vineyards.

Link Your Trip

15 Three Capes Loop

Head back through Portland and go west on Hwy 26 toward the coast.

17 Journey Through Time Scenic Byway

From The Dalles, it's about 30 miles east along Hwy 84 and the Columbia River Gorge to Maryhill.

01 TROUTDALE

Although the metal arch over Troutdale isn't the official entrée to the Historic Route 30 (which starts a few miles west from here), this is the logical place to turn off I-84 from Portland and begin a journey into the Columbia Gorge's moss-covered wonderland. Troutdale's center is adorably early 20th century and a pleasant place to stretch your legs before the drive.

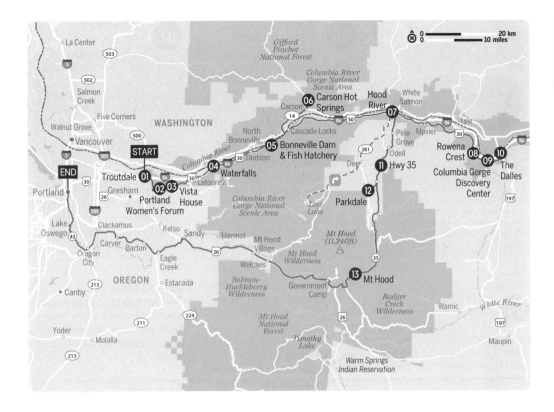

THE DRIVE

Continue through town then turn right (inland) after the bridge, following the signs for Historic Route 30 toward Corbett. The road follows the forested Sandy River before veering left. Follow this road through a few sleepy hamlets.

02 PORTLAND WOMEN'S FORUM

Pull into this parking lot for your first view of the Columbia Gorge. This spot was once the site of the Chanticleer Hotel, built in 1912. It was here, in 1913, that the plans were made for building Hwy 30, which would become Oregon's first modern paved road.

Unfortunately the hotel burned down in 1931, but the panoramas are as splendid as ever. This is arguably the best drive-to viewpoint in the Columbia Gorge.

THE DRIVE

Turn left from the parking lot, drive along the ridge and watch as Hwy 30 turns into classic Columbia Gorge country, with increasing mossy lushness.

03 VISTA HOUSE

Built between 1916 and 1918, this stone roadside rotunda sits atop Crown Point, 733ft above the Columbia River, and offers magnificent 180-degree views. From the outside, the building looks like it only houses a small information center, but there's a worthwhile historical **museum** (vistahouse.com) and gift shop hidden down a staircase underground. Weather permitting, you can also go upstairs to the fabulous outdoor viewing deck. Be warned: the winds here can be outrageously strong.

THE DRIVE

Take a right directly out of the parking lot and head downhill as the road winds along the old highway and its stone barriers give way to increasing greenery.

WHY I LOVE THIS TRIP

Celeste Brash, writer

Few routes take in this much beauty in such a small space – and it all starts only a half-hour from Portland! The waterfall strip of the Columbia Gorge is one of the most beautiful places I know, and Mt Hood's sharp snowy peak is symbolic of the region. The hiking is phenomenal, the people are down to earth, and you can pick fruit and drink fabulous beer and wine.

04 WATERFALLS

Welcome to a land so lush and vibrantly green that it looks more like something described in a fantasy novel than reality. This 9-mile section of Hwy 30 could easily be nicknamed 'Waterfall Alley' for the excessive number of spectacular cascades tumbling over mossy basalt cliffs. The falls are at their gushiest in spring. If you're into hiking, you could easily spend a day or two exploring this area, or you can take short walks to the easier-access places. **Multnomah Falls** is the highest in Oregon and the busiest stop – you'll find more peace and quiet around the lesser-known spots.

THE DRIVE

Keep heading east on Hwy 30 until it merges with I-84 shortly after Ainsworth State Park. After a few miles, take exit 40 toward Bonneville Dam.

05 BONNEVILLE DAM & FISH HATCHERY

Upon its completion in 1938, Bonneville became the first dam on the Columbia River, permanently altering one of the continent's mightiest rivers, as well as one of the world's most important salmon runs. It's worth stopping here to check out the **visitor center**, which has good exhibits, free tours to the powerhouse throughout the day and a theater showing videos of the dam's history. The underwater viewing room into the fish ladder is a highlight. Afterwards, stroll the nearby fish hatchery, making sure to visit the 11ft-long sturgeon named Herman, who has survived a kidnapping, a knife attack and even recent wildfires.

THE DRIVE

Get back on I-84 and drive about 3.5 miles upstream to exit 44, which leads you to the Bridge of the Gods (toll $2 each way) into Washington State. Turn east on Hwy 14, then left on Wind River Rd from the highway, and finally right on Hot Springs Ave.

06 CARSON HOT SPRINGS

Feel like a nice warm soak to ease your car-stiff bum? Carson Hot Springs Resort is hardly fancy, but its modesty is its finest feature; the first-come, first-served mineral baths are a true escape from any kind of hype.

THE DRIVE

Backtrack over the Bridge of the Gods, then head east on I-84.

07 HOOD RIVER

Your next stop is the windy riverside town of Hood River, one of the world's top windsurfing and kiteboarding destinations. It's also one very attractive town, thanks to its old homes and stunning setting on the Columbia River. Plus Mt Hood, with its hiking trails and ski runs, is only a stone's throw away. It should come as no surprise that Hood River has a youthful, adrenaline-hungry population and a main drag packed with good restaurants, boutique shops and adventure sports stores.

THE DRIVE

Get back on I-84 E for around 10 miles, then take exit 69 to Mosier. This links you back up with Historic Route 30 for another incredibly scenic 9 miles.

DETOUR

Lost Lake
Start: 07 Hood River

For a classic Mt Hood photo op, detour 25 miles south of Hood River to the spectacular Lost Lake. Flanked by forest, this stunning blue body of mountain water frames the white cone of Mt Hood like a perfect postcard. Along with fabulous views, the detour offers respite from the heat when the gorge gets too hot. To get there from Hood River, take Hwy 281 to Dee and follow the signs. Allow at least half a day for the excursion.

08 ROWENA CREST

The summit of this portion of Historic Route 30 has a parking lot with views over the Columbia Gorge, which at this point is losing its lushness to windy, barren hillsides and steep, stratified cliff faces. There are two hiking trails: the **Tom McCall Point Trail** (3 miles round-trip) will get you glimpses over the rolling hills of the plateau and Mt Adams; and the easier **Rowena Plateau Trail** (2.5 miles round-trip) is a particularly good spot for May wildflowers and leads to the waterfowl-filled **Rowena Pond**.

THE DRIVE
Historic Route 30 winds down the hill back to river level. Follow the signs to the Columbia Gorge Discovery Center.

09 COLUMBIA GORGE DISCOVERY CENTER
The informative **Columbia Gorge Discovery Center** (gorgediscovery.org) covers the history of the gorge from its creation by cataclysmic floods, through its Native American inhabitants, to the early pioneers, settlers and eventual damming of the river. Whether you're a gorge fanatic or a first-time visitor, the center will undoubtedly increase your appreciation for one of the Pacific Northwest's most amazing natural landscapes.

THE DRIVE
Go back out to Historic Route 30 or I-84 (they run parallel to each other from here, but Historic Route 30 is more scenic), then east a couple of miles to The Dalles.

10 THE DALLES
Though steadfastly unglamorous, The Dalles offers decent camping and hiking, and the fierce winds are excellent for windsurfing

Multnomah Falls

TOP WATERFALLS
The following are all off Hwy 30, listed from west to east.

Latourell Falls (249ft) The first major waterfall as you come east on Hwy 30. Hike 10 minutes to reach it, or go a mile to the top.

Bridal Veil Falls (140ft) Two-tiered falls reached via an easy half-mile walk. A separate wheelchair-accessible trail passes through a meadow.

Wahkeena Falls (242ft) Hike up the Wahkeena Trail, join Trail No 441 and head down to Multnomah Falls. Return via the road for the 5-mile loop.

Multnomah Falls (642ft) The gorge's top attraction. Trail No 411 leads to the top (1 mile). Continue up foresty Multnomah Creek and the top of Larch Mountain (another 7 miles).

Oneonta Falls (75ft) Located within the lovely half-mile Oneonta Gorge. Carefully scamper over logjams and wade in water up to waist-high. Fun and worth it!

Horsetail Falls (176ft) Just east of Oneonta Gorge. A 4.5-mile loop begins here, passing through Ponytail Falls and Triple Falls. Walk a half-mile east on Hwy 30 (passing the Oneonta Gorge) to return.

Elowah Falls (289ft) More isolated but pretty falls, located about a mile off the highway. Hike to the top, then take a 0.7-mile side trail to McCord Creek Falls (2.5 miles round-trip).

FIIPHOTO/SHUTTERSTOCK ©

and kiteboarding. Sights here include the fascinating **Fort Dalles Museum** (fortdalles museum.org), Oregon's oldest museum, which is full of historical items. Built in 1957, **The Dalles Dam & Lock** produces enough electricity to power a city of a million inhabitants. The **Dalles Dam Visitor Center** contains the expected homage to hydroelectricity, along with a fish cam to view migratory salmon – it's east on the frontage road from exit 87 off I-84.

 THE DRIVE
From here you'll backtrack on Historic Route 30 or I-84 (the faster option) to Hood River. Take exit 64 and follow the signs for Hwy 35, which leads inland toward Mt Hood.

11 HIGHWAY 35
The first 16.5 miles of Hwy 35 to Parkdale is the first leg of the 'Fruit Loop,' named for all its agriculture. Wind past scenic fertile lands, easy-to-spot family fruit stands, U-pick orchards, lavender fields, alpaca farms and winery tasting rooms. There are blossoms in spring, berries in summer, and apples and pears in fall – with plenty of festivals and celebra-

 Photo opportunity
Multnomah Falls: one of the country's highest cascades.

tions throughout the seasons (except for winter). It's a good way to sample the area's agricultural bounties while appreciating the local scenery too – try not to get in an accident from ogling the larger-than-life Mt Hood when it's in view.

 THE DRIVE
Enjoy the scenery of endless orchards and vineyards, and stop whenever you feel the whim – there are over 30 businesses to choose from.

12 PARKDALE
Your ascent ends at the little town of Parkdale, a great stop for lunch. You can also visit the tiny **Hutson Museum** in a country-perfect red farmhouse. It has displays of rocks and minerals, Native American artifacts and local memorabilia – plus a garden of native plants.

 THE DRIVE
Return to Hwy 35 and follow it south for 27 miles around grand, white-capped Mt Hood to Hwy 26.

13 MT HOOD
At 11,240ft, Mt Hood is the highest peak in Oregon. Its pyramid shape makes it peek out from behind many hills, enhancing the view. The best place to enjoy this alpine world is **Timberline Lodge**, a handsome wooden gem from the 1930s, offering glorious shelter and refreshments to both guests and nonguests (and yes, some exterior shots of *The Shining* were filmed here). In summer, wildflowers bloom on the mountainsides and hidden ponds shimmer in blue, making for some unforgettable hikes; in winter, downhill and cross-country skiing dominates people's minds and bodies. From here there's also convenient access to the **Pacific Crest Trail** (PCT). Whether you hike 2 miles or 12 miles along the PCT, the views of Mt Hood are incredible. The trail is easy to find – follow the signs to the right of the lodge.

MT HOOD RAILROAD
If you're tired of the road, the Mt Hood Railroad (mthoodrr.com) also starts here and runs scenically from Hood River up a similar route to Hwy 35, past the towns of Odell and Dee before its terminus in Parkdale. The views are spectacular, the cars are beautifully restored and the food is memorable. You can also choose to go on special train excursions that include wine tastings and visits to museums.

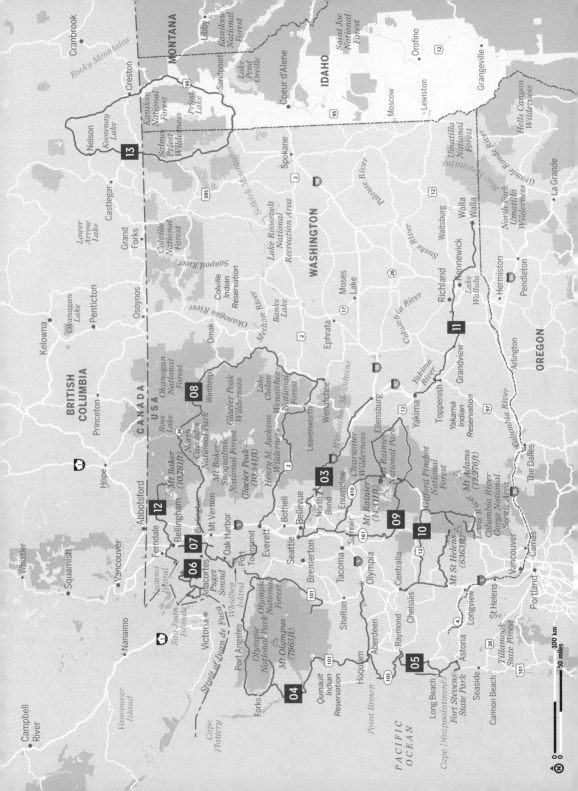

JAY YUAN/SHUTTERSTOCK ©

Sunrise Day Lodge (p72)

Washington

Explore

Washington

Washington State has more than its share of epic drives, whether your ideal scenery consists of winding roads through thick forest, high cliffs overlooking a frothy sea, or wide-open wheat fields across rolling hills. In a few hours you can drive from the wet, urban, liberal, evergreen coast, via a dramatic volcano-punctuated mountain range, to the arid, conservative, vineyard-patterned and scrublike east. On the way you'll find literary inspiration in the footsteps of Jack Kerouac, geological epiphanies near Mt St Helens, mighty rainforests on the Olympic Peninsula and miles and miles of expertly engineered strips of winding asphalt that seem to defy the icy, precipitous terrain.

Seattle

Most visitors to Washington will arrive via Seattle-Tacoma International Airport, known locally as 'Sea-Tac'. All major car rental companies have kiosks at the airport. Light-rail trains from the airport to downtown Seattle leave about every 10 minutes and get you into the heart of the city in about 40 minutes.

Seattle is the region's biggest city (though not its capital – that's comparatively tiny Olympia, 60 miles south) and has every amenity a road-tripper might want. Choosing your neighborhood is important, as the city tends to sprawl: to unfairly summarize, go to Capitol Hill for fun, Queen Anne for dignified quiet, Belltown for bars, Downtown for shopping, Pioneer Square for history, West Seattle for the beach, and Georgetown

to relive the 1990s. There are convenient places to stay in most areas, from chain hotels to AirBnB rentals to character-filled B&Bs. Be sure to ask about overnight parking fees when booking accommodations (free parking is gold in this city).

The city's dining scene is vast and worth exploring, but if you only have one night here, go for seafood. Before leaving town, combine your grocery shopping and sightseeing with a stop at Pike Place Market for farm-fresh produce and fish, and don't forget to grab a bag of locally roasted coffee.

Bellingham

Laid-back Bellingham has a salty, seafaring character along the waterfront, as well as a nice downtown core and a popular greenspace trail network. One of

WHEN TO GO

Mid-June through September and into October are usually the best times. Many high-elevation roads, including those to Mt Rainier and its surroundings, are closed November–May due to heavy snow. Early season (May to June) brings wildflowers and waterfalls, but also frequent rains. The peak summer and fall seasons typically mean warm weather, dry roads and abundant scenic beauty.

its four main sections, the historic town of Fairhaven is now a well-preserved and slightly upscale neighborhood. This historic district of handsome redbrick Victorians testifies to the city's rich, if sometimes rambunctious, past. Today, Fairhaven is home to an excellent bookstore with an attached cafe, Colophon. Fairhaven is also an important transport nexus, home to Bellingham's Amtrak station and ferry terminal, with regular ferries up the Inside Passage to Alaska.

Leavenworth

An adorable faux-Bavarian village, Leavenworth also has the advantage of a stunning mountain backdrop and proximity to some of the best outdoor activities in the state. Take your pick between roadside motels (all done up in 'German' drag, of course) or high-end lodges. The compact town center is easy to walk around, and visitors will have no trouble finding a place for a bratwurst and a beer. Stock up at the supermarket, fill up the gas tank and get a hearty breakfast before setting out, all in buildings decorated with ornate flower boxes and Old World–style exteriors.

TRANSPORT

Most visitors to Washington fly into Seattle-Tacoma International Airport ('Sea-Tac'). Rental cars are the most practical way to get around, although there are bus lines between major cities. Many of the drives here include ferry travel, and it's important to book ahead for car ferries, especially in July and August.

 WHAT'S ON

Seattle International Film Festival

This month-long festival brings delights from around the world for cinephiles. (April)

Skagit Valley Tulip Festival

Fields of colorful tulips stretch as far as the eye can see. (April)

Makah Days

Join celebrations of the Makah people's culture and history in Neah Bay. (August)

Wooden Boat Festival

Port Townsend fills with wooden boat fans during this marine-themed festival. (September)

Resources

Washington State Tourism (stateofwatourism.com) Information portal for the state overall.

Visit Seattle (visitseattle.org) Information about the state's largest city.

Washington State Ferries (wsdot.wa.gov/travel/washington-state-ferries) Source for ferry crossing schedules, prices, guidelines, routes and advance reservations.

Washington State Department of Transportation (wsdot.com/traffic) Road conditions.

 WHERE TO STAY

Car campers will love Washington, with its deep forests and wild coastline full of excellent campgrounds, some with camping yurts available. Be sure to reserve ahead or plan to arrive early and be flexible, and note that most campgrounds are closed in winter. Budget digs are hard to come by, but you'll find high-end 'rustic' lodges and resorts in many parts of the state, as well as fixed-up historic hotels and B&Bs. The urban hubs and major highways have plenty of midrange chain hotels, if all you need is a comfortable, no-nonsense room and somewhere to park for the night.

03

WASHINGTON

Mountains to Sound Greenway

BEST FOR FAMILIES

Northwest Railway Museum and its train rides

DURATION	DISTANCE	GREAT FOR
1–2 days	193km / 120 miles	History, Outdoors

BEST TIME TO GO	May to September: open museums and predictable weather

Ellensburg Rodeo

Dramatic changes in scenery and radically contrasting ecosystems are par for the course in Washington, a land bisected by the climate-altering Cascade Mountains. With I-90 as its main artery, this drive ferries you from the dry east to the wet west via the 3046ft Snoqualmie Pass on an ostensibly busy road. But a mile or two off the interstate a parallel 'greenway' of bucolic trails and small-town preservation societies prevails.

Link Your Trip

8 Cascade Drive

Both ends of this trip will deposit you close to entry points for the Cascade Drive, another mountain-punctuated driving extravaganza.

11 Washington Wine Tour

Do this drive backward, starting in Seattle, and the essence of local wine in Ellensburg might inspire you to travel on to Yakima and beyond.

01 ELLENSBURG

Take an archetypal American rodeo town with a smattering of historic buildings and add a stately college. Welcome to Ellensburg, a place of juxtapositions. Here, erudite college undergraduates rub shoulders with weekend cowboys in a small yet salubrious collegiate town where two-thirds of the 18,000 population are registered students. Ellensburg is at its busiest during the annual **rodeo** (ellensburgrodeo.com), the biggest of its kind in the Pacific Northwest. Like most Washing-

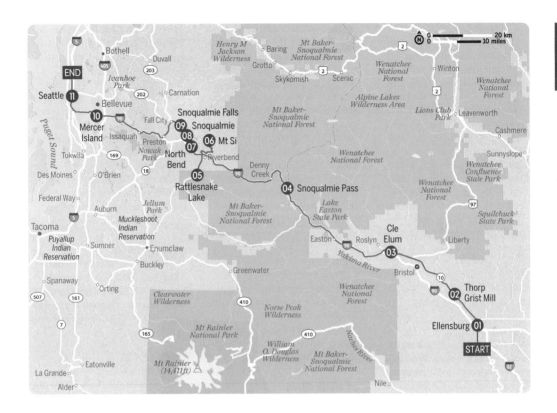

ton towns, Ellensburg has its fair share of peripheral motel/mall infestations, but body-swerve the familiar big boxes and you'll uncover a compact but select cluster of venerable red-brick buildings in a downtown **historic district**. Also worth checking out is the **Kittitas County Historical Museum** (kchm. org), housed in the 1889 Cadwell Building, known mostly for its petrified-wood and gemstone collections, but also hosting a cleverly laid out history section documenting the backgrounds of Croatian, Arabic and Welsh immigrants.

 THE DRIVE
To avoid the clamor of the busy interstate, take US 97 northwest out of town before branching onto SR 10 to the small rural settlement of Thorp, 9 miles from Ellensburg.

02 **THORP GRIST MILL**
In the small town of Thorp (population 297), the **Thorp Grist Mill** (thorp. org) was once a de facto meeting place for local farmers. Today, its well-preserved shell gives an interesting insight into the pioneer farmers who plowed the fields of the Kittitas Valley in the late 19th century. Converted to a rural museum, the mill originally

dates from 1873 when its primary purpose was to grind flour using water power from the nearby Yakima River. It ceased operation in 1946, but, thanks to the foresight of local community activists, was placed on the National Register of Historic Places in 1977.

 THE DRIVE
Continue northwest on SR 10 through quiet bucolic farmland to Cle Elum, 18 miles from Thorp.

03 **CLE ELUM**
Cle Elum's location on the cusp of the Eastern Cascades and the bald treeless grasslands of the Kittitas Valley pulls

in two radically different types of visitor. Seattleites regularly cross Snoqualmie Pass to sup the local wine and enjoy seemingly endless summer sunshine. Easterners stop by to gaze west at the snowier, more topographically interesting mountains. A posh resort, the **Suncadia** (suncadia resort.com), just west of Cle Elum and complete with golf, spa and winery, caters for both groups. Though small, the town has a couple of esoteric museums conceived and maintained by vivacious community groups. Up the road 3.5 miles, **Roslyn** stood in for Alaska in the 1990s TV show *Northern Exposure* (plot spoiler: there's more TV nostalgia four stops further on).

THE DRIVE
Time to brave I-90! Access the road at exit 84 and motor 30 miles progressively uphill to Snoqualmie Pass. Just before the summit you'll pass Keechelus Lake, the source of the Yakima River, on your left.

WHY I LOVE THIS TRIP
Becky Ohlsen, writer

This trip takes in a good sampling of Washington's unusually varied pleasures, from the cowboy town of Ellensburg to the skiing and hiking haven of Snoqualmie Pass; from a waterfall made famous by a trippy TV show to a rewardingly tough mountain hike. (The route has several great hiking opportunities, in fact.) And it all wraps up in the world-class city of Seattle.

04 SNOQUALMIE PASS
One of the easier routes across the Cascades and the only one to carry an interstate (I-90), Snoqualmie was first prospected by white settlers in the 1850s. By the 1930s a fledgling road was being plowed year-round and the pass had spawned a nascent ski area, which has since morphed into four separate areas known (and managed) communally as the **Summit at Snoqualmie** (summitatsnoqualmie.com). This is the nearest day-use ski area to Seattle (read: there will be long lines).

Should you summit the pass in summer, consider a hike. The **Pacific Crest Trail** briefly descends to the hustle of the interstate here but blissful tranquility stretches for many miles in either direction.

THE DRIVE
Descend on I-90 until exit 32, 22 miles from the pass. Go south on 436th Ave SE, which becomes Cedar Falls Rd. Within 3 miles you will be deposited at Rattlesnake Lake.

05 RATTLESNAKE LAKE
An important nexus on the Mountains to Sound Greenway, tranquil Rattlesnake Lake was once a more tumultuous place. A town called Moncton existed here until 1915 before it was flooded, evacuated and condemned after an abortive damming project. From 1906 to 1980 an erstwhile railway, the 'Milwaukee Road,' passed through. The railroad bed has been reworked into a non-motorized thoroughfare

known as the **John Wayne Pioneer Trail**, which is popular with cyclists. From here, with a bike or walking, you can descend to the lake, a journey that includes careering through the 2.3-mile Snoqualmie tunnel (bring headlamps). The lake is also the starting point for the **Snoqualmie Valley Trail** and a 4-mile round-trip hike up to Rattlesnake Ridge. There are toilets and a kayak launch lakeside, and a small interpretive center.

THE DRIVE
Return to I-90 but this time, rather than join it, head underneath on 436th Ave SE to the junction with E North Bend Way. Turn left and then go right on SE Mt Si Rd. This leg of the trip is 10 miles.

06 MT SI
Brooding moodily behind the town of North Bend, 4167ft Mt Si is allegedly the most climbed mountain in the state (approximately 40,000 hike it every year) and an annual fitness test for many Seattleites. The trail starts 2.5 miles down SE Mt Si Rd from a parking lot and is an 8-mile round-trip, including 3150ft of ascent. Though popular and predictably crowded in summer, the switchbacking path is no piece of cake. Dress appropriately for the mountains and bring water. The lofty meadow that acts as the summit for most walkers (the actual summit is a precipitous haystack-shaped rock) is revered for its hard-earned Puget Sound views.

THE DRIVE

Retrace your route along SE Mt Si Rd to the intersection with E North Bend Way, where you turn right into North Bend, about 4 miles away.

07 NORTH BEND

If you're one of the many fans of a certain cult-classic TV show, your first sight of North Bend might make you do a double-take. This is where David Lynch's weird and wonderful *Twin Peaks* was filmed, both the original run in the early 1990s and the final season in 2017. The town – a sleepy, if salubrious, place these days – is still milking its fame. **Twede's** (twedescafe. com), the 'Double R Diner' in

Photo opportunity

Snoqualmie Falls' raw power and *Twin Peaks* flashbacks.

the TV show, proudly advertises its *Twin Peaks* credentials with cherry pie and 'a damn fine cup o' coffee,' along with 50 – yes, 50 – different types of burger. Down the road, the **Snoqualmie Valley Historical Museum** (snoqualm ievalleymuseum.org) charts the pre-Lynchian history of the valley with pioneer and Native American exhibits.

THE DRIVE

From North Bend take Bendigo Blvd, cross the South Fork of the Snoqualmie River and continue 3 miles into Snoqualmie.

08 SNOQUALMIE

Located a mile east of the famous falls, Snoqualmie is a diminutive town of eclectic shopfronts that ply hardware, organic coffee and Native American art. Across the tracks, the lovingly restored **Northwest Railway Museum** (train museum.org) is the largest of its type in Washington. Its hook is its retro steam-train trips (adult/child $20/10), which chug (Saturdays and Sundays from April

Snoqualmie Falls

to October) 5 miles down the line to North Bend and another equally cute Thomas-the-Tank-Engine station. Snoqualmie is also an ideal place to jump onto the **Snoqualmie Valley Trail**, the region's longest greenway (31 miles), which parallels the Snoqualmie River along the course of an old railway line. Access is best gained from the north end of Meadowbrook Way SE.

 THE DRIVE
From Snoqualmie follow Railroad Ave northwest out of town and within a mile you'll be at Snoqualmie Falls.

09 SNOQUALMIE FALLS
Come between April and June during the spring snow melt and you'll see why this 268ft mini Niagara has been producing hydroelectric power since 1899. Observation decks and an overlook park stand face-on against the supersonic spray, while perched awfully close to the giant falls' rim is the luxurious **Salish Lodge & Spa**, the second incarnation of a hotel that was first built here in 1918. A half-mile trail drops down through spray-fed rainforest to the **Snoqualmie Falls Hydroelectric Museum**, housed in the old train depot and chronicling the history of the power plant.

THE DRIVE
Take the Fall City–Snoqualmie Rd to Fall City, where you turn left onto the Preston–Fall City Rd opposite the Fall City Roadhouse and Inn. Merge west onto I-90 again at Preston (exit 22) to reach Mercer Island, 23 miles from Snoqualmie Falls.

Twede's Cafe, North Bend

TWIN PEAKS

Recognize *that* Snoqualmie Valley mountain, *that* waterfall, *that* cafe and *that* hotel? If so, you're not alone. By now, *Twin Peaks* probably needs very little introduction. The TV drama series conceived, written and directed by Mark Frost and legendary US film director David Lynch has long since moved beyond cult status to become an almost mainstream cultural phenomenon. Laura Palmer, Agent Cooper and the log lady are widely beloved characters. David Lynch *(Blue Velvet, Wild at Heart)* has become so influential that he has his own adjective: 'Lynchian' denotes anything that's surreal, dreamy, unsettling and – occasionally – freakishly funny.

Twin Peaks originally ran for 30 episodes over two seasons between 1990 and 1991, then returned for a final season in 2017. The show was set in a fictional Washington town of the same name (and filmed in North Bend and Snoqualmie). It starred Kyle MacLachlan as FBI agent Dale Cooper, investigating the mysterious death of a homecoming queen. The series, with its complex plot and surreal, but suspenseful, storyline, quickly gained a large audience and won numerous Golden Globe and Emmy nominations and several awards. Time has done little to diminish its appeal. The third season was wildly anticipated, and praised by fans and critics alike.

As for those recognizable landmarks? The mountain (the fictional 'Twin Peaks') is Mt Si, the waterfall (seen in the show's opening credits) is Snoqualmie Falls, the cafe (where Kyle MacLachlan extolled the virtues of hot black coffee) is Twede's and the hotel (the Great Northern in the show) is the Salish Lodge & Spa.

HAY IS FOR HORSES

As you drive the rural roads around Ellensburg and then again as you descend into the Snoqualmie Valley, you're sure to see fields of Timothy grass, a tall, rolled-form grass farmed for hay that's considered top-notch cattle and horse feed as well as tasty grub for rabbits and guinea pigs. Surprisingly, hay is one of the highest-valued crops in Washington and around 35% of the harvest is shipped internationally, mostly to Asia. The grass is cut two times per year, usually in June and September.

10 MERCER ISLAND

You don't have to get out of your car to experience Mercer Island's greatest engineering marvel. The community's two colossal parallel bridges that carry traffic over to metro Seattle are the second- and fifth-longest floating bridges in the world. An older bridge was destroyed by a storm in 1990. The **Homer M Hadley Memorial Bridge** (westbound traffic) and the **Lacey V Murrow Memorial Bridge**

(eastbound) were built in 1989 and 1993, respectively.

THE DRIVE

Coming off the floating bridges, traffic is directed through the Baker Tunnel before coming out with surprising suddenness in Seattle's downtown core close to King Street Station.

11 SEATTLE

Put aside some time to enjoy Seattle at the end of this drive, which deposits you

on the cusp of downtown and its cluster of craning skyscrapers, great to explore on foot. For dazzling city views ascend the **Columbia Center** (skyviewobservatory.com), which, at 932ft high, is the loftiest building in the Pacific Northwest and a lot cheaper than the Space Needle.

Pioneer Square is Seattle's oldest quarter and home to the **Klondike Gold Rush National Historical Park** (nps.gov/klse), a shockingly good free museum about the 1897 Alaska gold rush. Another good family-orientated attraction is the **aquarium** (seattleaquarium.org), the centerpiece of which is a glass-domed room. For a post-drive picnic, decamp to **Pike Place Market** (pikeplacemarket.org) for artisan cheeses, Russian pastries and Italian deli meats.

CREDIT/CREDIT ©

Parallel bridges, Mercer Island

Pike Place Market, Seattle

04

WASHINGTON

Olympic Peninsula Loop

DURATION	DISTANCE	GREAT FOR
4 days	365 miles / 585km	Nature

BEST TIME TO GO	June to September, when deluges are slightly less likely.

Lake Quinault Lodge

Imagine pine-clad beaches fused with an American Mt Olympus, with a slice of Stephenie Meyer's *Twilight* saga thrown in for good measure and you've got an approximation of what a drive around the Olympic Peninsula looks like. This is wilderness of the highest order, where thick forest collides with an end-of-the-continent coastline that hasn't changed much since Juan de Fuca sailed by in 1592. Bring hiking boots – and rain gear!

Link Your Trip

5 Graveyard of the Pacific Tour

Continue down the coast from Aberdeen, where you'll begin a coastal drive along a watery ship cemetery.

7 Chuckanut Drive & Whidbey Island

Across from Port Townsend, Whidbey is a gentler and – traditionally – drier contrast to the Olympics.

01 OLYMPIA

Welcome to Olympia, city of weird contrasts, where street-side buskers belt out acoustic grunge, and stiff bureaucrats answer their ringtones on the lawns of the expansive state legislature. A quick circuit of the Washington State Capitol (olympiawa.gov/community/events___activities/ visiting_the_capitol.php), a huge Grecian temple of a building, will give you a last taste of civilization before you depart. Then load up the car and head swiftly for the exits.

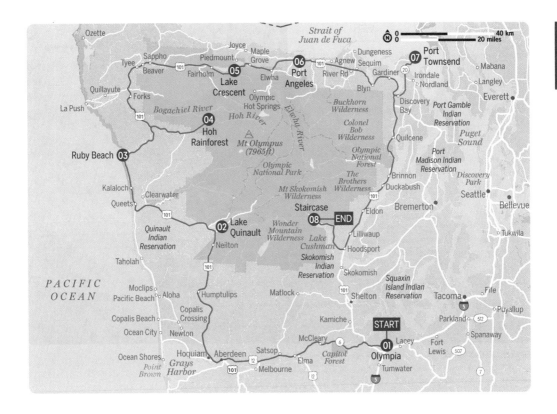

 THE DRIVE
Your basic route is due west, initially on US 101, then (briefly) on SR 8 before joining US 12 in Elma. In Grays Harbor, enter the twin cities of Aberdeen and Hoquiam, famous for producing William Boeing and the grunge group Nirvana. Here, you swing north on US 101 (again!) to leafier climes at Lake Quinault, 88 miles from Olympia.

02 LAKE QUINAULT
Situated in the extreme southwest of the Olympic National Park (nps.gov/olym), the thickly forested Quinault River Valley is one of the park's least-crowded corners. Clustered on the south shore of deep-blue glacial Lake Quinault is the tiny village of Quinault, complete with the luscious Lake Quinault Lodge, a US Forest Service (USFS) office and a couple of stores.

A number of short hiking trails begin just below Lake Quinault Lodge; pick up a free map from the USFS office. The shortest of these is the Quinault Rain Forest Nature Trail, a half-mile walk through 500-year-old Douglas firs. This brief trail adjoins the 3-mile Quinault Loop Trail, which meanders through the rainforests before circling back to the lake. The Quinault region is renowned for its huge trees. Close to the village is a 191ft Sitka spruce tree (supposedly over 1000 years old), and nearby are the world's largest red cedar, Douglas fir and mountain hemlock trees.

 THE DRIVE
West from Lake Quinault, US 101 continues through the Quinault Indian Reservation before entering a thin strip of national park territory that protects the beaches around Kalaloch (klay-lock). This is some of the wildest coastal scenery in the US accessible by road; various pullovers allow beach forays. After a total of 40 miles you'll reach Ruby Beach.

03 RUBY BEACH
Inhabiting a thin coastal strip that was added to the national park in 1953, Ruby

RS SMITH PHOTOGRAPHY/SHUTTERSTOCK ©

Photo Opportunity

The Hoh Rainforest to see greens you've never imagined.

Olympic National Park

Beach is accessed via a short 0.2-mile path that leads down to a large expanse of windswept coast embellished by polished black stones and wantonly strewn tree trunks. To the south toward Kalaloch, other accessible beaches include unimaginatively named Beach One through to Beach Six, all of which are popular with beachcombers. At low tide, rangers give talks on tidal-pool life at Beach Four and on the ecosystems of the Olympic coastal strip.

THE DRIVE

North of Ruby Beach, US 101 swings sharply northeast and inland, tracking the Hoh River. Turn right off US 101 onto the Hoh River Rd to explore one of the national park's most popular inner sanctums, the Hoh Rainforest. It's 14 miles from Ruby Beach to the turnoff, then 19 miles further to the Hoh visitor center.

04 HOH RAINFOREST

Count yourself lucky if you arrive on a day when it isn't raining! The most popular detour off US 101 is the 19-mile paved road to the Hoh Valley, the densest, wettest, greenest and most intensely surreal temperate rainforest on earth. The essential hike here is the short but fascinating Hall of Moss Trail, an easy 0.75-mile loop through the kind of weird, ethereal scenery that even JRR Tolkien couldn't have invented. Old-man's beard drips from branches above you like corduroy fringe, while trailside licorice ferns and lettuce lichens overwhelm the massive fallen trunks of maple and Sitka spruce. Rang-

ers lead interesting free guided walks here twice a day during summer and can help you spot some of the park's 5000-strong herd of Roosevelt elk.

THE DRIVE

Rejoining US 101, motor north to the small and relatively nondescript but handy settlement of Forks. Press on through as US 101 bends north then east through a large logging area before plunging back into the national park on the shores of wondrous Lake Crescent, which is 66 miles from the Hoh Rainforest visitor center.

05 LAKE CRESCENT

Before you've even had time to erase the horror of teenage vampires from your mind, the scenery shifts again as the road winds along the glittering pine-scented shores of glacier-carved Lake Crescent. The lake looks best from water level, on a rental kayak, or from high above at its eastern edge on the Storm King Mountain Trail (named after the peak's wrathful spirit), accessible via a steep, 1.7-mile ascent that splits off the Barnes Creek Trail. For the less athletic, the Marymere Falls Trail is a 2-mile round trip to a 90ft cascade that drops down over a basalt cliff. Both hikes leave from a parking lot north of US 101 at the Storm King Ranger Station. The area is also the site of the Lake Crescent Lodge, the oldest of the park's trio of celebrated lodges, which opened in 1916.

 THE DRIVE
From Lake Crescent take US 101 22 miles east to the town of Port Angeles, a gateway to Victoria, Canada, which is reachable by ferry.

06 PORT ANGELES
Up above the clouds, stormy Hurricane Ridge lives up to its name with fickle weather and biting winds made slightly more bearable by the park's best high-altitude views. Its proximity to Port Angeles is another bonus; if you're heading up here be sure to call into the museum-like Olympic National Park Visitor Center (nps.gov/olym) in Port Angeles first. Hurricane Hill Trail and the Meadow Loop Trails network are popular and moderately easy. The

THE TWILIGHT ZONE

It would have been impossible to envisage 20 years ago: diminutive Forks, a depressed lumber town full of hard-nosed loggers, reborn as a pilgrimage site for 'tweenage' girls following in the ghostly footsteps of two fictional sweethearts named Bella and Edward. The reason for this weird metamorphosis was, of course, the *Twilight* saga, a four-part book series by US author Stephenie Meyer about love and vampires on the foggy Olympic Peninsula that in just a few years shifted more than 100 million books and spawned five Hollywood movies. With Forks acting as the book's main setting, the town was catapulted to international stardom, and the cachet has yet to wear off.

first half-mile of these trails is wheelchair accessible.

 THE DRIVE
Press east through the retirement community of Sequim (pronounced 'skwim'). Turn north on SR 20 to reach another, more attractive port, that of Port Townsend.

07 PORT TOWNSEND
Ease back into civilization with the cultured Victorian comforts of Port Townsend, whose period charm dates from the railroad boom of the 1890s, when the town was earmarked to become the 'New York of the West.' That never happened, but you can pick up a historic walking tour map from the visitor center (enjoypt.com) and wander the waterfront's collection of shops, galleries and antique malls. Don't miss the gorgeously renovated Rose Theatre (rosetheatre.com), which has been showing movies since 1908, and the fine Victorian mansions on the bluff above town, where several

charming residences have been turned into B&Bs.

 THE DRIVE
From Port Townsend, head back to the junction of US 101, but this time head south passing Quilcene, Brinnon and the Dosewallips Park entrance. You get more unbroken water views here on the park's eastern side courtesy of the Hood Canal. Track the watery beauty to Hoodsport, where signs point west off US 101 to Staircase, 67 miles from Port Townsend.

08 STAIRCASE
It's drier on the park's eastern side and the mountains are closer. The Staircase park nexus, accessible via Hoodsport, has a ranger station, a campground and a decent trail system that follows the drainage of the North Fork Skokomish River and is flanked by some of the most rugged peaks in the Olympics. Nearby Lake Cushman has a campground and water sports opportunities.

05

WASHINGTON

Graveyard of the Pacific Tour

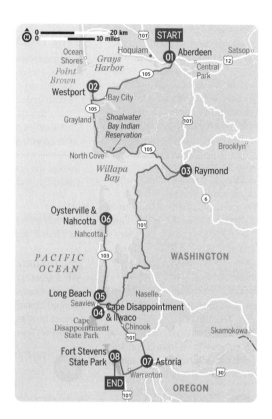

DURATION	DISTANCE	GREAT FOR
2 days	212km / 132 miles	History

BEST TIME TO GO	April to September for the best weather.

They call it the Graveyard of the Pacific. The area from northern Oregon to Vancouver Island is known for its unpredictable weather, unforgiving coastline and bad habit of gobbling up ships. Thousands of vessels have been lost, from war ships to barges to countless smaller craft. Dive in to this area with its unique seafaring character and fascinating maritime history.

Link Your Trip

04 Olympic Peninsula Loop

From Aberdeen, pick up this loop that features the best of northwest Washington, including more coastline and Olympic National Park.

14 Highway 101 Oregon Coast

Hook up with this trip at Fort Stevens State Park, continuing down the coast for seafood, razor clams, tide pools and lighthouses.

01 ABERDEEN

Start your trip in Aberdeen's Grays Harbor, home port of the tall ship **Lady Washington** (historicalseaport.org), the official ship of the State of Washington. This impressive reproduction of a 1788 tall ship – featured in *Pirates of the Caribbean* if that helps give you a visual – is available for dockside tours and adventure sails all along the state's coast. Check the website to find out where along the way you might catch her.

Fans of Nirvana might be interested in several sites dedicated to Kurt Cobain, including the **Kurt**

BEST SHIP SIGHTING

The tall ship *Lady Washington* docks along the coast

Grays Harbor Lighthouse

Cobain Memorial Park, his childhood home and the town's 'come as you are' sign.

 THE DRIVE
From Aberdeen, take US 101 across the Chehalis River bridge, then follow Grays Harbor southwest on SR 105 for 20 miles to reach the coastal town of Westport.

02 WESTPORT
The seaside town of Westport has two worthwhile stops. First, head to **Grays Harbor Lighthouse**, the tallest lighthouse in Washington. It's always there for photo ops, and tours up the 135-step circular staircase (pant, wheeze) are available seasonally. Next, head over to the **Westport Maritime Museum** (westport maritimemuseum.com), a noteworthy Cape Cod–style building at the northern tip of town. It offers your typical array of nautical knickknacks, but most impressive is the authentic Fresnel lighthouse lens. It's a first-order lens, which as anyone who knows about lens rankings will attest, is really impressive; loosely translated, that means it's big enough to need its own separate building.

 THE DRIVE
Continue on SR 105, following the coast 30 miles southeast to Raymond.

03 RAYMOND
Raymond is home to the **Willapa Seaport Museum** (willapaseaportmu seum.com). It looks more like a cross between a fisherperson's garage sale and Disney's *Pirates of the Caribbean* ride than a formal museum, but that's part of its charm, and it's a good leg-stretch on your way to your next stop. Let the salty ol' museum owner lead you around if you've got an hour or more.

Before you leave, though, you might want to stop to pay your respect to Willie Keils at **Willie Keils Grave State Park**, just south of town. Nineteen-year-old Willie died in 1855 right before his family left Missouri, but they couldn't bear leaving him; instead, they filled his coffin with whiskey and brought him along, turning their wagon train into a very slow funeral procession.

THE DRIVE
Pick up US 101 west and head 45 miles south. When you get to Seaview, follow the signs for Cape Disappointment, 2 miles further south.

04 CAPE DISAPPOINTMENT & ILWACO
Although little remains of the original Fort Canby that once stood in **Cape Disappointment State Park** (parks.state.wa.us/486), 2 miles southwest of Ilwaco, the area does hold the excellent **Lewis & Clark Interpretive Center** (capedisappointment.org); some wild beach; around 8 miles of coastal, forested hiking trails; and two dramatic lighthouses. It's a short walk from the interpretive center to the small **Cape Disappointment Lighthouse**, perched on a particularly vertiginous cliff over crashing seas. You could also take a short trail on the other side of the park to **North Head Lighthouse**, which offers tours in summer and is the oldest lighthouse in use on the west coast. Just north, you'll pass through the cute seaside village of Ilwaco, decorated with driftwood, glass floats and fishing nets. It's an

WHICH WAY TO THE PETER IREDALE?
Shipwrecks don't have addresses: here's how to find the *Peter Iredale*. Cross the bridge from Astoria to Hammond and turn right on East Harbor Dr, which becomes Pacific Dr. Take a left at Lake Dr then a right at the KOA campground and go straight until you see the signs.

excellent place to stop for fresh seafood.

THE DRIVE
Head back north on US 101, which continues on to become SR 103; Long Beach is just 6 miles north of Cape Disappointment.

05 LONG BEACH
Need a break from all the nautical history? Wee Long Beach packs in the roadside fun and is a big hit with road-weary kids. **Marsh's Free Museum** (marshsfree museum.com) dates back to the 1930s and isn't a museum so much as a place where souvenirs and seashells intermingle with sideshow-worthy attractions and oddities. The real star of the show is **Jake the Alligator Man**, media darling of the *Weekly World News*. Half-alligator, half-man, his suspiciously plaster-like remains hold packs of tweens in his thrall. Across the street from Marsh's is the **World's Largest Frying Pan**, measuring over 18ft tall. Want to find out just how long Long Beach is? Primary beach access points in Long Beach are off 10th St SW and at the end of Bolstad Ave; a 0.25-mile boardwalk links the two entryways.

THE DRIVE
Head north up the peninsula for 15 miles to find the quiet, undeveloped part of Willapa Bay.

06 OYSTERVILLE & NAHCOTTA
Purists might prefer the Willapa Bay side of the peninsula, with its old towns, oyster beds and wildlife viewing. The charm of these old communities – the only ones on the bay side of the Long Beach Peninsula – derives not only from their history but also from the absence of the beachfront towns' carnival atmosphere. Tiny Oysterville stands largely unchanged since its heyday in the 1870s, when the oyster boom was at its peak. The town is filled with well-preserved Victorian homes, including the 1863 **Red Cottage**, near Clay St, which served as the first Pacific County courthouse, and the **Big Red House**, built in 1871. Other historic buildings include a one-room schoolhouse and the 1892 **Oysterville Church** (oysterville.org); pick up a walking-tour brochure here.

THE DRIVE
Head back south down the Long Beach Peninsula, then take US 101 south. After 9 miles you'll cross the Columbia River and arrive in Astoria.

07 ASTORIA
Astoria sits at the mouth of the Columbia River, where you'll find some of the most treacherous waters of the Pacific, thanks to river

currents rushing out where ocean tide is trying to get in. The town has a long seafaring history and has seen its old harbor attract fancy hotels and restaurants in recent years, thanks in part to Astoria's popularity as a film location. *Kindergarten Cop, Free Willy* and *Into the Wild* were all filmed here, and fans of the cult hit *The Goonies* can seek out the house where Brandon and Mikey Walsh lived.

You can explore both flotsam and jetsam at **Columbia River Maritime Museum** (crmm. org). It sits right on the edge of the Columbia River, offering a look at everything from old boats to maritime mementos

that have washed up in the area. A Coast Guard exhibit – featuring a rescue boat plying dramatic, fake waves – makes you really appreciate the danger of their job.

THE DRIVE
Head west for the 10-mile drive to Hammond and Fort Stevens State Park.

08 FORT STEVENS STATE PARK

Thousands of vessels have been lost in the Graveyard of the Pacific, from warships to barges to freighters, and those are just the ones on record. There are likely countless

smaller craft littering the ocean floor. A few are still visible occasionally at low tide, but the easiest one to spot is the **Peter Iredale**, resting peacefully at Fort Stevens State Park. The ship was driven onto the shore by rough seas on October 25, 1906, and the wreckage has sat embedded in the sand for over a century. Today, kids have made a jungle gym out of the rusted skeleton and families picnic and build sandcastles on the nearby sand at low tide. (As a reassuring side note, no lives were lost in the shipwreck, so don't let the thought of ghostly sailors dampen your fun.)

Peter Iredale wreck, Fort Stevens State Park

06

WASHINGTON

San Juan Islands Scenic Byway

BEST FOR WILDLIFE

Whale-watching trips from Friday Harbor

Orca, San Juan Island

DURATION	DISTANCE	GREAT FOR
3 days	220km / 136 miles	Nature

BEST TIME TO GO	April to September for calmer seas and regular whale sightings

A thousand metaphorical miles from the urban chaos surrounding Puget Sound, the San Juan archipelago conjures up flashbacks from another era (the 1950s, perhaps?). Crime barely registers here, fast-food franchises are a nasty mainland apparition, and cars are an optional luxury on the three ferry-reachable islands of Orcas, Lopez and San Juan.

Link Your Trip

7 Chuckanut Drive & Whidbey Island

A short hop from Anacortes, this pastoral trip acts like a decompression chamber before re-entering metro Puget Sound.

28 Southern Vancouver Island Tour

Located a handful of watery miles from Vancouver Island, the San Juans provide an ideal opportunity to visit Canada by sea.

01 ANACORTES

This voyage starts at **Anacortes Ferry Terminal** (wsdot.wa.gov/ferries), where you'll board the ferry for Friday Harbor. Drivers might end up waiting for hours in the busy summer months (hint: reserve ferry tickets online). Two alternatives are to spend the night in Anacortes and get to the ferry early, or park at the terminal and make the trip on foot or by bike.

THE DRIVE

If you're taking your car, today's drive is limited to sliding in slow motion onto the ferry where you'll be

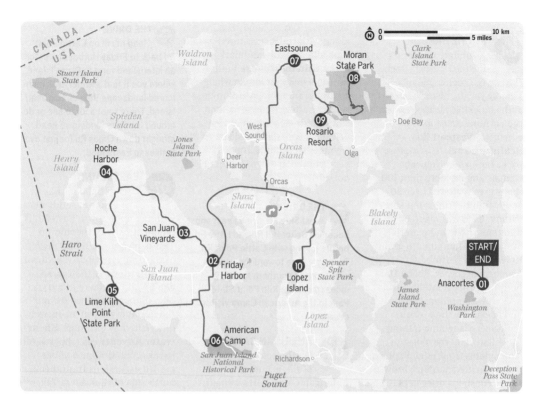

packed tightly in with several hundred others. Don't stay put; climb upstairs and enjoy the 80-minute journey (and it is a great journey) from the passenger lounge.

 02 **FRIDAY HARBOR**
You'll land at Friday Harbor, the San Juans' only real town and a blueprint for the archipelago as a whole, where the worst kind of hassle you're likely to face is a badly pitched baseball. Restaurants, shops and a couple of interesting museums embellish the settlement's diminutive grid. San Juan Island has the good fortune to be right in the migration path of three pods of orcas (aka killer whales),

unimaginatively named the J, K and L pods. (Pod members' names aren't much better: 'K-17, meet L-9.') To learn more about the island's unofficial mascots, stop by the **Whale Museum** (whale-museum.org). To see the real thing – a regional highlight – hook up with **San Juan Excursions** (watchwhales.com), which stands by its boast: 'see whales or come again free.'

THE DRIVE
Navigation on San Juan Island is a no-brainer. Take Roche Harbor Rd northwest out of Friday Harbor as far as Sportsmans Lake. It's 3 miles from the harbor to the vineyards.

 03 **SAN JUAN VINEYARDS**
The premier **vineyard** (sanjuanvineyards.com) in the islands has a tasting room adjacent to its on-site, 1896-vintage schoolhouse. The vineyard also has an outlet in town. For the real homegrown stuff, you're looking at Siegerrebe and Madeleine Angevine varietals, with the occasional Pinot Noir thrown in. The vineyard also makes wines using grapes imported from East Washington.

THE DRIVE
Continue northwest on Roche Harbor Rd. At the T-junction with West Valley Rd, 4.5 miles from the vineyard, turn right.

04 ROCHE HARBOR

A sublime rurally inclined 'resort,' Roche Harbor is a scenic mix of swanky yachts, historic houses and picnicking vacationers. At the entrance gate sits the eccentric **Westcott Bay Sculpture Park** (sjisculpture park.com) where you can wander among more than 100 sculptures scattered over 20 acres. Half the fun is the sheer variety: each was made by a different artist, and materials range from aluminum to granite to recovered redwood. Around the corner, Roche Harbor proper has a lovely marina packed with millionaires' boats and backed by the historic buildings of the lime-mining McMillan clan, the oldest of which dates from 1886. Explore the manicured gardens, browse the plush shops or even play boules.

THE DRIVE

Roche Harbor to Lime Kiln Point State Park is about 10 miles. Heading back down the Roche Harbor Rd, take the West Valley Rd south at the first junction. Just past the alpaca farm, turn right on Mitchell Bay Rd and then left on West Side Rd, which skirts the lapping waters of Haro Strait.

05 LIME KILN POINT STATE PARK

Clinging to the island's rocky west coast, this beautiful park overlooks the deep Haro Strait and is one of the best places in the world to view whales from the shoreline. There is a small **interpretive center** in the park, open from Memorial Day to Labor Day, along with trails, a restored lime kiln and the landmark **Lime Kiln lighthouse** built in 1919. Orca and minke whale sightings are more common in summer after the June salmon run. Offering exceptional views of Vancouver Island and the Olympic Mountains, the park is best enjoyed at sunset, camera poised.

THE DRIVE

West Side Rd swings east and becomes Bailer Hill Rd and Little Rd before joining with Cattle Point Rd. Turn right here toward the island's wild treeless southern tip. It's 9 miles from Lime Kiln Point State Park to the American Camp visitor center.

06 AMERICAN CAMP

On the southern flank of the island, the American Camp hosts a small **visitor center** and is a good place to learn about the islands' history and the infamous 'Pig War' with Britain in 1859, a military standoff ignited after an American settler shot a pig belonging to a homesteading Irishman on San Juan Island. The ensuing squabble led to a border dispute and near conflict between Britain and the US. Among the remnants of an old fort are the officers' quarters and a laundress' house, while a series of interpretive trails lead to earthwork fortifications, a British farm from the dispute era and desolate **South Beach**. The 1.8-mile trail along the ridge of **Mt Finlayson** makes for a pleasant hike, with splendid views and unlimited birdwatching potential.

THE DRIVE

Head north on Cattle Point Rd back to Friday Harbor and catch an interisland ferry to Orcas Island, where you'll find a wilder, less manicured landscape than on San Juan Island. There's not a lot to see or do around the ferry landing so head straight down Orcas Rd for just over 8 miles to Eastsound.

07 EASTSOUND

Orcas Island is shaped like a pair of saddlebags, with the main town, Eastsound, diplomatically in the middle. This is where you'll find most of the dining options. The town shuts down early though, so don't wait till you're hungry to plan dinner. Paddling around the island gives you an entirely different view of things. **Shearwater Adventures** (shearwater kayaks.com/all-tours) offers guided excursions from the north side of the island. Take anything from a quick, one-hour splash-about to an all-day outing in its hand-crafted, Aleut-style kayaks.

THE DRIVE

East of Eastsound, Olga Rd gives access to the island's eastern saddlebag, dominated by Moran State Park, 4.5 miles from Eastsound.

DETOUR
Shaw Island
Start: 07 Eastsound

The quietest and smallest of the four main San Juan Islands, tranquil Shaw is famous for its restrictive property laws and handsome Benedictine monastery. Ferries arrive here daily from Orcas Island (car and driver $28), but with only one campsite offering just 12 overnight berths, opportunities to linger are limited. For the curious, Shaw is worth a slow spin on a mountain bike or an afternoon of quiet contemplation on a pebbly beach. History buffs can break the reverie at the **Shaw Island Historical Museum**, while perennial peace-seekers can find lazy solace on quiet South Beach in **Shaw Island County Park** (sanjuanco.com/523), a stop and potential camping spot on the aquatic Cascadia Marine Trail – doable on nonmotorized boats and kayaks – which starts in southern Puget Sound.

08 **MORAN STATE PARK**
Ex-Seattle mayor Robert Moran's generous gift to the island was **Moran State**

Park, where more than 5000 acres of forest lie draped over two mountains. On a clear day, the view from **Mt Constitution** is incomparable; you can see mountains, islands, even Vancouver. Sadly, on a foggy day, you can only see the person standing next to you. Thirty miles of trails give you ample opportunity to explore on foot, but there's also a road straight to the top if you have a ferry to catch.

 THE DRIVE
Just after exiting the park's northern gate a road turns left to the Rosario Resort, 1.5 miles south.

09 **ROSARIO RESORT**
Orcas' resort is a refined place, unsullied by modern clamor, where seaplanes dock, kayaks launch and discerning vacationers bask in a heady kind of F Scott Fitzgerald–style romance. Its centerpiece is the seafront Rosario mansion, built by former shipbuilding magnate Robert Moran in 1904. A **museum** encased in the mansion tells the life and times of Moran, a former Seattle mayor who lived here from 1906 until 1938. Look out for the ship memorabilia and the huge custom-made organ.

 THE DRIVE
There's only one way back to the ferry terminal – the way you came! Interisland ferries leave five times daily for Shaw and Lopez Islands.

10 **LOPEZ ISLAND**
Lopez – or *Slow-pez* as it's sometimes known – is the ultimate friendly isle where local motorists give strangers the 'Lopezian wave' (two fingers raised from the steering wheel) and you can leave your bike outside the village store and it'll still have both wheels when you return several hours later. A leisurely pastoral spin can be tackled in a day with good overnight digs available in the clustered settlement that passes for the main village. If you arrive bike-less, call up **Lopez Bicycle Works** (lopezkayaks.com), which can deliver a bicycle to the ferry terminal for you.

Lime Kilm lighthouse

07

WASHINGTON

Chuckanut Drive & Whidbey Island

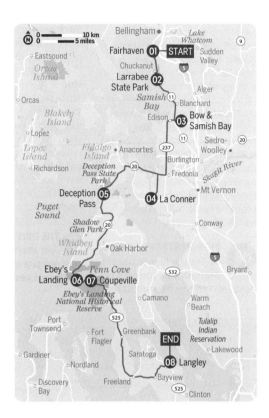

DURATION	DISTANCE	GREAT FOR
1-2 days	143km / 89 miles	Food & wine, Nature

BEST TIME TO GO	March to June when spring flowers bloom.

Short but sweet, this winding sojourn along Chuckanut Dr and through Whidbey Island is the kind of dreamy drive you see in car commercials: sunlight through trees, sparkling ocean and a dozen broccoli-colored islands shimmering in the mid-distance. If you've got a convertible, it's roof-down time, weather permitting, as you glide between oyster restaurants, beaches and scenic state parks.

Link Your Trip

6 San Juan Islands Scenic Byway

The San Juan archipelago is never out of view as you breeze down Chuckanut Dr and across Whidbey Island, begging you to visit.

8 Cascade Drive

Bisected by SR 20, Whidbey Island, though physically flat, is actually part of the official Cascade Drive. Join it in Burlington.

01 FAIRHAVEN

Of Bellingham's four original towns, Fairhaven is the best preserved; a four-square-block historic district of handsome red-brick Victorians testifies to a rich, if sometimes rambunctious, past. Today, the same buildings harbor bookstores, cafes and arty nooks – they're lovely to explore on foot. Fairhaven is also an important transport nexus, and home of Bellingham's Amtrak station and ferry terminal, with regular ferries up the Inside Passage to Alaska.

CL SHERLEY/SHUTTERSTOCK ©

BEST FOR FOOD

Fresh oysters in Samish Bay

Larrabee State Park

THE DRIVE

You don't have to wait long for the beauty of Chuckanut Dr to unfold. Vistas open out immediately south of Fairhaven, where homes hug million-dollar lots high above Puget Sound. Cut into the cliff, the road winds spectacularly through trees that frame island-speckled water views; to the right is the railway. After 6 miles you come to Larrabee State Park.

02 LARRABEE STATE PARK

At the southern end of the Interurban Trail sits **Larrabee State Park** (parks. wa.gov/536/Larrabee), a square chunk of emerald-green forest that spills into the bay at popular Clayton Beach and Wildcat Cove. Poking around in the tide pools or hiking up to **Fragrance Lake Trail** (5.1 miles return) are the most popular activities, though the trails can be crowded at weekends.

THE DRIVE

Chuckanut's precipitous topography continues for a few miles after Larrabee. Then, with dramatic suddenness, the landscape opens out into the flat agricultural pastures of the Skagit River Valley. Pass the Oyster Bar and Chuckanut Manor (both on the right) and, almost 9 miles from Larrabee State Park, you'll arrive at Bow Hill Rd, the first main intersection since Fairhaven.

03 BOW & SAMISH BAY

As you continue the drive south, several pullouts lure you with fine views over Samish Bay as they explain the history of the road and its oyster industry. Oysters adore the brackish waters of the bay, and nearby **Taylor Shellfish Farms** (taylorshellfish.com) has been hand harvesting and shucking 1800 acres of seabed here since the 1880s. Staff can lead you through oyster etiquette as you learn to differentiate between a buttery Shigoku or a creamy Kumamoto. Both Taylor and nearby Blau, across the bay on Samish Island, deliver their freshest catch to a pair of Chuckanut Dr restaurants that between them boast the region's most hypnotic views: the **Oyster Bar** (theoysterbar. net) and **Chuckanut Manor** (chuckanutmanor.com). South of Blanchard Mountain, Bow junction holds a few surprises, including the gourmet Goudas (and other treats) of **Samish Bay Cheese** (samish baycheese.com), available for tasting at its tiny store.

 THE DRIVE
Back at the Bow Hill Rd–Chuckanut Dr intersection, take the W Bow Hill Rd through the pinprick community of Edison, whose artisan bread store and Tweets Café merit a quick stopover. Continue south on the ruler-straight Farm to Market Rd to busy SR 20, which you join briefly heading west before turning left onto the La Conner–Whitney Rd. This section of the drive is 16 miles.

 04 LA CONNER
Celebrated for its tulips, wild turkeys, erudite writer's colony and (among other culinary treats) soccer-ball-sized cinnamon buns, La Conner's myriad attractions are hard to categorize. Jammed with gift shops and classy B&Bs, it also has three decent museums; the best is the **Museum of Northwest Art** (monamuseum.org). The zenith of La Conner's cultural calendar is during the annual **Tulip Festival** and surrounding months, when the nearby fields are embellished with a colorful carpet of daffodils (March), tulips (April) and irises (May). To see the flowers in all their artistic glory, detour a few miles to the **Roozengaarde Display**

INTERURBAN TRAIL
For a break from the car, you can join Bellingham's fleece-wearing weekend warriors and savor a bit of Chuckanut Dr by bike along the 6-mile Interurban Trail, a deliciously flat former electric trolley bed that parallels the tarmac passing deep forest and lovely views of Chuckanut Bay to Larrabee State Park. **Fairhaven Bicycles** (fairhavenbicycles. com) will set you up with a bike ($25 for four hours) for the easy two-hour ride.

Garden (tulips.com), halfway between La Conner and Mt Vernon. This renowned 3-acre garden plants 250,000 tulip bulbs annually and, with Mt Baker in the background, photo opportunities abound.

 THE DRIVE
Retrace your tracks north to SR 20 and turn left with the Anacortes traffic toward the San Juan Islands ferry terminal. After crossing the Swinomish Channel, turn left to stay on SR 20, following signage to Whidbey Island. Deception Pass is 13 miles from La Conner. You're now on Fidalgo Island, separated from the mainland by a narrow sea channel.

05 DECEPTION PASS
Emerging from the flat pastures of Fidalgo Island, Deception Pass leaps out like a mini Grand Canyon, its precipitous cliffs overlooked by a famous bridge made all the more dramatic by the sight of the churning, angry water below. The bridge consists of two steel arches that span Canoe Pass and Deception Pass, with a central support on Pass Island between the two. Visitors to the 5.5-sq-mile **Deception Pass State Park** (parks.state. wa.us/497) usually introduce themselves to the spectacular

land- and seascape by parking at the shoulders on either end and walking across the bridge. Built during the 1930s by the Civilian Conservation Corps, the bridge was considered an engineering feat in its day. Besides the dramatic bridge overviews, the park's attractions include over 15 miles of saltwater shoreline and 27 miles of forest trails. **Deception Pass Tours** (deceptionpasstours.com) organizes jet-boat tours through the turbulent waters daily.

 THE DRIVE
Deception Pass disappears almost as quickly as it materialized and you're soon in the pastoral fields that characterize Whidbey Island. After passing the entrance to the Naval Air station on your right, you'll skirt the rather ugly mall infestations of Oak Harbor. Traffic lights will slow your progress. Keep on SR 20 to Ebey's Landing, 16 miles from Deception Pass.

06 EBEY'S LANDING
The nation's first National Historic Reserve, listed in 1978, was created in order to preserve Whidbey Island's historical heritage from the encroaching urbanization that had already partly engulfed Oak Harbor. Still 90% privately owned,

Ebey's Landing (nps.gov/ebla) comprises 17,400 acres encompassing working farms, four historic blockhouses, two state parks and the small historic town of Coupeville. A series of interpretive boards shows visitors how the patterns of croplands, woods and even roads reflect the activities of those who have peopled this scenic landscape, from its earliest indigenous inhabitants to 19th-century settlers. The museum in Coupeville distributes a brochure on suggested driving and cycling tours through the reserve. Highly recommended is the 3.6-mile **Bluff Trail**, which starts from a small parking area at the end of Ebey Rd. The energetic can walk or cycle here from

Photo opportunity

The daffodil and tulip fields around La Conner are the best this side of Holland.

Coupeville, thus crossing the island at one of its narrowest points.

 THE DRIVE
Veer off SR 20 just past Penn Cove to visit Coupeville, just 2.5 miles north.

07 COUPEVILLE
Tiny Coupeville is Whidbey Island personified: fresh mussels and clams, old-world B&Bs, historic clapboard shop fronts, and instant access to a National Historical Reserve. Call in at the **Island County Historical Society Museum** for the lowdown on Washington State's second-oldest settlement (founded in 1852) and walking-tour maps of the town's handsome vintage homes.

 THE DRIVE
SR 20 veers east at the southern end of Ebey's Landing toward the Keystone Ferry and Fort Casey State Park. The latter was part of an early 1900s military defense system and features old cement batteries, tunnels and a lighthouse. Continue south on SR 525 through Freeland to Bayview, where you take a left for Langley, 26 miles from Coupeville.

08 LANGLEY
Langley, like Coupeville, is a small seafront community that is little changed since the late 19th century. Encased in its attractive historical center are small cafes, antique furniture shops, funky boutiques and a couple of decent B&Bs. While there's little to do here activity-wise, Langley provides a perfect antidote to the hustle and bustle of nearby Seattle and is a great place to relax and unwind.

Langley is 8 miles north of **Clinton** and the 20-minute ferry service from **Mukilteo** (wsdot.com/ferries), making this the closest of the Whidbey Island communities to the urban areas of northern Seattle.

2009FOTOFRIENDS/SHUTTERSTOCK ©

Ebey's Landing

08

WASHINGTON

Cascade Drive

BEST FOR HIKING

The Maple Pass Loop Trail from Rainy Pass

DURATION	DISTANCE	GREAT FOR
4–5 days	350 miles / 563km	Outdoors

BEST TIME TO GO	June to September when roads are snow-free and passable.

Leavenworth

Nature defies modern engineering in the North Cascades, where high-altitude roads succumb to winter snow storms, and the names of the mountains – Mt Terror, Mt Fury, Forbidden Peak – whisper forebodingly. Less scary are the scattered settlements, small towns with eclectic distractions such as Bavarian Leavenworth and 'Wild West' Winthrop. Fill up the tank, put on your favorite Springsteen track and prepare for one of the rides of your life

Link Your Trip

7 Chuckanut Drive & Whidbey Island

For a break from the mountain madness, veer north in Burlington to Bellingham and sample the coastal and pastoral joys of Puget Sound.

12 Mt Baker & Lummi Island

For more mountain madness, head north to Bellingham and then inland into another North Cascadian wilderness.

01 EVERETT

This drive incorporates four-fifths of the popular 'Cascade Loop.' You can complete the other fifth by taking in the second half of the trip through Whidbey Island. There's not much to detain you in Everett, the route's starting point, 30 miles north of Seattle. It's known mainly for its Boeing connections and as the genesis of countless Seattle-region traffic jams. Head directly east and don't stop until Stevens Pass.

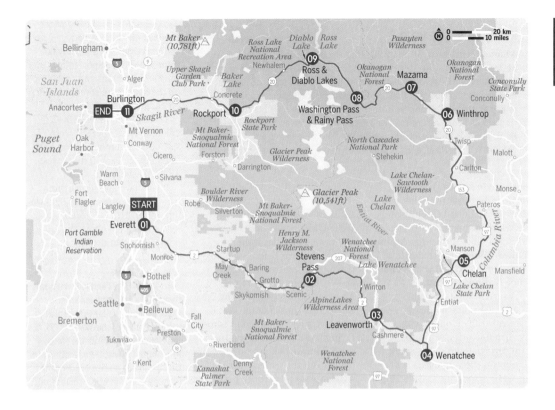

 THE DRIVE
Everett marks the starting point of US 2, a 2579-mile cross-continental road that terminates in Maine. Crossing I-5, the route, which parallels the Great Northern Railway and Skykomish River for much of its journey, passes the towns of Startup, Sultan and Index, climbing toward Stevens Pass, 66 miles away. There are a number of drive-through espresso huts en route.

02 STEVENS PASS
Accessible year-round thanks to its day-use **ski area** (stevenspass.com), Stevens Pass was only 'discovered' by white settlers as recently as 1890. Despite its lofty vantage – at

4061ft it is over 1000ft higher than Snoqualmie Pass – it was chosen for the Great Northern railroad's cross-Cascade route, but you won't see any train tracks here. Instead, the railway burrows underneath the pass via North America's longest rail tunnel (7.8 miles). The long-distance Pacific Crest Trail also crosses the highway here. Tempted?

 THE DRIVE
From Stevens Pass the descent begins immediately with subtle changes in the vegetation; the cedars and hemlocks of the western slopes are gradually replaced by pine, larch and spruce. For 35 miles, the road threads through the steep-sided Tumwater

canyon alongside the turbulent Wenatchee River. Suddenly, German-style houses start to appear against an eerily familiar alpine backdrop.

03 LEAVENWORTH
Blink hard and rub your eyes. This isn't some strange Germanic hallucination. This is Leavenworth, a former lumber town that underwent a Bavarian makeover in the 1960s after the re-routing of the cross-continental railway threatened to put it permanently out of business. Swapping loggers for tourists, Leavenworth today has successfully reinvented itself as a traditional *Romantische Strasse* village, right down to the

KEROUAC & THE VOID

A turnout at milepost 135 on US 20 offers the drive's only roadside views of Desolation Peak. The peak's lookout tower was famously home to Zen-influenced Beat writer Jack Kerouac who, in 1956, spent 63 days here in splendid isolation, honing his evolving Buddhist philosophy, raging at 'the Void' of nearby Hozomeen Mountain (also visible from the turnout) and penning drafts of *Desolation Angels*. It was the last time Kerouac would enjoy such anonymity; the following year saw the publication of *On the Road*, and his propulsion to the status of literary icon.

beer and bratwurst. *The Sound of Music*–style setting helps, as does the fact that Leavenworth serves as the main activity center for sorties into the nearby **Alpine Lakes Wilderness** (recreation. gov/permits/233273) and **Wenatchee National Forest**.

A surreal stroll through the gabled alpine houses of Leavenworth's Front St with its dirndl-wearing waitstaff, wandering accordionists and European cheesemongers is one of Washington state's oddest, but most endearing, experiences. For white-water rafting trips, call by **Osprey Rafting Co** (ospreyrafting.com).

THE DRIVE

The 22 miles between Leavenworth and Wenatchee highlight one of the most abrupt scenery changes in the state. One minute you're in quasi-Bavaria surrounded by crenellated alpine peaks, the next you're in a sprawled couldn't-be-anywhere-but-America town amid bald hills and a wide river valley. East of Leavenworth, US 2 shares the road briefly with US 97.

04 WENATCHEE

Fruit stands start peppering the highway soon after you leave Leavenworth, paving your entry into Wenatchee, the self-proclaimed Apple Capital of the World. Something of an ugly sister after cute Leavenworth, Wenatchee's a place to go local and taste the apples from the nearby orchards before swinging north. The best fruit stands enliven US 2/97 on the way to Chelan. As an overture to your tasting experience, check out the Washington Apple Commission Visitors Center (bestapples.com) on the way into town, where you can bone up on the relative merits of a Gala versus a Braeburn over a surprisingly interesting video.

THE DRIVE

US 2/97 plies the east side of the Columbia River for 39 miles between Wenatchee and Chelan. This is one of the best places to 'shop' at impromptu seasonal fruit outlets run by enterprising local farmers who haul their freshly plucked produce from the nearby fields and orchards to sell roadside from semi-permanent stores, carts or just plain old boxes.

05 CHELAN

Lake Chelan shelters some of the nation's cleanest water and has consequently become one of Washington's premier water recreation areas. The place is packed in summer, with speedboats, Jet Skis and power-craft battling it out for their own private slice of water. To avoid any high-speed collisions, try renting a kayak from Lake Rider Sports (lakeridersportschelan.com) and paddling up the lake to see some undiluted Cascadian nature firsthand.

There are public beaches at Lakeside Park, near the west side of Chelan town, and at Lake Chelan State Park, 9 miles west on S Lakeshore Rd.

If you have kids, don't think they'll let you sneak past Slidewaters Water Park (slidewaters.com), located on a hill above the *Lady of the Lake* boat dock.

THE DRIVE

Rejoin US 97 and follow it north through the grand coulees of the Columbia River Valley to the small town of Pateros. From here SR 153, aka the Methow Hwy, tracks the Methow River north to Twisp. At a junction with US 20 turn left, and continue on the highway into Winthrop, 61 miles from Chelan.

06 WINTHROP

Winthrop is – along with Leavenworth – one of two themed towns on this Cascade Drive. Once a struggling mining community, it avoided ghost town status in the 1960s when it was made over to look like a cowboy settlement out of the Wild West. Although on paper it sounds like a corny Hollywood gambit, the Gary Cooper touches feel surprisingly authentic. Winthrop's *High Noon* shopfronts hide a genuine frontier spirit (the road ends in winter not far beyond here), along with some fantastic accommodations and places to eat.

The facades of downtown Winthrop are so realistic that it's easy to miss the collection of

Maple Pass Loop Trail (p65)

homesteader cabins that make up the **Shafer Museum** (shafermuseum.org). But best of all is the unmissable **Sun Mountain Lodge**, a sporting and relaxation dreamscape 10 miles out of town overlooking the valley.

THE DRIVE
Out of Winthrop, SR 20 enters the most bucolic and endearing stretch of the Methow Valley. Here, the broad valley floor, scattered with farms, gives little hint of the jagged wilderness that lies beyond. If you thought Winthrop was small, don't blink when, in 14 miles, you reach Mazama, a small cluster of wooden buildings reminiscent of a gunslinger movie.

Photo Opportunity
View from the Sun Mountain Lodge.

07 MAZAMA
The last outpost before the raw, desolate, occasionally terrifying North Cascades, Mazama's half-dozen wooden abodes sit at the western end of the Methow Valley. Fuel up on brownies at the Mazama Store (themazamastore.com), a deli/espresso bar for outdoorsy locals that's a great place to pick up trail tips.

THE DRIVE
You'll be working through your gears soon after Mazama as the North Cascade Mountains start to close in. This part of US 20 is unlike any other trans-Cascade road. Not only is the scenery more spectacular, but the road itself (closed November to May) is a major engineering feat. You have 22 miles to enjoy it before reaching Rainy Pass.

08 WASHINGTON PASS & RAINY PASS
Venture less than 100yd from your car at the Washington Pass overlook (5477ft) and you'll be rewarded with fine views of the towering Liberty Bell and its Early Winter Spires, while the highway drops below you in ribbonlike loops. By the time the highway reaches Rainy Pass (4875ft) a couple of miles further

Diablo Lake

west, the air has chilled and you're well into the high country, a hop and a skip from the drive's highest hiking trails. The 6.2-mile **Maple Pass Loop Trail** is a favorite, climbing 2150ft to aerial views over jewel-like Lake Ann. The epic Pacific Crest Trail also crosses US 20 nearby, so keep an eye open for wide-eyed and bushy-bearded through-hikers popping out of the undergrowth. Perhaps the best choice if you want to shake the crowds is the excellent climb up to Easy Pass, hardly 'easy,' but offering spectacular views of Mt Logan and the Fisher Basin below.

THE DRIVE
Surrounded by Gothic peaks, the North Cascades Scenic Hwy makes a big swing north shadowing Granite Creek and then Ruby Creek, where it swings back west and, 20 miles from Rainy Pass, enters the Ross Lake National Recreation Area near Ruby Arm.

09 ROSS & DIABLO LAKES
The odd thing about much of the landscape on this trip is that it's unnatural, born from the construction of three huge dams that still supply Seattle with a large share of its electricity. The wilderness that surrounds it, however, is the rawest you'll get outside Alaska. Ross Lake was formed in the 1930s after the building of the eponymous dam. It stretches north 23

miles into Canada. Soon after the Ross Lake overlook, a path leads from the road to the dam. You'll see the Ross Lake Resort floating on the other side.

A classic photo op comes a couple of miles later at the **Diablo Lake overlook**. The turquoise lake is the most popular part of the park, offering beaches, gorgeous views and a boat launch at Colonial Creek Campground (nps.gov), with nearby hikes to Thunder Knob and Thunder Creek.

THE DRIVE
From Diablo, head west alongside the sinuous Gorge Reservoir on US 20. Pass through Newhalem (where you can stop at the North Cascades Visitor Center). Look out for rafters, floaters and bald eagles along the Skagit River.

10 ROCKPORT
As the valley widens further you'll touch down in Rockport. A 10-mile stretch of the Skagit River is a wintering ground for over 600 bald eagles who come here from November to early March to feast on spawning salmon. January is the best time to view them, ideally on a winter float trip with **Skagit River Guide Service** (skagitriverfishingguide.com), whose boats use propane heat and are equipped with comfy cushioned seats. Three-hour trips run from mid-November to early February.

THE DRIVE
From Rockport, head west for 37 miles on US 20 through the Cascade Mountain foothills and the ever-broadening Skagit River Valley to the small city of Burlington, which sits just east of busy I-5.

11 BURLINGTON
The drive's end, known as the 'Hub City,' is not a 'sight' in itself (unless you like shopping malls), although the settlement's location in the heart of the Skagit River Valley means it acts as a hub for nearby attractions, including the tulip fields of La Conner, Chuckanut Dr (which officially ends here) and the San Juan Islands.

09

WASHINGTON

Mt Rainier Scenic Byways

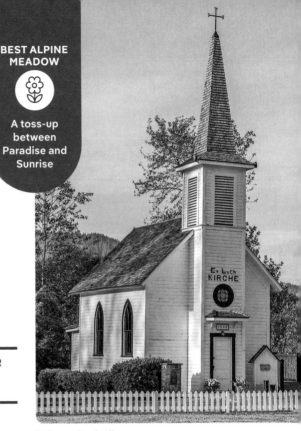

BEST ALPINE MEADOW

A toss-up between Paradise and Sunrise

Lutheran church, Elbe

DURATION	DISTANCE	GREAT FOR
2–3 days	570km / 354 miles	Families, Outdoors

BEST TIME TO GO	June to October, when alpine flowers bloom

Wrapped in a 368-sq-mile national park, and standing 2000ft higher than anything else in the Pacific Northwest, Rainier is a mountain of biblical proportions. Circumnavigate it by car and you'll swap the urban melee of Seattle for forest-covered mountain foothills strafed with huge trees and imbued with Native American myth. Closer to Paradise, flower meadows shimmer beneath Rainier's summit during an intense summer season.

Link Your Trip

10 Mt St Helens Volcano Trail

A logical link and an easy one given the proximity of the two mountains – Packwood, near Rainier's Ohanapecosh entrance, serves both drives.

3 Mountains to Sound Greenway

Seattle is the finish point of this roller-coaster drive, which is equally spectacular if done in reverse.

01 SEATTLE

Seattle is an appropriate place to start this epic circuit around what locals refer to reverentially as 'the Mountain.' Before heading off, take some time to walk around, seeking out the soul of the city at Pike Place Market. On the days when Rainier reveals itself from the cloudy heavens (a minority annually), you can also wander down to the waterfront for a glimpse of the high-altitude glories to come.

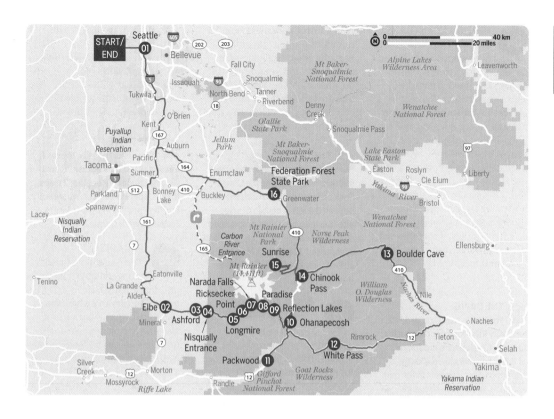

 THE DRIVE
There is little to delay you beyond Seattle until the tiny town of Elbe, 72 miles away. Drive south on I-5 to exit 154A, then east on I-405, and south again on SR 167 and SR 161. Just southwest of Eatonville, SR 161 merges with SR 7; follow this road into Elbe on the cusp of the national park.

02 ELBE
The pinprick settlement of Elbe has two claims to fame: its tiny white **Lutheran church** built by German immigrants in 1906 (and positively ancient by Pacific Northwest standards) and the heritage **Mt Rainier Scenic Railroad** (mtrainierrailroad.com) that

runs summer steam trains between Elbe and Mineral (7 miles south). Trips depart three times daily from May to September. Aping the railway theme is the **Hobo Inn & Diner** (rrdiner. com/the-hobo-inn), whose restaurant, bar and rooms all inhabit vintage, but lovingly tended, cabooses (train carriages).

 THE DRIVE
From Elbe take SR 706 (the National Park Hwy) 8 miles due east to Ashford.

 03 ASHFORD
Situated a couple of miles outside the busy Nisqually entrance, Ashford is

the national park's main service center with some standard accommodations, an info center and **Whittaker's Motel & Bunkhouse**, a hostel-cafe conceived by legendary local mountaineer Lou Whittaker in the early 1990s. It would be heresy to leave town without popping inside for an espresso before grabbing brunch (or lunch) down the road at the **Copper Creek Inn**, where the wild blackberry pies have fuelled many a successful summit attempt.

 THE DRIVE
Two miles east of Ashford on SR 706 you'll encounter the park entrance gate.

04 NISQUALLY ENTRANCE

The southwestern Nisqually entrance (named for the nearby river, which in turn is named after a local Native American tribe) is the busiest in **Mt Rainier National Park** (nps.gov/mora) and the only year-round entry gate. The simple entrance arch was built in 1922. Pay your park fee at the ticket window. As you drive through the entrance, you'll notice how, almost immediately, the trees appear denser and older. Many of these moss-covered behemoths date back over 700 years and measure up to 200ft in height.

THE DRIVE
Follow the road alongside the Nisqually River for a couple of miles to Kautz Creek, where the summit of Rainier appears like a ghostly apparition. Six miles east of the park entrance, you'll reach Longmire.

05 LONGMIRE

Worth a stop to stretch your legs or gain an early glimpse of Rainier's mossy old-growth forest, Longmire was the brainchild of a certain James Longmire who first came here in 1883 during a climbing trip when he noticed the hot mineral springs that bubbled up in a lovely meadow opposite the present-day National Park Inn. He and his family returned the following year and established Longmire's Medicinal Springs, and in 1890 he built the Longmire Springs Hotel. Since 1917 the National Park Inn has stood on this site – built in classic 'parkitecture' style – and is complemented by a small store, the tiny **Longmire Informa-tion Center & Museum** and a number of important trailheads. For a laid-back look at some old-growth forest and pastoral meadows, try the **Trail of the Shadows** loop, a 0.8-mile circuit that begins across the road from the museum.

THE DRIVE
After Longmire the road slowly starts to climb, passing the Cougar Rock campground and Christine Falls, both on the left. A couple of miles after the falls, bear right onto a short stretch of summer-only one-way road (signposted 'Viewpoint') for a view stop at Ricksecker Point, 6.5 miles from Longmire.

06 RICKSECKER POINT

One of the park's premier viewpoints, beloved by photographers, professional or otherwise, Ricksecker Point is a fine place to study five of Rainier's 26 glaciers – Nisqually, Pyramid, Success, Kautz and Wilson. The summit you see here is actually a false one (Point Success); the obscured *true* summit is 257ft higher. Equally majestic to the southeast is the sawtoothed Tatoosh range.

THE DRIVE
Rejoin the main road and continue uphill for 2.5 miles.

07 NARADA FALLS

Eight miles east of Longmire, a parking area marks the starting point for a steep 0.2-mile trail that leads down through flowers and ferns to the misty 168ft Narada Falls. The falls, often embellished by brilliant rainbows, carry the Paradise River over a basalt cliff. In high season, expect to get a face-full of water spray and an earful of oohing and ahhing as this is the park's most popular waterfall. In winter the falls freeze over and attract daring ice-climbers.

THE DRIVE
Soon after the falls, the road forks; stay left for Paradise. Follow the winding asphalt for another 2 miles to the Upper Parking Lot, where you'll find the Paradise Inn and Henry M Jackson Visitor Center.

08 PARADISE

The daughter of park pioneer James Longmire unintentionally named this high mountain nirvana when she exclaimed what a paradise it was on visiting the spot for the first time in the 1880s. Suddenly, the area had a name, and a very apt one at that. One of the snowiest places on earth, 5400ft-high **Paradise** remains the park's most popular draw with its famous flower meadows backed by dramatic Rainier views on the days when the mountain decides to take its cloudy hat off.

Aside from hiding numerous trailheads and being the starting point for most summit hikes, Paradise guards the iconic Paradise Inn (built in 1916) and the informative **Henry M Jackson Visitor Center**. Park naturalists lead free interpretive hikes from the visitor center daily in summer, and snowshoe walks on winter weekends.

THE DRIVE
Drive out of the east end of the Paradise Upper Parking Lot, cross

the Paradise River (looking out for marmots) and descend the one-way road for 2 miles to a junction. Turn left and rejoin the main two-way road for 1.5 miles toward Reflection Lakes and Steven's Canyon.

09 REFLECTION LAKES

Rainier eyes itself in the mirror on calm cloudless days at Reflection Lakes, formed during a violent volcanic eruption nearly 6000 years ago. You can pull over for double-vision photos of the mountain framed by tufts of precious wildflowers. The main lake used to have a boat concession, but now it's deliciously tranquil bar the odd passing tour bus.

THE DRIVE

Avalanche chutes plague the U-shaped Steven's Canyon Rd in

Photo opportunity

Rainier's snow-topped summit reflected in Reflection Lakes.

winter, ensuring it remains closed outside peak season (unlike Paradise on the western side). Seen from above, the canyon is rather spectacular. Stop for a bird's-eye view a mile or so after Reflection Lakes before the trees close in. From here it's downhill to Ohanapecosh, 20 miles from the lakes.

10 OHANAPECOSH

Ohanapecosh (o-*ha*-nuh-peh-*kosh*) – the name means 'at the edge' – in the park's southeastern corner

is usually accessed by the small settlement of Packwood, 11 miles to the southwest on US 12, which harbors a small number of eating and sleeping options. Shoehorned between Mt Rainier and its two southern neighbors, Mt St Helens and Mt Adams, this is a good base for travelers wanting to visit two or more of the mountains. Just inside the Steven's Canyon gate, you'll find the 1.5-mile **Grove of the Patriarchs Trail**, one of the park's most popular short hikes. The trail explores a small island in the Ohanapecosh River replete with craning Douglas fir, cedar and hemlock trees, some of which are over 1000 years old. To reach the **Ohanapecosh Visitors Center**, turn right at the Steven's Canyon entrance onto SR 123 and drive 1.5 miles

TUSHAR KOLEY/SHUTTERSTOCK ©

Mt Rainier

south. Alternatively, you can hike down from the Grove of the Patriarchs.

THE DRIVE
Go right at the Steven's Canyon entrance and follow SR 123 south past the visitor center to the intersection with US 12. For Packwood, bear right for 11 miles.

11 PACKWOOD
A service center for Mt St Helens, Mt Rainier and the nearby ski area of White Pass, Packwood is what in the Old West they called a 'one-horse town.' A few low- to mid-ranking eating joints and accommodations glued to US 12 provide a good excuse to pull over and mingle with other road-trippers. Chin-waggers congregate at **Mountain Goat Coffee**, where you may run into a park ranger or two.

THE DRIVE
Retrace your route to the intersection of US 12 and SR 123. The 20-mile climb to White Pass begins here. Stop at a pullover soon after the intersection to appreciate the indelible sight of Mt Rainier as it appears briefly above the trees.

12 WHITE PASS
Higher than Snoqualmie and Stevens Passes to the north, White Pass carries a quieter, open-year-round road that, at various points, offers glimpses of three Cascadian volcanoes: Mt Rainier, Mt Adams and Mt St Helens. The pass itself, perched at 4500ft, is home to an understated **ski area** (skiwhitepass.com), which has one condo complex for overnighters. Otherwise, people stay

FOTO-JAGLA.DE/SHUTTERSTOCK ©

Wonderland Trail

SUMMER WONDERLAND

You've circumnavigated it in a car; now how about walking it? Rainier is not only encircled by a road; you can also hike around it via the long-distance **Wonderland Trail**. Laid out in 1915, the 93-mile-long precipitous path initially served as a patrol beat for park rangers and in the 1930s it was briefly earmarked as a paved ring road for cars. Fortunately, the plan never reached fruition and today the unbroken trail (which gains 21,000ft in cumulative elevation) is one of the most challenging and iconic hikes in the Pacific Northwest. You'll need food, camping gear, eight to 12 free days and a permit from the Longmire Information Center (p68) to do Wonderland. Longmire is a popular start point. There are 18 backcountry campgrounds en route; reservations ($20) are advisable in peak season (July and August). The official park page (nps.gov/mora) has more information.

in nearby Packwood or drive up for the day from Yakima.

THE DRIVE
A classic east–west Washington scenery shift kicks in soon after White Pass as you follow US 12 amid increasingly scattered trees and bald, steep-sided river coulees. At the intersection with SR 410, swing north on the Chinook Scenic Byway just west of the town of Naches to reach

Boulder Cave, 65 miles from White Pass.

13 BOULDER CAVE
Among the many excuses to pull over on this stretch of the Chinook Scenic Byway is Boulder Cave, a rarity in the relatively cave-free terrain of the Pacific Northwest and doubly unique due to its formation through a combination

of volcanic and erosive processes. A 2-mile round-trip trail built by the Civilian Conservation Corps in 1935 leads into the cave's murky interior, formed when Devil's Creek cut a tunnel through soft sedimentary rock, leaving hard volcanic basalt on top. Up to 50 rare big-eared bats hibernate in the cave each winter, when it is closed to the public. Bring a flashlight.

 THE DRIVE
Continue west and uphill toward Chinook Pass, 25 miles from Boulder Cave, as the air cools and the snowdrifts pile up roadside.

14 CHINOOK PASS
Closed until May and infested with lingering snowdrifts well into July, Chinook Pass towers at 5430ft on Rainier's eastern flank. The long-distance **Pacific Crest Trail** crosses the highway here on a pretty stone bridge, while nearby **Crystal Mountain** (skicrystal.com) comprises Washington's largest ski area and only bona fide overnight 'resort.' Rather than stop at the pass, cruise a few hundred yards further west to **Tipsoo Lake**, another reflective photographer's dream where a paved trail will return the blood to your legs.

THE DRIVE
From Tipsoo Lake the road winds down to relatively 'low' Cayuse Pass (4694ft). Turn north here and descend a further 1000ft in 3 miles to the turning for Mt Rainier's White River entrance. This is the gateway to Sunrise, 16 miles uphill via a series of switchbacks.

15 SUNRISE
Sunrise, at 6400ft, marks the park's highest road. Thanks to the superior elevation, the summer season is particularly short and snow can linger into July. It is also noticeably drier than Paradise, resulting in an interesting variety of subalpine vegetation, including masses of wildflowers. The views from Sunrise are famously spectacular and – aside from stunning close-ups of Rainier itself – you can also, quite literally, watch the weather roll in over the distant peaks of Mt Baker and Mt Adams. Similarly impressive is the glistening Emmons Glacier, which, at 4 sq miles, is the largest glacier in the contiguous USA. A trailhead directly across the parking lot from the **Sunrise Day Lodge** cafeteria provides access to **Emmons Vista**, with good views of Mt Rainier, Little Tahoma and the glacier. Nearby, the 1-mile **Sourdough Ridge Trail** leads to pristine subalpine meadows for stunning views over other volcanic giants.

THE DRIVE
Coast downhill to the White River entrance and turn north onto the Mather Memorial Pkwy in order to exit the park. In the small community of Greenwater on SR 410 you can load up with gas and food. Federation Forest State Park is 36 miles from Sunrise.

16 FEDERATION FOREST STATE PARK
Just when you thought you'd left ancient nature behind, up springs Federation Forest State Park, created by a foresighted women's group in the 1940s in order to preserve a rapidly diminishing stock of local old-growth forest from logging interests. Today its fir, spruce, hemlock and cedar trees cluster around the lackadaisical White River, while the **Catherine Montgomery Interpretive Center** (parks.state. wa.us/502) offers a rundown of the contrasting ecosystems of east and west Washington State. There's also a bookstore and 12 miles of trails, most of them family-friendly.

 DETOUR
Carbon River Entrance
Start: 16 Federation Forest State Park

The park's northwest entrance is its most isolated and undeveloped corner, with two unpaved (and unconnected) roads and little in the way of facilities, save a lone ranger station and the very basic **Ipsut Creek Campground**. But while the tourist traffic might be thin on the ground, the landscape lacks nothing in magnificence.

Named for its coal deposits, Carbon River is the park's wettest region and protects one of the few remaining examples of inland temperate rainforest in the contiguous USA. Dense, green and cloaked in moss, this verdant wilderness can be penetrated by a handful of interpretive trails that fan off the Carbon River Rd.

Getting here takes you part of the way back to Seattle. Take US 410W to 116S (Carbon River Rd) then turn left. After about 15.5 miles you'll come to the Carbon River ranger station just before the entrance.

Sunrise Day Lodge

10

WASHINGTON

Mt St Helens Volcano Trail

BEST FOR FAMILIES

Mt St Helens Visitor Center's interactive exhibits

DURATION	DISTANCE	GREAT FOR
3 days	589km / 366 miles	Nature

BEST TIME TO GO	July to October – the mountain's best sights and roads are open

Silver Lake Wetlands Trail

The name Mt St Helens has a fearful resonance for anyone who was alive on May 18, 1980, when a massive volcanic eruption set off the largest landslide in human history. Nearly 40 years later, you can drive through the embattled but slowly recovering landscape that makes up the Mt St Helens National Monument, stopping at interpretive centers that document the erstwhile environmental carnage. It's a unique, if sometimes disconcerting, ride.

Link Your Trip

9 Mt Rainier Scenic Byways

St Helens' taller, potentially more lethal mountain twin is easily accessible via its southeastern Ohanapecosh entrance.

11 Washington Wine Tour

Head east in Randle and continue on to Yakima on the cusp of a sunny valley full of grapes and wineries. Say no more.

01 CENTRALIA

The main reason to make this rather mundane mining and lumber town the starting point for your volcanic excursion is to stay at a converted brothel. The **Olympic Club Hotel** (mcmenamins.com/olympic-club) – a 'venue hotel' run by Portland's McMenamin brothers – dates from 1908 when it opened as a 'gentlemen's resort' designed to satisfy the various drinking, gambling and sexual vices of transient miners and loggers. In 1996 the turn-of-the-century building was taken

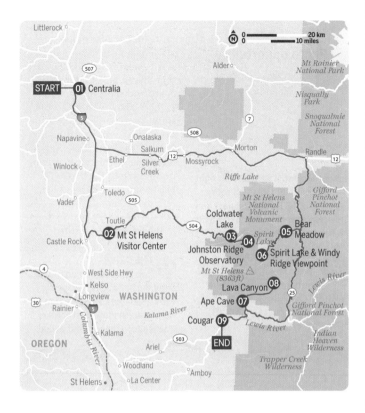

Mt St Helens National Volcanic Monument

Mt St Helens is one of only two National Volcanic Monuments in the nation. The unique park, which measures 110,000 acres, was set aside in 1982 and is mostly comprised of land in the so-called 'blast zone' – the plan being that anything inside the park boundary is to be left to recover as nature intends. The monument, which is closely monitored, acts like a massive outdoor scientific laboratory.

over by the McMenamins, who restored the brothel to its former glory complete with creaking floorboards, Tiffany lamps and art deco murals (but without the nighttime shenanigans).

THE DRIVE
Steer south out of Centralia on I-5 for 32 miles to exit 49, where you proceed east 6 miles on SR 504, aka the Spirit Lake Memorial Hwy.

02 MT ST HELENS VISITOR CENTER
Situated 5 miles east of Castle Rock on SR 504, the **Mt St Helens Visitor Center** (parks.state.wa.us/245) at Silver Lake is the best introduction

to the monument. There's a classic film and various exhibits, including a mock-up of the volcano; duck beneath the cone for displays on the subterranean workings of the mountain. Outside is the mile-long **Silver Lake Wetlands Trail**. If you're in need of a break, try the Fire Mountain Grill located on the 504.

THE DRIVE
Continue east on the Spirit Lake Memorial Hwy (SR 504) until you get to the Forest Learning Center at milepost 33. The center runs an interesting film about the eruption. Soon after, you enter the blast zone near Elk Rock viewpoint.

About 16 miles from Hoffstadt Bluffs you'll reach Coldwater Lake.

03 COLDWATER LAKE
You're now categorically in the blast zone. Coldwater Lake, 43 miles east of Castle Rock, was created in 1980 when water backed up behind a dam caused by debris brought down by the eruption. The recreation area here (rest rooms, phone, boat launch) is the starting point of the 0.6-mile **Birth of a Lake Trail** (No 246), a paved interpretive hike that demonstrates the regrowth of vegetation in the area. Look out for beavers and their handiwork.

THE DRIVE
Follow the increasingly winding Spirit Lake Memorial Hwy (SR 504) 5.8 miles through the denuded landscape to the end of the road.

04 JOHNSTON RIDGE OBSERVATORY

Situated at the end of SR 504 and looking directly into the mouth of the crater, this famous **observatory** (fs.usda.gov) has exhibits that take a more scientific angle than the Mt St Helens Visitor Center, depicting the geological events surrounding the 1980 blast and how they advanced the science of volcano forecasting and monitoring. The paved 1-mile round-trip **Eruption Trail** (No 201) offers once-in-a-lifetime views over toward the crater.

THE DRIVE
Retrace your steps 52 miles to Castle Rock. Go north on I-5 and, at exit 68, east on US 12. Refuel in the

Photo opportunity

Mountain view from Bear Meadow.

tiny settlement of Randle. Turn right off US 12 onto SR 131, which soon becomes USFS Rd 25. Just past Iron Creek Falls, turn right onto USFS Rd 99. This section is 124 miles total.

05 BEAR MEADOW

Bear Meadow, just outside the blast zone, is where Gary Rosenquist took his iconic photographs of Mt St Helens erupting on May

18, 1980. The four quick-succession shots that Rosenquist started snapping at 8:32am are reproduced on an interpretive board and show the mountain, 11 miles away, with its northern slopes literally sliding away. Rosenquist, who was camping in the area at the time, was lucky and got out alive, driving north through thick ash. The blast zone stopped less than a mile away from the meadow, as the stands of still healthy trees in the foreground testify.

THE DRIVE
Two miles further on, you'll enter the blast zone marked by eerie dead trees. Press on 12 miles from Bear Meadow, past various trailheads to the end of the road.

MICHELLE BAUMBACH/SHUTTERSTOCK ©

Johnston Ridge

SPIRIT LAKE & WINDY RIDGE VIEWPOINT

06 More remote but less crowded than Johnston Ridge is the harder-to-reach **Windy Ridge viewpoint** on the mountain's eastern side, accessed via USFS Rd 99. Here visitors get a palpable, if eerie, sense of the destruction that the blast wrought, with felled forests, desolate mountain slopes and the rather surreal sight of lifeless **Spirit Lake**, once one of the premier resorts in the South Cascades. There are toilets and a snack bar at the viewpoint parking lot, which is often closed until June. More than 350 steps ascend the hillside for close-up views of the crater 5 miles away. A stubbly green carpet covers the ridge slopes in summer as dwarf plants struggle back to life more than 30 years later. A few miles down the road you can descend 600ft on the 1.5-mile **Harmony Trail** (No 224) that leads to Spirit Lake.

THE DRIVE
Retrace your steps to USFS Rd 25; turn right (south) and drive over Elk Pass and past the Clearwater viewpoint to Pine Creek information center. Turn west on USFS Rd 90 and drive along the north shore of Swift Reservoir before going

right onto USFS Rd 83 and left onto USFS Rd 8303, a total distance of 56 miles.

APE CAVE

07 Ape Cave, on the south flank of Mt St Helens, is a 2-mile-long lava tube formed 2000 years ago by a lava flow that followed a deep watercourse. It's the longest lava tube in the western hemisphere. Hikers can walk and scramble the length of the cave on either the 0.8-mile **Lower Ape Cave Trail** or the 1.5-mile **Upper Ape Cave Trail**, which requires a certain amount of scrambling over rock piles and narrower passages. Bring your own light source. Free ranger-led explorations depart from **Apes' Headquarters**, located at the entrance to the caves, several times daily in summer.

THE DRIVE
Retrace your route to USFS Rd 83. Turn left and drive to the road's terminus at Lava Canyon, 14 miles from Ape Cave.

LAVA CANYON

08 The geology class continues on Mt St Helens' southeast side. Although the mountain's 1980 lateral blast blew north, the heat of the massive explosion melted its eastern glaciers and created a

huge mud flow. Water, boulders and trees came flooding down **Muddy Creek**, scouring it out and revealing much older lava basalt underneath. This fascinating geological demolition can be seen at Lava Canyon, where a short 0.5-mile **interpretive trail** leads through new-growth trees to an overlook. To get closer, take a steeper path that zigzags down into the canyon, which you can cross on a bouncy suspension bridge built in 1993. **Lava Canyon Falls** crashes below. The trail continues further along the Canyon (though it's extremely exposed) to Smith Creek.

THE DRIVE
Track back along USFS Rd 83 to the junction with USFS Rd 90. Turn right (west) and head into the small settlement of Cougar, 21 miles from Lava Canyon, on Yale Lake.

COUGAR

09 A 'town' with virtually no residents, Cougar (population 120-ish), the nearest settlement to Mt St Helens, was mercifully spared the carnage of the 1980 eruption – though it was temporarily evacuated. Since 1953 it has sat on the shores of **Yale Lake**, a reservoir created after the construction of the Yale Dam on the Lewis River. It is a good pit stop courtesy of its **Lone Fir Resort & Café**, convenience store (with gas), grill restaurant and peaceful lakeside tranquility. Climbers making a St Helens summit bid often psyche up here.

MT ST HELENS INSTITUTE

The not-for-profit **Mt St Helens Institute** (mshinstitute.org) in Amboy is one of the most admired educational and conservation groups in the nation. Look out for the institute's expert volunteers at various interpretive sites around the mountain, where they organize hikes, talks, films and fundraisers, all related to the volcano and its geology.

11

WASHINGTON

Washington Wine Tour

DURATION	DISTANCE	GREAT FOR
3 days	225km / 140 miles	Food & drink

BEST TIME TO GO	April to October for weather and flowers

American Hop Museum

Napa? Too crowded. France? Too far. Fortunately, the Yakima and Walla Walla valleys have emerged as major wine-making destinations. Learn about terroir and viticulture, or dedicate yourself to sampling lush reds and crisp whites in your search for your favorite appellation (you can always spit to manage consumption). For now this is still an unpretentious, small-town scene with bucolic scenery all around, but the wines are nothing less than extraordinary.

Link Your Trip

1 On the Trail of Lewis & Clark

From Pasco, you can head west through the Yakima Valley or east to Walla Walla.

3 Mountains to Sound Greenway

Drive 36 miles from Yakima to Ellensburg via the Yakima River valley.

01 YAKIMA

Yakima is a sprawling, flat mid-century-feeling city that doesn't have much allure, but it's a pleasant enough place to start your trip. It's also home to some of the only bubbles available in this region. Start the day at **Treveri Cellars** (trevericellars.com), whose sparkling wines are so good they've been served at the White House.

THE DRIVE

From I-82E, take exit 50 toward Toppenish. Turn right on Buena Way off the exit and continue about 3 miles to

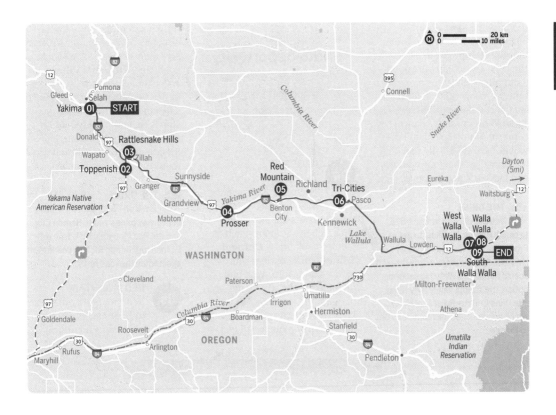

1st St, the main drag of downtown Toppenish.

 TOPPENISH
02 Toppenish makes up for its lack of wineries with a kooky personality. The antique, distinctly Wild West brick-and-timber buildings are further beautified by some 70 **murals** within the downtown area. Scenes include Native Americans, cowboys and early settlers as well as artistic hat-tipping to the majority Latinx population. Country-and-western music is pumped via loudspeaker into the streets.Stop at the **American Hop Museum** (americanhop museum.org) to think about beer

for a while, and the **Yakama Nation Museum & Cultural Center** (yakamamuseum.com) to see crafts from the area's original artists.

THE DRIVE
Go back toward I-82E but instead of getting on the freeway, cross over it. Cross the Yakima Valley Hwy, then at the crossroads turn left (this is still Buena Way). Take the third right on Highland Rd, up a hill through orchards to Bonair Winery in Rattlesnake Hills, 18 miles from Toppenish.

DETOUR
Yakama Scenic Byway
Start: 2 Toppenish
This byway leads 63 miles down US

97 from Toppenish to Maryhill. You'll pass through native Yakama country and up through the desolate Simcoe Mountains. Highlights between them include the **St John's Monastery & Bakery** (stjohnmonastery.org) and **Goldendale Observatory State Park** (goldendaleobservatory.com).

 RATTLESNAKE HILLS
03 Lazing next to the tiny town of Zillah, the warm, rolling Rattlesnake Hills grow thick with grapevines and apple orchards. Nary a rattlesnake has been found in recent memory but you will find plenty of smooth and delicious Bordeaux reds at any of the dozen or so wineries. Start at wonderfully welcoming **Bonair Winery**

(bonairwine.com), one of the oldest in the area, where you're heartily encouraged to picnic on the lawn overlooking the pond – or grab a table in front of the buttery-yellow chateau for tapas. Just north of Bonair, **Silver Lake Winery** (silverlakewinery.com) sits at the top of a hill overlooking the whole valley, making it a prime location for weddings and fancy-schmancy events.

THE DRIVE
You can choose to take I-82E to exit 80 (about 30 miles) to get to Prosser, or take the Yakima Valley Hwy, which leads more slowly through scenic farmlands. With this second option, the Yakima Valley Hwy turns into Wine Country Rd at Grandview, which parallels I-82 and continues on to Prosser.

Photo opportunity
Terra Blanca – views over grapevines from a grand villa.

04 PROSSER
The historic center of Prosser is a small grid of brick buildings worthy of a 1950s-era movie set – it's a choice stop for lunch at picture-book pretty **Chinook Wines** (chinookwines.com), with a flower-filled yard and picnic area. The winery has been in operation since 1983 and is known for its classy Chardonnay and sauvignon blanc. It's just off Wine Country Rd to the east out of town. Prosser sprawls less scenically across I-82, where you'll find **Vintner's Village**, a collection of excellent wineries in flat, housing-community-like surroundings. If you make one stop here, make it **Airfield Estates** (airfieldwines.com), known for esteemed whites including a zesty unoaked chardonnay.

THE DRIVE
Back on I-82E, another 17 miles of highway brings you to Benton City and the Red Mountain AVA. Take exit 96 then turn left on SR 224, veering left again when the road forks.

05 RED MOUNTAIN
Red Mountain, just next to Benton City, is the tiniest American Viticultural

BPPERRY/STOCK/GETTY IMAGES ©

Vineyard, Red Mountain

Area (AVA) in the state, coveted for its vintages brought to perfection on sun-drenched slopes. It's a California-esque landscape of hills covered in vineyards, golden grass and sagebrush. Meander up N Sunset Rd, making your first stop at **Cooper Wine Company** (cooperwinecompany. com), whose L'Inizio Bordeaux blend is anything but boring. Next, sample the highly regarded Bordeaux blends at **Hedges Family Estate** (hedgesfamily estate.com) in a French-inspired mansion; then drive up further to **Tapteil Estate** (tapteil.com), where you'll find delicious syrah and cabernet sauvignons to sip over views of the valley. Last, take a detour to the grandest estate on this trip, **Terra Blanca** (terrablanca.com), on N DeMoss Rd, which runs parallel to N Sunset Rd toward Benton. Try the reds and dessert wines in the castle-like tasting room or out on the terrace overlooking manicured gardens, a pond, the valley and mountains.

THE DRIVE
It's about 12 miles from Red Mountain to Richland. Go back out to your friend I-82, take the I-182 exit toward Richland and then take exit 3. Turn right on Queensgate Dr and an immediate left onto Columbia Park Trail, then another left onto Tulip Lane.

06 TRI-CITIES
Next stop? The Tri-Cities: Richland, Kennewick and Pasco. Nicknamed the Tri-Windies for the pushy gusts of wind that scoot you into the tasting rooms, this trio of towns is home to another batch of wineries just off the freeway, among them **Barnard Griffin** (barnardgriffin.com). You don't have to ask if they've won any awards; the medals are practically used as decor.

THE DRIVE
Get ready for a change of scenery and wine style. Take US 12 south then east for about an hour to the Walla Walla Valley.

07 WEST WALLA WALLA
About 11 miles before you get to Walla Walla you'll find **L'Ecole No 41** (lecole.com). The building alone, an early-1900s schoolhouse, is worth a visit, but the syrah and Bordeaux earn an easy 'A' among wine lovers. Back on the road about another mile toward Walla Walla is **Waterbrook Winery** (waterbrook. com) with an afternoon-devouring outdoor patio by a pond and authentic, mouthwatering tacos available on Friday and Saturday. Imbibe a long selection of wines in the fresh air.

THE DRIVE
Continue east on US 12 for about 10 miles into central Walla Walla. The center of town is Main St and 2nd Ave.

08 WALLA WALLA
Walla Walla, more than any Washington town, has fermented the ingredients to support a burgeoning wine culture, including a historic Main St, a handsome college, a warm summer climate and a growing clutch of wine-loving restaurants. If it's time to let the pedal off the metal for a day or two, this is where to do it. The downtown area has lots of tasting rooms. A good one if you're on a stroll is **Otis Kenyon** (otiskenyonwine.com) – ask about its quirky story.

THE DRIVE
Take SR 125 south out of town and turn right on Old Milton Hwy. In just a couple of miles you'll find yourself passing numerous orchards and wineries.

DETOUR
Dayton & Waitsburg
Start: **08** Walla Walla

Dayton (32 miles north of Walla Walla on US 12) and Waitsburg (21 miles from Walla Walla on the same highway) are a pair of quiet small towns with well-preserved buildings and a handful of places to eat and drink – though the expected boom in chic eateries from a few years back doesn't seem to have panned out, and several pioneering establishments have closed. They're more ghost towns than lively hubs now, but the countryside is pretty enough to make it well worth driving out.

09 SOUTH WALLA WALLA
The southern part of the Walla Walla wine-growing region is the most scenic, with wineries off the highway and tucked within apple orchards or within their own vineyards. Fabulous wines are served in a low-key garden patio and tasting room (actually a part of the owner's home) at **Dusted Valley Wines**. Just down the road is the not-to-be-missed **Amavi Cellars** (amavi cellars.com), whose wines make headlines in the viticulture world. Indulge in its addictive syrah and cabernet sauvignon on the classy yet comfortable outdoor patio, admire the view out to the Blue Mountains and toast to the end of your tour.

12

WASHINGTON

Mt Baker & Lummi Island

BEST FOR HIKING

Heliotrope Ridge Trail

Lummi Island

DURATION	DISTANCE	GREAT FOR
1-2 days	135km / 84 miles	Outdoors

BEST TIME TO GO	Mid-July to September, when the whole road is open.

The 57-mile Mt Baker Scenic Byway that winds east from metropolitan Bellingham to the otherworldly flower meadows of Artist Point is one of the Northwest's most magic-invoking drives, replete with moss-draped forests and gurgling creeks. Affix Lummi Island onto the start of the trip with its slow-motion traffic and feisty insularity, and you have pretty much every facet the Pacific Northwest has to offer.

Link Your Trip

7 Chuckanut Drive & Whidbey Island

If you enjoyed Lummi Island, veer off along Chuckanut Drive for more pastoral scenery.

8 Cascade Drive

You'll find plenty more Cascade giants starting in Everett, 60 miles south down I-5

01 LUMMI ISLAND

Not technically one of the San Juan Islands but with them in spirit, Lummi acts as a bucolic buffer to the fast-spreading tentacles of American outlet-mall culture that plagues I-5. A slender green finger of land measuring approximately 9 miles long by 2 miles wide, and supporting a population of just under 1000, this tranquil dose of rural realism is home to the world's only reef-net salmon fishing operation, a pioneering agritourism project and an unhurried tempo of life best epitomized by the island's maximum speed

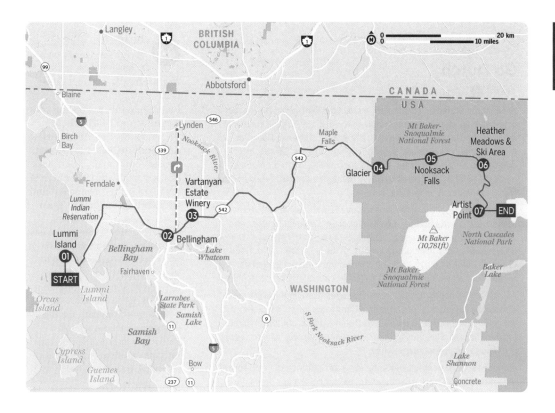

limit – a tortoise-like 25mph. One of the main reasons to come to Lummi is to sample the food at the reservations-only **Willows Inn** (willows-inn.com). The chefs forage for many of the locally grown ingredients, and the place has garnered international accolades in recent years.

🚗 THE DRIVE
Take the island's loop road to Lummi's small ferry terminal on the east shore. The five-minute crossing runs every 20 minutes (hourly at weekends) to Gooseberry Point on the mainland. From here, head north on Haxton Rd and right on Slater Rd to join I-5. Head south and exit to Bellingham, 17 miles from Gooseberry Point.

02 BELLINGHAM
Imagine a slightly less eccentric slice of Portland, Oregon, broken off and towed 250 miles to the north. Welcome to laid-back Bellingham, a green, liberal and famously livable settlement that has taken the libertine, nothing-is-too-weird ethos of Oregon's largest city and given it a peculiarly Washingtonian twist. Mild in both manners and weather, the 'city of subdued excitement,' as a local mayor once dubbed it, is historically four different towns – Fairhaven, Sehome, Whatcom and Bellingham – that amalgamated into a single metro area in the late 19th century. Despite vestiges of

an ugly industrial past along the waterfront, and a flirtation with an out-of-town 1980s mall development directed mainly toward bargain-hunting Canadians, Bellingham's downtown has been revitalized in recent years with intra-urban trails, independent food co-ops, fine brunch spots and – in genteel Fairhaven – a rejuvenated historic district. It's an ideal place to stretch your legs.

🚗 THE DRIVE
The Mt Baker Scenic Byway officially begins at exit 255 of I-5 on Sunset Dr, which, within a mile, becomes the Mt Baker Hwy. Here the road dips into the pastoral Baker foothills. At the Hannegan Rd intersection you can

DETOUR:

Go Dutch

START: ② BELLINGHAM

Washington State has an interesting stash of small towns that harbor a palpable European influence. Leavenworth, in the Eastern Cascades, draws in thousands of tourists annually with an authentic Bavarian look (not to mention its beer and sausages); Poulsbo, near Seattle, has a detectable Norwegian flavor. Lynden, meanwhile, located a few miles north of the Mt Baker Scenic Byway in the agricultural lowlands of the Nooksack Valley, is unmistakably Dutch.

First settled in the 1850s, the area received its first wave of Dutch settlers in the early 1900s – a steady trickle of Calvinist farmers who arrived from the Netherlands via brief stopovers in the Midwest. United by raspberries (the town produces 60% of the US crop), they formed a Christian Reform Church and set up mixed farms on the kind of flat pastoral fields that would have had Van Gogh reaching for his paint palette.

As well as competing for the prize of 'cleanest town in the US,' Lynden also excels in historical preservation. Handsome Front St includes a 72ft windmill, a mall with a canal, various Dutch eateries and the inspired **Lynden Pioneer Museum** (lyndenheritagemuseum.org), which eloquently catalogs the pioneer experience.

Rumor has it that people from as far away as California plan pie sorties to **Lynden Dutch Bakery** (lyndendutchbakery.com) a few doors down. Try the split-pea soup or humongous rhubarb and raspberry pie.

detour north to the town of Lynden. Otherwise, continue 6 miles to Noon Rd and turn north for half a mile.

03 VARTANYAN ESTATE WINERY

Wrong side of the Cascade Mountains for grape-growing, you're thinking. Think again! The **Vartanyan Estate Winery** (vewinery.com) is one of dozens of wineries that form the Puget Sound AVA (American Viticultural Area), the state's only wine-growing region west of the Cascade Mountains. The cool, wet, year-round climate here favors the sowing of mainly white grape varietals such

as siegerrebe and madeleine angevine. Wine-tasting here is a mellow, understated affair. Let curiosity get the better of you and check out Vartanyan's tasting room for a general sense of the region's offerings.

THE DRIVE

Retrace your steps south to the well-signposted Scenic Byway (SR 542), which tracks the North Fork of the Nooksack River from where it splits near Denning. Ignore various turnoffs in the small settlements of Kendall and Maple Falls, and continue due east to Glacier, 30 miles from Vartanyan Winery. Maple Falls is your last potential gas stop until you return.

04 GLACIER

A tiny service center and the last proper settlement before Mt Baker, Glacier is basically a ranger station, two restaurants, a ski shop and a small store. This is where SR 542 enters the **Mt Baker-Snoqualmie National Forest**. Consequently, many of Mt Baker's best trails start near here. A highlight is the 7.4-mile out-and-back **Heliotrope Ridge Trail**, which begins 8 miles down unpaved USFS Rd 39, 1 mile east of Glacier. The trail takes hikers from thick old-growth forest to flower-filled meadows and, ultimately, a breathtaking Coleman Glacier overlook. At the 2-mile point, the path for the Coleman Glacier ascent of Mt Baker branches to the left. Call into the excellent ranger station for maps, trail information and forest passes ($5).

THE DRIVE

You're now in the Mt Baker-Snoqualmie National Forest, where the trees tell a different story: tall moss-covered behemoths that look like ghostly old men sporting green beards. Keep straight on the highway for 6 miles to the Wells Creek Rd. Turn right here and follow the forest road for half a mile to a parking area and the Nooksack Falls viewpoint.

05 NOOKSACK FALLS

Powerful Nooksack Falls drops 175ft into a deep gorge. This was the site of one of the oldest hydropower facilities in the US, built in 1906 and abandoned in 1997. Sharp-eyed movie nerds will recognize it from one of the hunting scenes in the 1978 film, *The Deer Hunter*.

THE DRIVE

Rejoin the Scenic Byway and continue east paralleling the Nooksack River. Beyond milepost 48, the road leaves the river valley and starts to climb via a series of switchbacks. Mt Shuksan soon comes into view and at the road's 52 milepost you'll spy the Mt Baker Ski Area's White Salmon Day Lodge on the left, 12 miles from the falls.

06 HEATHER MEADOWS & SKI AREA

Receiving record-breaking annual snowfall and enjoying one of the longest seasons in the US, the **Mt Baker Ski Area** (mtbaker.us) prides itself on being the classic 'nonresort' ski area and a rustic antidote to Whistler in Canada. While luxury facilities are thin on the

Photo opportunity

Mt Shuksan with Picture Lake in the foreground.

ground, the fast, adrenaline-fueled terrain has garnered many dedicated admirers. It was also one of the first North American ski locations to accommodate and encourage snowboarders. There are two day lodges, both equipped with restaurants/cafeterias: the Cascadian-flavored **White Salmon Day Lodge** at milepost 52 and the **Heather Meadows Day Lodge**, 4 miles higher up. In

high summer, Picture Lake is the object of most people's affections. The view of Mt Shuksan reflected in its iridescent waters is an Instagram staple. You can wander for a half-mile around its shore taking follow-up snaps, or drive 1 mile further up to the **Heather Meadows Visitor Center** and plenty more trailheads.

THE DRIVE

Stay right when the road forks at Picture Lake. The last 3 miles (mileposts 55 to 58) of the byway are only open from around mid-July to September and subject to a $5 fee. The road terminates at a parking lot at Artist Point, 3.5 miles from the ski area.

07 ARTIST POINT

A picnic-spot extraordinaire, surrounded by perhaps the best high-altitude wilderness area in the US that is accessible by road, Artist Point at 5140ft is *high* – so high that in 2011 it remained snowed-in all year. Various hikes fan out from here, overlooked by the dual seductresses of Mt Baker and Mt Shuksan. Some are appropriate for families and most are snow-free by mid-July. The interpretive **Artist Ridge Trail** is an easy 1-mile loop through heather and berry fields with the craggy peaks of Baker and Shuksan scowling in the background. Other options are the 0.5-mile **Fire and Ice Trail** adjacent to the Heather Meadows Visitor Center, which explores a valley punctuated by undersized mountain hemlock, and the 7.5-mile **Chain Lakes Loop** that starts at the Artist Point parking lot before dropping down to pass a half-dozen icy lakes surrounded by huckleberry meadows.

CASCADE CREATIVES/SHUTTERSTOCK ©

Mt Baker Ski Area

Artist Ridge Trail

13

WASHINGTON

International Selkirk Loop

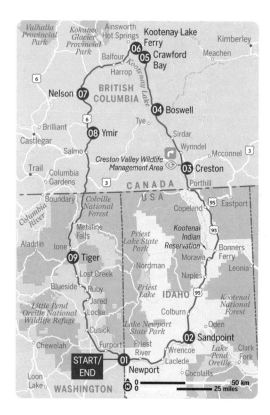

DURATION	DISTANCE	GREAT FOR
3 days	462km / 387 miles	Families, Nature

BEST TIME TO GO	May to October for sun-dappled lake views

Borders are arbitrary in the Selkirks, a more remote and geologically older antidote to the Rockies, where curious roadside attractions verge on the esoteric and the word 'clamorous' means the occasional moose blocking your views of so-clear-you-can-drink-it Kootenay Lake. Pack your passport, shake off the crowds and plunge into this wildly scenic two-nation loop through the forgotten corners of Washington, Idaho and British Columbia.

Link Your Trip

3 Mountains to Sound Greenway

Drive west via Spokane and I-90 to the next spectacular mountain range, the snow-enveloped Cascades. From Spokane it's 172 miles to Ellensburg, where this trip begins.

32 Around the Kootenays

Since you brought your passport all this way, you might as well use it further north and keep the rugged mountain theme going.

01 NEWPORT

Newport, a Washington State lavender-growing and logging town, faces off against Oldtown (the town's original incarnation), which sits across the state line in Idaho. The visitor center is situated next to the **Pend Oreille County Historical Museum** (pochsmuseum.org), housed in a 1908 train depot and filled with local farming and railway paraphernalia. Both look out onto carefully manicured Centennial Plaza, which sits majestically at the head of Washington Ave (US 2), your ticket out of town.

BEST FOR ROADSIDE ATTRACTIONS

The Glass House, an icon made completely of glass bottles

Lake Pend Oreille

THE DRIVE
Follow US 2 east for 29 miles (47km) on the north bank of the Pend Oreille River through the town of Priest River to Sandpoint.

02 SANDPOINT
Within 45 minutes of leaving Washington at Newport you hit one of the Northwest's rarest jewels, Sandpoint, whose 7500 Idahoans make up the largest US town on this loop. Squeezed between the downhill runs of Schweitzer Mountain and the deep waters of Lake Pend Oreille, Sandpoint is the most discovered 'undiscovered' town in the nation. Budget a couple of hours to stroll the bars, restaurants and shops of 1st Ave and sup vino and enjoy fresh fare at the **Pend D'Oreille Winery** (powine.com), which also offers tours of its production process. Sandpoint is right on Lake Pend Oreille ('hanging from the ears,' pronounced 'ponderay'), and the white sand and Jet Skis of City Beach are the closest the Idaho Panhandle ever gets to Miami. Bring a swimsuit and preferably some kind of boat.

THE DRIVE
US 95 heads to Bonners Ferry, originally built on stilts during the gold rush, and continues north past ranches, Christmas-tree farms and the world's largest hop farm at Elk Mountain. Branch onto SR 1 and cross into Canada at the Porthill–Rykerts border crossing, where you join Canadian Hwy 21 to Creston. The total journey is 67 miles (108km).

03 CRESTON
Creston advertises its premier business with a statue of a 7ft Sasquatch (Bigfoot) making off with a six-pack. Fear not: this is the home of the **Columbia Brewery** (kokanee beergearstore.ca), creator of the mass-market Kokanee and Kootenay brands. The brewery offers tours (four to six daily) and visits to the sample room.

These mild lagers are consumed by the barrel during hockey season. Creston's other pulls are fruit (apples and cherries dominate) and murals (there's an art walk and mural tour). The downtown's art deco–heavy architecture is interrupted by two grain elevators – the only two city-center silos left in Canada.

 THE DRIVE
The long, shimmering fjord of Kootenay Lake bursts into view a few miles outside Creston. This 90-mile slice of sapphire framed by the peaks of the Selkirk and Purcell ranges has water pure enough to drink. The 30-mile (48km) Creston–Boswell section is the most stunning of the drive and is enjoyed by drivers and riders for its curves.

DETOUR
Creston Valley Wildlife Area
Start: **03** Creston

Nature lovers and birders should detour 6 miles (9.7km) west of Creston to the **Creston Valley Wildlife Management Area** (crestonwildlife.ca), part of the region's most important wildlife corridor. Walk the boardwalks and spot osprey, tundra swans, pelicans or great blue herons from the two birding towers, or sign up for an hour-long guided canoe paddle through the wetlands. Dawn and dusk are the best times to spot wildlife, including the occasional moose chomping in the shadows. Don't miss the very sweet 'turtle crossing' road sign.

04 **BOSWELL**
The wackiest sight on Kootenay Lake's eastern shore is without doubt Boswell's **Glass House**. With a mortician's sense of humor, funeral director David H Brown decided to build his dream retirement home out

of used embalming-fluid bottles – half a million of them in total (and, more incredibly, then persuaded his wife this was a good idea). The result is a whimsy of turrets, towers, bridges and even a garden shed, all made from recycled bottles. Brown then topped this off with an interior decorated with fearless 1970s panache and a small army of garden gnomes.

 THE DRIVE
Keep on lake-hugging Hwy 3A for 17.4 miles (28km) to Crawford Bay.

05 **CRAWFORD BAY**
Wizards and muggles (non-wizards) with a penchant for Harry Potter will find empathy in Crawford Bay at **North Woven Broom** (north wovenbroom.com), maker of traditional brooms since 1975. One can only assume that orders have gone through the roof since the late 1990s when the word 'Quidditch' (a fictional sport in the *Potter* books that is played on broomsticks) entered the language. Numerous US colleges, including Harvard, now compete in real-life Quidditch cups and the workshop's owners once made 50 Nimbus 2000s (Harry Potter's prized broomstick) for a Vancouver book launch. The workshop's feathery golden hues and musky broomcorn fragrance are surprisingly beguiling, and there's something comforting

about its almost total lack of modernity. While you're here, check out the glassblowers, blacksmith's forge and weavers' studio across the road.

 THE DRIVE
The highway runs out 3 miles (5km) west of Crawford Bay, and it's time for the ferry.

06 **KOOTENAY LAKE FERRY**
Bridges are overrated. Go slow on the world's longest free ferry ride, courtesy of the Canadian government and the Kootenay Lake Ferry. The scenic crossing departs every hour or so and offers 40 minutes of superb lake views before docking at Balfour, some 20 miles northeast of Nelson. If you have some time to kill before departing, drive south from the ferry terminal for 3 miles (5km) to a turnout that marks a section of Pilot Bay Provincial Park, a shoreline haven punctuated with walking trails and the charming white clapboard 1907 **Pilot Bay lighthouse**.

THE DRIVE
At the ferry landing, take SR 31 alongside Kootenay Lake's West Arm for around 20 miles (32km) to Nelson.

07 **NELSON**
Nelson has always flirted with contrarianism. It kept its early 20th-century boomtown buildings when

everyone else was tearing theirs down, and it's happy to pursue anything outside of the mainstream. Outdoorsy, alternative and organic, the historic former mining town has a tangible Victorian air, and is considered by many to be the most interesting and creative hangout east of Vancouver. Pick up a free **architectural walking tour** pamphlet to track down the most interesting of the town's 360 heritage buildings and stroll the waterfront pathway 1.2 miles to the lovely beaches of Lakeside Park, returning on the restored century-old 'Streetcar No 23.' Revel in the mélange of cultures on Baker St, enjoying sitar music and intriguing boutiques. Pause to absorb the lake and mountain views. Choose from cafes with superb coffee, browse a farmers market, try some creative seasonal cuisine and hear local talent at one of Nelson's bars (where you'll also find some fine microbrews).

THE DRIVE
Leaving Nelson in your rear-view mirror, the final day's drive takes you 18 miles (29km) south along Hwy 6 to Ymir, past remote, forested (and slightly odd) communities.

08 YMIR
The oddest of the odd is historic Ymir (pronounced 'why-mur,' though grinning locals may well try to persuade you the name stands for 'Why Am I Here?'). It's weirdly named after a hermaphroditic giant from Norse mythology, though its history has more to do with gold mining than an Icelandic creature.

Photo opportunity

Anything with the sapphire waters of Kootenay Lake in it.

Boomtown Ymir – founded as Quartz Creek in 1897 – once listed 10,000 inhabitants. Now there's little more than two hotels and a store. Check out the unusual **Hotel Ymir** (hotelymir.com), built in 1916.

THE DRIVE
After completing your US border formalities at the low-key

Nelway–Metaline border crossing, 23.5 miles (38km) from Ymir, continue straight down the Washington SR 31 for 26.5 miles (42.6km) through the town of Metaline Falls to the Tiger junction.

09 TIGER
The fiercely named ex-town of Tiger, 4 miles (5.4km) south of Ione, has been reduced to one last remnant, the 1912 clapboard **Tiger Historical Center & Museum** (facebook.com/tigerhistorical), which functions as a gift shop, cafe, information center and museum of the milling/railway town that once was. Glued to the junction of SR 31 and SR 20, it serves as a welcome apparition on this final part of the loop, aka the Pend Oreille Scenic Byway.

NALIDSA/SHUTTERSTOCK ©

Kootenay Lake Ferry

UNEXCEPTIONAL ADVENTURER/SHUTTERSTOCK ©

Cape Lookout State Park (p106)

Oregon

Explore

Oregon

Oregon's landscape ranges from rugged coastline and thick evergreen forests to barren-seeming, fossil-strewn deserts. Then there are the towns: funky Portland, dramatic Ashland, beer-loving Bend and beyond. Only two interstate highways offer fast lanes across the state, and that's as it should be: driving in Oregon is all about meandering along back roads and scenic byways. The Cascades are dense with natural wonders, including mountains, waterfalls, mighty rivers, forests and hot springs. The Oregon coast offers miles and miles of coastal highway stringing together charming seaside towns. Or head to the remote eastern part of the state, where high desert and empty roads await.

Portland

Portland has acquired something of a reputation lately, and that's just fine with Portlanders. Oregon's largest city has a long history of public demonstrations and protests, including the one in 1991 that led then-President George HW Bush to dub it 'Little Beirut.' It's a haven for countercultural thought, even though these days the sidewalks are also crowded with tent cities and the signs of gentrification are everywhere.

Visitors should take advantage of the city's many beautifully landscaped parks and gardens, especially when the rhododendron trees flower in the spring. Supermarkets and farmers' markets make it fun to stock up on local produce for your road trip. Fuel up with excellent coffee at Stumptown or any number of cafes, and you can't go wrong with a meal at a Vietnamese or Thai restaurant. Vegetarians and vegans will be spoiled for choice. And make sure to sample some of the famous Portland microbrews, from the sour ales at Cascade Barrel House to the boundary-pushing brews at Ecliptic, Breakside or Culmination.

If you fly into Oregon, you'll most likely end up at Portland International Airport. There are plentiful chain hotels around the airport, but it's also a quick 20-minute cab ride or light-rail trip into town. Likewise, car rentals are easily available at the airport but are also dotted around town. Budget accommodations are hard to find and often sketchy, so budget and book accordingly.

WHEN TO GO

Mid-June through September/October is usually the best time with warm temperatures (often hot and humid) and dry roads. Many mountain roads, such as those near Sisters and Bend into the Oregon Cascades, are closed November–May. Early season (May–June) brings wildflowers and waterfalls, but also frequent rains.

Bend

Bend has grown rapidly in recent years, but the downtown core maintains a friendly, laid-back vibe and a small-town feel. This is one of the best places to visit if you're a fan of Northwest-style beers – there's even a tourist brochure that maps out a walk through the town's major breweries. The Deschutes River slides lazily through town, pooling briefly at Drake Park, and the greenway on either side of the river makes for a delightful leg-stretcher. (You can also float and paddle this beginner-friendly section of river.) Accommodations of all types are strung along 3rd St, parallel to Hwy 97.

Ashland

Home of the Oregon Shakespeare Festival, Ashland is a pretty town full of parks. A good selection of old-school motels line its main drag. The closer you get to the downtown stretch of Main St, the fancier and more expensive the accommodations become. Lithia Park, with its fountains and tree-lined trails, is right beside the town center, making a fine escape from busy shopfronts and restaurants surrounding the Town Plaza.

TRANSPORT

Most people arrive in Oregon at Portland International Airport (PDX). From here, light-rail trains connect to various parts of the city. Bus lines cover most of Portland and its suburbs. There are also regional bus lines along the coast and into the Columbia River Gorge. But driving a car is the most practical way to get around Oregon.

WHERE TO STAY

As elsewhere in the region, car campers will love Oregon, with its forested peaks and rugged coastline full of excellent campgrounds. Look for camping yurts for extra luxury. Reserve ahead or plan to arrive early and be flexible, and note that most campgrounds are closed in winter.

Budget digs are hard to come by, but you'll find high-end 'rustic' lodges and resorts, as well as hipsterized motor inns and fixed-up historic hotels and B&Bs. Urban hubs and major highways have plenty of midrange chain hotels, if a comfortable room and free parking will suffice.

👍 WHAT'S ON

Portland Rose Festival

A summer-long festival with parades, floats, carnival rides and waterfront activities. (May/June)

Waterfront Blues Festival

One of the area's biggest music festivals, with big-name headliners. (July)

Pickathon Experimental Music Festival

A beloved family-friendly music festival campout on the outskirts of Portland. (August)

Portland International Film Festival

Highly regarded films from around the world are screened in Portland theaters. (March)

Resources

Travel Portland (travelportland.com) For planning and getting around the state's largest city.

Oregon Tourism Commission (traveloregon.com) For statewide maps, suggestions, event tickets and bookings.

TripCheck (tripcheck.com) Up-to-date road conditions statewide.

14

OREGON

Highway 101 Oregon Coast

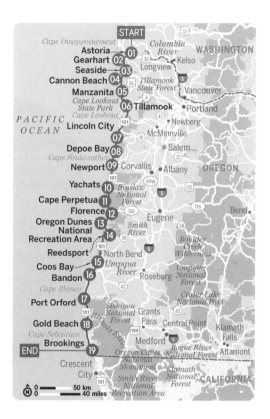

DURATION	DISTANCE	GREAT FOR
7 days	547km / 340 miles	Outdoors, Families

BEST TIME TO GO	July to October, when the weather is more cooperative.

Scenic, two-lane Hwy 101 follows hundreds of miles of shoreline punctuated with charming seaside towns, exhilarating hikes, and ocean views that remind you you're on the edge of the continent. On this trip, it's not about getting from point A to point B. Instead, the route itself is the destination. And everyone from nature lovers to gourmands to families can find their dream vacation along this exceptional coastal route.

Link Your Trip

1 On the Trail of Lewis & Clark

Do the Hwy 101 trip backwards and you can pick up the trail of Lewis and Clark in Astoria.

23 Crater Lake Circuit

Continue south to Crescent City then take US-199 northeast to Grant's Pass.

01 **ASTORIA**

We begin our coastal trek in the northwestern corner of the state, where the Columbia River meets the Pacific Ocean. Ever so slightly inland, Astoria doesn't rely on beach proximity for its character. It has a rich history, including being a stop on the Lewis and Clark trail. Because of its location, it also has a unique maritime history, which you can explore at the **Columbia River Maritime Museum** (crmm.org).

Astoria has been the location of several Hollywood movies, making it a virtual Hollywood by the sea: it's

BEST FOR HIKING

Cape Perpetua offers several breathtaking hikes

GORDON MONTGOMERY/SHUTTERSTOCK ©

Highway 101

best known as the setting for cult hit *The Goonies*. Fans can peek at the **Historic Clatsop County Jail**.

THE DRIVE
Head south on Hwy 101 for 14.5 miles to Gearhart.

02 GEARHART
Check your tide table and head to the beach; Gearhart is famous for its razor clamming at low tide. All you need are boots, a shovel or a clam gun, a cut-resistant glove, a license (available in Gearhart) and a bucket for your catch. Watch your fingers – the name razor clam is well earned. Boiling up a

batch will likely result in the most memorable meal of your trip. For information on where, when and how to clam, visit the Oregon Department of Fish & Wildlife's online guide (myodfw.com/ crabbing-clamming).

THE DRIVE
Don't get too comfortable yet: Seaside is just 2.4 miles further down the coast.

03 SEASIDE
Oregon's biggest and busiest resort town delivers exactly what you'd expect from a town called Seaside, which is wholesome, Coney Island–esque fun. The 2-mile board-

walk – known as 'the Prom' – is a kaleidoscope of seaside kitsch, with surrey rentals, video arcades, fudge, elephant ears, caramel apples, saltwater taffy and more. It's also where you'll find the **Seaside Aquarium** (seasideaquarium .com). Open since 1937, the privately owned aquarium isn't much more than a few fish tanks, a touch pool and a small indoor seal tank where you can feed the splashy critters, but it's a fun stop for inquisitive kids.

THE DRIVE
Leave the beach behind for a bit as you veer inland for the 8.8-mile drive to Cannon Beach.

04 CANNON BEACH

Charming Cannon Beach is one of the most popular beach resorts on the Oregon coast. The wide sandy beach stretches for miles, and you'll find great photo opportunities and tide-pooling possibilities at glorious **Haystack Rock**, the third-tallest sea stack in the world. (What's a sea stack, you might ask? It's a vertical rock formation – in this case, one that's shaped like a haystack.) For the area's best coastal hiking, head immediately north of town to Ecola State Park, where you can hike to secluded beaches.

THE DRIVE
Follow the coast 14.4 miles through Oswald West State Park to reach your next stop.

05 MANZANITA

One of the more laid-back beach resorts on Oregon's coast is the hamlet of Manzanita – smaller and far less hyped than Cannon Beach. You can relax on the white-sand beaches, or, if you're feeling more ambitious, hike on nearby **Neahkahnie Mountain**, where high cliffs rise dramatically above the Pacific's pounding waves. It's a 3.8-mile climb to the top, but the views are worth it: on a clear day, you can see 50 miles out to sea.

THREE CAPES LOOP

South of the town of Tillamook, Hwy 101 veers inland from the coast. An exhilarating alternative route is the slow, winding and sometimes bumpy Three Capes Loop, which hugs the shoreline for 30 miles and offers the chance to go clamming. En route you'll traverse Cape Meares, Cape Lookout and Cape Kiwanda – three stunning headlands that you'd otherwise miss entirely.

Photo Opportunity

Silhouette of Haystack Rock in Cannon Beach.

THE DRIVE
Drive 27 miles from Manzanita along Nehalem and Tillamook Bays to reach inland Tillamook.

06 TILLAMOOK

Not all coastal towns are built on seafood and sand. Tillamook has an entirely different claim to fame: cheese. Thousands stop annually at the **Tillamook Cheese Factory** (tillamook.com) for free samples. You might choose to skip the dairy altogether and head to the two interesting museums: the **Pioneer Museum** (tcpm.org) has antique toys, a great taxidermy room (check out the polar bear) and a basement full of pioneer artifacts; and just south of town, the **Tillamook Naval Air Museum** (tillamookair.com) has a large collection of fighter planes and a 7-acre blimp hangar.

THE DRIVE
South of Tillamook, Hwy 101 follows the Nestucca River through pastureland and logged-off mountains 44 miles to Lincoln City.

07 LINCOLN CITY

The sprawling modern beach resort of Lincoln City serves as the region's principal commercial center. In addition to gas and groceries, the town does offer a unique enticement to stop: from mid-October to late May, volunteers from the Visitor and Convention Bureau hide brightly colored glass floats – which have been hand-blown by local artisans – along the beaches, making a memorable souvenir for the resourceful and diligent vacationer.

THE DRIVE
It's back to the coast for the 12-mile drive south to Depoe Bay.

08 DEPOE BAY

Though edged by modern timeshare condominiums, Depoe Bay still retains some original coastal charm. It lays claim to having the 'world's smallest navigable harbor' and being the 'world's whale-watching capital' – pretty big talk for such a pint-sized town. Whale-watching and charter fishing are the main attractions in the area, though 5 miles south of town there is the **Devil's Punchbowl**, an impressive collapsed sea cave that churns with waves and offers good tide pools nearby.

THE DRIVE
Another 12.8 miles brings you to the lively tourist city of Newport.

09 NEWPORT

Don your marine-biologist cap and head to **Yaquina Head Outstanding Natural Area** (blm.gov/learn/interpretive-centers/yaquina), a giant spit of land that protrudes

YAQUINA HEAD LIGHTHOUSE

If Yaquina Head Lighthouse in Newport seems a little creepier than a lighthouse ought, that's because it featured in the 2002 horror film starring Naomi Watts, *The Ring*. Built in 1873, it was originally called Cape Foulweather Lighthouse, but in the movie it was known as the Moesko Island Lighthouse. The lighthouse was also in the 1977 masterpiece *Nancy Drew: Pirate's Cove*.

nearly a mile into the ocean. This headland is home to some of the best touch pools on the Oregon coast. You'll also get a good look at the tallest lighthouse in Oregon, Yaquina Head Lighthouse (not to be confused with Yaquina Bay Lighthouse, 3 miles south).

Also worth a stop: the cutting-edge **Oregon Coast Aquarium** (aquarium.org). The sea otters are cute as can be, and the jellyfish room is a near-psychedelic experience. But what really knocks this

place off the charts is the deep-sea exhibit that lets you walk along a Plexiglas tunnel through sharks, rays and other fish.

THE DRIVE
It's 24 miles to Yachats along the edge of the Siuslaw National Forest.

10 YACHATS
One of the Oregon coast's best-kept secrets is the friendly little town of Yachats (ya-hots), which kicks off about

20 miles of spectacular shoreline. This entire area was once a series of volcanic intrusions, which resisted the pummeling of the Pacific long enough to rise as ocean-side peaks and promontories. Acres of tide pools are home to starfish, sea anemones and sea lions. Definitely stop in at the delicious **Yachats Brewing & Farmstore** for a bite to eat and some local flavor.

THE DRIVE
Just 3 miles down the coast the dramatic Cape Perpetua begins.

11 CAPE PERPETUA
Whatever you do, don't miss the spectacular scenery of the **Cape Perpetua Scenic Area** (fs.usda.gov). You could easily spend a day or two exploring trails that take you

DANITA DELIMONT/SHUTTERSTOCK ©

Sea Lion Caves

MATTL_IMAGES/SHUTTERSTOCK ©

Cape Perpetua Scenic Area

through moss-laden, old-growth forests to rocky beaches, tide pools and blasting marine geysers.

At the very least, drive up to the **Cape Perpetua Overlook** for a colossal coastal view from 800ft above sea level – the highest point on the coast. While you're up there, check out the historic West Shelter observation point built by the Civilian Conservation Corps in 1933.

If you have more time to spend, stop at the **visitor center** (fs.usda.gov/siuslaw) to plan your day. High points include Devil's Churn, where waves shoot up a 30ft inlet to explode against the narrowing sides of the channel, and the Giant Spruce Trail, which leads to a 500-year-old Sitka spruce with a 10ft diameter.

THE DRIVE
It's 22 miles to Florence, but only 12 to the Sea Lion Caves.

12 FLORENCE
Looking for a good, old-fashioned roadside attraction? North of Florence is the **Sea Lion Caves** (sealion caves.com), an enormous sea grotto that's home to hundreds of groaning sea lions. Open to the public since the 1930s, the cave is accessed by an elevator that descends 208ft to the sea lions' stinky lair.

Here's the deal: it can be fascinating, but you might feel a little taken in when you realize that the view is exactly the same as what was on the monitor up in the gift shop – and there's not even free fudge samples down there. But if money's no object,

you'll enjoy watching the sea lions cavort, especially if you have kids in tow.

THE DRIVE
The Oregon Dunes start just south of Florence and continue for the next 50 miles.

13 OREGON DUNES NATIONAL RECREATION AREA
As you drive south, you start to notice something altogether different: sand. Lots of it. Stretching 50 miles, the Oregon Dunes are the largest expanse of oceanfront sand dunes in the US. Sometimes topping heights of 500ft, these mountains of sand undulate inland up to 3 miles. Hikers and bird-watchers stick to the peaceful northern half of the dunes, and the southern half is

WHY I LOVE THIS TRIP

Celeste Brash, writer

There's nowhere else on the West Coast that matches the road-tripping perfection of this curving route alongside empty beach coves and waves of evergreen forest. Pull over and find a silent patch of sandy bliss, a mountain trail to climb or trundle along admiring the views with the windows open. I love looking for whales offshore and experiencing the changes in weather, from wild and stormy to perfect sunshine.

dominated by dune buggies and dirt bikes.

At Mile 200.8, the Oregon Dunes Overlook is the easiest place to take a gander if you're just passing through. To learn more about trails and off-road vehicles, visit the **Oregon Dunes Visitors Center** (fs.usda.gov/siuslaw). For the area's biggest dunes, the 6-mile John Dellenbeck Trail (at Mile 222.6) loops through a wilderness of massive sand peaks.

THE DRIVE
Reedsport is about halfway into the dunes area, some 22 miles south of Florence.

14 REEDSPORT
Reedsport's location in the middle of the Oregon Dunes makes it an ideal base for exploring the region. Check out the **Umpqua Lighthouse State Park**, offering summer tours of a local 1894 lighthouse (oregonstateparks.org). Opposite is a

whale-watching platform, and a nearby nature trail rings freshwater Lake Marie, which is popular for swimming.

Want to see how Oregon's largest land mammal spends its free time? You can spy a herd of about 120 Roosevelt elk meandering about at the Dean Creek Elk Viewing Area, 3 miles east of town on Hwy 38.

THE DRIVE
Enjoy the sand for another 27.5 miles, until you reach Coos Bay and the end of the dunes.

15 COOS BAY
The no-nonsense city of Coos Bay and its modest neighbor North Bend make up the largest urban area on the Oregon coast. Coos Bay was once the largest timber port in the world. The logs are long gone, but tourists are slowly taking their place.

In a historic art deco building downtown, the **Coos Art Museum** (coosart.org) provides a hub for the region's art culture with rotating exhibits from the museum's permanent collection.

Cape Arago Hwy leads 14 miles southwest of town to **Cape Arago State Park** (stateparks.oregon.gov), where grassy picnic grounds make for great perches over a pounding sea. The park

protects some of the best tide pools on the Oregon coast and is well worth the short detour.

THE DRIVE
Hwy 101 heads inland for a bit then gets back to the coast 24 miles later at Bandon.

16 BANDON
Optimistically touted as Bandon-by-the-Sea, this little town sits happily at the bay of the Coquille River. Its Old Town district has been gentrified into a picturesque harborside shopping location, offering pleasant strolling and window-shopping.

Along the beach, ledges of stone rise out of the surf to provide shelter for seals, sea lions and myriad forms of life in tide pools. One of the coast's most interesting rock formations is the much-photographed **Face Rock**, a huge monolith with some uncanny facial features that does indeed look like a woman with her head thrown back – giving rise to a Native American legend.

THE DRIVE
Follow the coastline another 24 miles south to Port Orford. This part of the drive isn't much to look at, but not to worry: there's more scenery to come.

WHALE-WATCHING

Each year, gray whales undertake one of the longest migrations of any animal on earth, swimming from the Bering Strait and Chukchi Sea to Baja California – and back. Look for them migrating south in winter (mid-December through mid-January) and north in spring (March through June).

17 PORT ORFORD

Perched on a grassy headland, the hamlet of Port Orford is located on one of the most scenic stretches of coastal highway, and there are stellar views even from the center of town. If you're feeling ambitious, hike the 3-mile trail up **Humbug Mountain** (stateparks.oregon.gov), which takes you up, up, up past streams and through prehistoric-looking landscapes to the top, where you'll be treated to dramatic views of Cape Sebastian and the Pacific.

Speaking of prehistoric scenery: your kids may scream at the sight of a Tyrannosaurus rex in front of **Prehistoric Gardens** (prehistoricgardens.com), 12 miles south of town. Life-size replicas of the extinct beasties are set in a lush, first-growth temperate rainforest; the huge ferns and trees set the right mood for going back in time.

🚗 THE DRIVE

The scenery starts to pick up again, with unusual rock formations lining the 28-mile drive to Gold Beach.

18 GOLD BEACH

Passing through the tourist hub of Gold Beach, you can take a jet boat excursion up the scenic Rogue River. But the real treat lies 13 miles south of town, when you enter the 12-mile stretch of coastal splendor known as the **Samuel Boardman State Scenic Corridor**, featuring giant stands of Sitka spruce, natural rock bridges, tide pools and loads of hiking trails. Along the highway are well over a dozen roadside turnouts and

Gold Beach

picnic areas, with short trails leading to secluded beaches and dramatic viewpoints. A 30-second walk from the parking area to the viewing platform at **Natural Bridge Viewpoint** (Mile 346, Hwy 101) offers a glorious photo op of rock arches – the remnants of collapsed sea caves – after which you can decide whether you want to commit to the hike down to China Beach.

🚗 THE DRIVE

It's just 34 miles from Gold Beach to the California border, and 28 to Brookings.

19 BROOKINGS

Your last stop on the Oregon coast is Brookings. With some of the warmest temperatures on the coast, Brookings is a leader in Easter lily-bulb production; in July, fields south of town are filled with bright colors and a heavy scent. In May and June you'll also find magnificent displays of flowers at the hilly, 30-acre **Azalea Park**.

History buffs take note: Brookings has the distinction of being the location of the only WWII aerial bombing on the US mainland. In 1942 a Japanese seaplane succeeded in bombing nearby forests with the intent to burn them, but they failed to ignite. The Japanese pilot, Nobuo Fujita, returned to Brookings 20 years later and presented the city with a peace offering: his family's 400-year-old samurai sword, which is now displayed at the **Chetco Community Public Library** (chetcolibrary.org).

15

OREGON

Three Capes Loop

DURATION	DISTANCE	GREAT FOR
2 days	283km / 176 miles	Families, Outdoors

BEST TIME TO GO	May to October to avoid chilling wind and rain

Cape Meares Lighthouse

Cape Meares, Cape Lookout and Cape Kiwanda are some of the coast's most stunning headlands, strung together on a slow, winding alternative to US 101. If you start from Portland, you'll drive through towering forests and salmon-filled river country on a loop with minimal backtracking. However you tackle this trip, strap on your boots for walks through spruce groves and over dunes to basalt and sandstone precipices.

Link Your Trip

14 Highway 101 Oregon Coast

Highway 101 leads straight into Tillamook. Follow this trip's directions from there.

16 Willamette Valley Wine Tour

Follow the directions from Robert Straub Scenic Park toward Portland and you'll hit McMinnville. From here you can follow the Willamette Valley Wine Tour.

01 TILLAMOOK FOREST CENTER

Learn about the stretch of forest between Portland and the sea at the **Tillamook Forest Center** (tillamookforestcenter.org), 51 miles from Portland. The interpretive center focuses on the history of wildfire in the region via hands-on exhibits, a 40ft replica fire tower to climb and a suspension bridge over an incredibly scenic part of the Wilson River; the film *Legacy of Fire* is worth watching. Also enjoy over 20 miles of hiking on the **Wilson River Trail**, which wends along this powerful, Douglas fir-

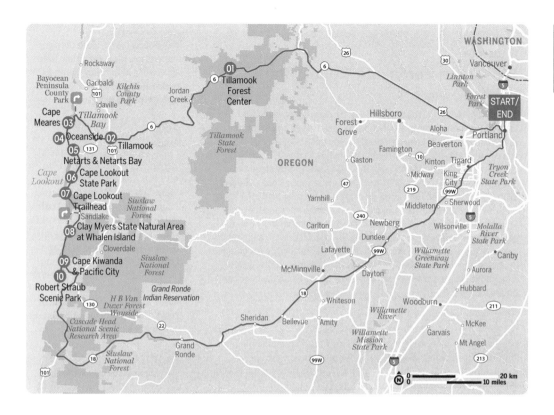

and maple-lined river renowned for its steelhead fishing. It's a 2-mile walk to Wilson Falls, where you can splash through rapids moving around big boulders – look for signs of beavers and listen for kingfishers.

 THE DRIVE
Head 22 miles west to Tillamook through the scenic Tillamook State Forest.

02 **TILLAMOOK**
Best known for its huge cheese industry, Tillamook is a nondescript town that's worth a stop to down some dairy. The famed **Tillamook Cheese**

Factory (tillamook.com), 2 miles north of town, produces more than 100 million pounds of the product every year. Line up for free cheese samples, lick down an ice-cream cone or peek into the factory-floor assembly line; there's a cafe too. Aircraft lovers should stop at the gargantuan **Tillamook Naval Air Museum** (tillamookair.com), 2 miles south of town on the way to the next stop.

THE DRIVE
Hwy 6 turns into Hwy 131 Scenic Route as it heads west. Shortly after the Tillamook Naval Air Museum take the right signposted for Cape Meares.

Drive a mile around the Tillamook Estuary then uphill 2 miles to the cape.

03 **CAPE MEARES**
The first trailhead of Cape Meares has two trails through luxurious spruce forest: a 2.1-mile trail down to rocky **Meares Beach** or a quarter-mile stroll to **Big Spruce**, heralded as the largest Sitka spruce in Oregon (it's 144ft tall and 15.5ft in diameter). A half-mile further down Hwy 131 leads you to a second, much more developed parking area with paved paths to the perhaps-haunted 1889 **Cape Meares Lighthouse** (friendsofcapemeareslighthouse.

⬦ DETOUR:

Bayocean Peninsula County Park

START: 02 TILLAMOOK

At a humble fork in the road, where Hwy 131 veers left toward Cape Meares, turn right to Bayocean Peninsula County Park and follow the road about 2 miles. Today you'd hardly guess that this was once the site of a very swanky planned resort community, built in 1906. In 1914 the town had 2000 residents, even though access was by steamship. The residents built a jetty in 1917 to ease the often-rough boat landings. Within a few years, shifting currents caused by the jetty made the beach begin to disappear; the townspeople extended the jetty and the problem amplified, with more and more structures getting devoured by the ocean. By the late 1930s most of the remaining houses were abandoned and in 1953 the post office closed. In 1971 the last building, a car garage, crumbled into the sea. Today a commemorative sign is all that is left. It's a beautiful, isolated sandy stretch, great for hiking along the beach and bird-watching.

com). There are many viewpoints and information panels along the quarter-mile walk. A shorter dirt path leads to the impressive **Octopus Tree**, a legendary eight-limbed spruce that mystifies science.

THE DRIVE
Descend 3 miles down the cape then turn right to Oceanside.

04 OCEANSIDE

This tiny village of cozy beach houses perched over a long, flat white-sand beach is the most charming on this route and a great stop for lunch, dinner or overnight. The **Three Arches Rocks Wildlife Reserve** can be seen at the far right if you're facing the ocean. With binoculars you'll be able to see the orange beaks and yellow head tufts of tufted puffins, one of this

coast's most recognizable birds, out on these towering rocks. Picnic or fly kites on the beach, search for agates in the winter months or just chill out in the seaside vibe.

THE DRIVE
Turn left onto Hwy 131 again and drive 2 miles to Netarts.

05 NETARTS & NETARTS BAY

Take a sharp turn on Happy Camp Rd to reach a small parking lot for a pretty stretch of white beach protected by a wide, flat sandbar island. Or you can continue on Hwy 131 another quarter mile to Crab Ave on the left to head into 'town,' which is a couple of ramshackle motels and deli markets. It's not the most scenic stop, but it may be easier to park here than the more popular beaches on busy weekends.

THE DRIVE
Follow the Scenic Route signs that lead to a road veering left, which winds along Netarts Bay, known for its clamming. After a few miles you'll rejoin Hwy 131 to Cape Lookout.

06 CAPE LOOKOUT STATE PARK

Besides great camping, there are several trails that fan out from this lovely, protected, white-sand beach area. Take the 2.3-mile (one-way) **North Trail** through lush forest and over cliffs to the summit of Cape Lookout, or the 2.4-mile (one-way) **Cape Trail** that goes through coastal rainforest to a panoramic lookout on the cape. Otherwise, try the easier 1.8-mile (one-way) **South Trail** over to a secluded beach off the cape.

THE DRIVE
Climb a little over a mile uphill then drive another 1.5 miles along the cape to the Cape Lookout Trailhead.

07 CAPE LOOKOUT TRAILHEAD

You can access the same trails (at different points) found at Cape Lookout State Park from here. If you're after a short stroll, take the trail to the far left of the parking lot then walk straight at the first junction about 300ft along. In half a mile you'll be rewarded with a viewpoint – on a clear, sunny day you can see all the way to Cape Kiwanda.

THE DRIVE
After descending about 5 miles from Cape Lookout you'll pass inland dunes on your right, a popular ATV spot. At the next junction turn right and continue about 4 miles.

DETOUR

Sandlake
Start: 07 **Cape Lookout Trailhead**

About 2 miles before Whalen Island is a turnoff leading to Sandlake, a spit of land that's home to 1076 acres of sand dunes. Folks from all over the Pacific Northwest come here to camp, drink beer and tool around in ATVs. You can join the fun watching the spills and thrills or, if that doesn't sound good, and race back to the highway.

08 **CLAY MYERS STATE NATURAL AREA AT WHALEN ISLAND**

Whalen Island is a wildlife-filled, wooded island that's surrounded by the **Sand Creek Estuary**. A trail makes a relatively flat but gorgeous 1.4-mile loop from the parking lot through low forest

Photo opportunity

Capture the lens of the Cape Lookout Lighthouse contrasting with the sea.

to fringing white-sand beaches. Wildlife that may be spotted here includes deer, otter, bear and (gulp!) cougar. It also has some of the best tent camping on this trip, but given the animal life, you probably don't want to leave out any food.

THE DRIVE
Go south 7 miles on Hwy 131 along the coast until the road veers inland at Cape Kiwanda.

09 **CAPE KIWANDA & PACIFIC CITY**

The best beach of the Three Capes sits in front of tiny Pacific City, south of the towering sandstone, dune-covered Cape Kiwanda. Wide and lush with sand space to spare, you can hike the cape via the dune (under a quarter of a mile, but straight up). Back on the beach, dory fishers haul their boats in or out from the beach around 6am and sunset when the weather is calm. You can buy fish from them or order it at one of many local restaurants.

THE DRIVE
Head south through Pacific City then turn right at the first crossroads.

CHECUBUS/SHUTTERSTOCK ©

Cape Kiwanda

GEORGE OSTERTAG/ALAMY ©

Clay Myers State Natural Area

10 ROBERT STRAUB SCENIC PARK

You can access the wild and rugged part of Cape Kiwanda Beach via this little park at the **Nestucca Sand Spit**, where the legendary – and Chinook salmon–friendly – Little Nestucca River meets the sea. The beach here is less protected and thus is windier and has stronger surf and currents. You can find shelter from the elements in the grass-covered dunes.

CLAMMING

If you're around Netarts Bay at a minus tide, you're likely to see groups of rubber-booted, bucket-wielding foragers combing the beach. Want to get in on the clamming action? First, everyone 14 and older needs a $10 shellfish license, available at sporting goods stores (there are a few in Tillamook) or through the Oregon Department of Fish & Wildlife (dfw. state.or.us) website, where you can also check the regulations, limits and seasonal closures. Cockles, little necks, gaper clams and other species are all present, but razor clams are the real prize. In all cases, show up about an hour before the lowest tide with a bucket, shovel and/or a clam gun, look for small holes in the sand, then dig fast!

BEST SCENERY

Dundee Hills

OREGON

Willamette Valley Wine Tour

DURATION	DISTANCE	GREAT FOR
2 days	80km / 50 miles	Food & wine, Outdoors

BEST TIME TO GO	April to August for sunshine on green hills

Vineyards, Willamette Valley

Oregon's Willamette Valley stretches over 100 miles from Eugene to Portland and more than 500 wineries lie within its six subappellations. Most of these are approachable, family-run operations dedicated to producing small quantities of high-quality pinot noir and sometimes other varietals. Organic, sustainable practices are the norm. This trip takes in the top half of the valley where you'll find the greatest concentration of wineries amid scenic farmlands.

Link Your Trip

2 Columbia River Gorge & Mt Hood

Head back through Portland and east on Historic Highway 30.

15 Three Capes Loop

Take the loop backwards by driving to Pacific City from Hwy 99W.

01 **NEWBERG**

The gateway to the Willamette Valley wine country was founded as a Quaker settlement and, ironically, was 'dry' for most of its early history. It's the biggest town in the area (population 23,600) and its historic architecture has been surrounded and overwhelmed by strip malls and fast-food joints. Still, it's a convenient place to stay and start your trip.

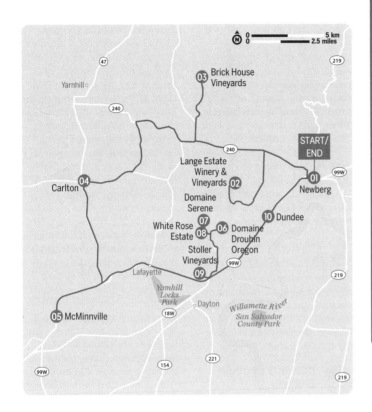

Mark Your Calendar

Many Willamette Valley wineries are open for tastings only on certain days of the week (usually Wednesday through Sunday or just the weekend), while others offer visits by appointment only. But on Memorial Day and Thanksgiving Day weekends, nearly all of the valley's wineries open their doors to the public – no reservations required. These are widely publicized and very busy weekends. Inside tip: most wineries also open their doors on the weekends prior to these...for those in the know.

THE DRIVE

Take Hwy 240 west where the landscape quickly turns into the beautiful vineyard-covered countryside you came here for. Turn right on Red Hills Rd and follow the signs up to Lange, 3.5 miles from the turnoff. The last half is on a well-maintained gravel road.

02 LANGE ESTATE WINERY & VINEYARDS

Your first tasting is at the **Lange Estate Winery & Vineyards** (langewinery.com), founded by one of the valley's earlier families. Here you'll find all the makings of an authentic Willamette Valley winery:

gorgeous views, good wines and shaggy dogs. It's very much a family affair and it's known for its good-value pinot noir called Three Hills Cuvee.

THE DRIVE

Head back down to Hwy 240, turn left, drive about 3 miles and turn right at Ribbon Ridge Rd. After about 2.5 miles, turn right on Lewis Rogers Lane to Brick House Vineyards.

03 BRICK HOUSE VINEYARDS

Within the Ribbon Ridge appellation, **Brick House Vineyards** (brickhousewines.com)

is another classically Oregonian winery. Brick House's owner, Doug Tunnell, is a former CBS foreign correspondent and an Oregon native. He's also one of the state's pioneers in organic farming. And the winery is great. Stand in the barn and look out over the vines and you'll get a sense of the unpretentious charm that makes the Willamette Valley so special. The winery itself occupies a converted barn and the pinot noir, chardonnay and gamay noir poured here are as fine as the experience is fresh.

THE DRIVE

Go back down Ribbon Ridge Rd and turn right on Hwy 240. After about 2 miles turn left onto Stag Hollow Rd, then right on Carlton–Chehalem Creek Rd, which eventually turns into Carlton's Main St.

04 CARLTON

It's hard to come up with a better descriptive word for Carlton than 'adorable.' Just a few streets wide, the town is made up almost entirely of pretty, historic buildings that house an impressive number of tasting rooms, great restaurants, antique shops, a jam maker and a fabulous French-style bakery. Nearby **Anne Amie Vineyards** (anne amie.com) has stellar sparkling rosé and dessert wines. Carlton makes a great stop for lunch, and it's also a lovely place to stay overnight. Be sure to wander around town aimlessly to turn up plenty of delicious surprises.

THE DRIVE

Go south on Tualatin Valley Hwy 47. After about 4.5 miles turn right on Hwy 19 which goes right into downtown McMinnville.

05 MCMINNVILLE

At the heart of the region's wine industry lies McMinnville. Stay within its historic, red-brick downtown district and you'll find older buildings, art galleries, boutiques and fine restaurants, along with a small-town feel as kids play on sidewalks and tourists stroll up and down the main artery of 3rd St; head outside this area and this image is dimmed by modern housing communities and shopping areas. It's a great place to

stay, eat and end your tour of the wine region.

As you'd expect, there are also several wineries and tasting rooms that you can easily find by taking a stroll around downtown. The most special is **Eyrie Vineyards** (eyrievineyards.com). The late owner, David 'Papa Pinot' Lett, planted the region's first vines (including the first pinot gris in the USA) in 1965 and the first wines were produced in 1970. Today David's son, Jason, runs the operation.

THE DRIVE

Head northeast on Hwy 99W. After 8 miles turn left at OR 18W/SE Dayton Bypass then take an immediate right onto NE MacDougall Rd. After half a mile turn left on NE Breyman Orchards Rd and follow the signs to Domaine Drouhin.

06 DOMAINE DROUHIN OREGON

You may be on day two at this point and it's time for a little more glamour. Owned by renowned the Burgundy producer Maison Joseph Drouhin,

TOP TIP:

Spit & Drive

Some words of advice: when tasting wine, learn to spit. That bucket is there for a reason. Spitting will actually mark you as a pro rather than an amateur.

Domaine Drouhin Oregon (domainedrouhin.com) is famed as much for its history as it is for its pinot noir. The winery owes its existence in part to the 1979 Gault Millau 'Wine Olympics,' a blind tasting held in France. In the competition, McMinnville's Eyrie Vineyards placed in the top 10, holding its own against France's most esteemed pinots, including one from the respected Maison Joseph Drouhin. This stoked Drouhin's already existing interest in the Willamette Valley (Drouhin first visited the valley in 1961), and he soon decided it was time to extend the family's operation. In 1988 he opened Domaine Drouhin Oregon under the management of his daughter, winemaker Véronique Drouhin. She still makes the wine and the top picks are named after her three children. Today the winery is one of the most elegant and scenically located in the valley and the wines, which are made from grapes planted in the French style with vines close together, have a distinct old-world touch.

THE DRIVE

Go straight out the driveway across Breyman Orchards Rd (don't turn) and follow the signs for Domaine Serene.

07 DOMAINE SERENE

Domaine Serene (domaineserene.com) is one of the Willamette Valley's best-known wineries heralded, as would be expected, for its pinot noir. It's a grand, modern place with a stunning wine cellar and lovely views over the rolling hills and vineyards that sweep

across the valley. Along with pinot noir, the winery produces highly regarded Chardonnays. You can go with the standard tasting-room-only wine tasting or tour the entire winery, including the cellar, as part of the VIP tour – that, however, will cost you extra.

THE DRIVE
Turn right out of the driveway and don't blink or you'll miss White Rose Estate, your next stop.

08 **WHITE ROSE ESTATE**
A short hop down the road is **White Rose Estate** (whiteroseestate.com), where you can take in wonderful views from the lawn before

Photo opportunity
Domaine Drouhin Oregon: take a picture of pinot noir vines with a view of the valley.

descending into the tasting room, which is built directly into the hillside and above the cellars, in order to maintain an optimal temperature for the barrels below. Jesús Guillén, Oregon's first-ever Latino head winemaker, put the winery on the map with its 'neo-classical' (whole-cluster fermentation)

pinot noirs. Before his passing in November 2018, Jesús was profiled in a documentary about the state's pioneering minority winemakers called 'Red, White and Black,' produced by Bertony Faustin of **Abbey Creek Vineyards** (abbeycreekvineyard.com).

THE DRIVE
Go back down Breyman Orchards Rd and turn right at NE MacDougall Rd. Stoller Vineyards is about a mile along.

09 **STOLLER VINEYARDS**
On the site of what was the biggest turkey farm in Oregon, **Stoller Vineyards** (stollerfamilyestate.com) is one of the most ecologically sustainable

PERNELLE VOYAGE/SHUTTERSTOCK ©

Stoller Vineyards

Grapes, Dundee Hills

wineries in the country, if not the world. The winery building holds the US Green Building Council's gold-level certification for Leadership in Energy and Environmental Design, plus the architecture (that looks like a cross between a grain elevator and a barn – but prettier) is true to the site's history. The winery produces some well-heralded pinot noirs and chardonnays.

 THE DRIVE
Backtrack east on NE Mac-Dougall Rd, drive a little over a mile then turn right onto Hwy 99W. You'll be in central Dundee in under 4 miles.

10 **DUNDEE**
Dundee is the hub of the **Dundee Hills**, the Willamette Valley's pre-eminent subappellation, where you've

already visited three superb wineries. Now it's time to see what the region can produce for lunch and chances are you won't be disappointed. Although Dundee isn't the most scenic of the region's towns, it's pleasant enough with a few parks and early 20th-century homes. The real draw here, however, is that it's teeming with fabulous restaurants.

17

OREGON

Journey Through Time Scenic Byway

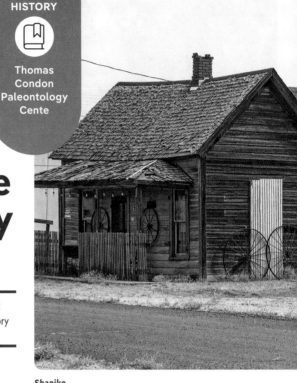

BEST FOR HISTORY

Thomas Condon Paleontology Cente

Shaniko

DURATION	DISTANCE	GREAT FOR
3 days	584km / 363 miles	Families, History

BEST TIME TO GO	June to September for warm temperatures and less rain

Unless you count the futuristic-looking windmills around the town of Wasco, a more precise name for this state scenic byway would be Journey Back in Time Scenic Byway. From the moment you leave Hwy 84 it's truly a time warp: ghost towns lie off the roadside, fossils expose millions of years of history, and even the restaurants and hotels make you feel you've driven into decades past.

Link Your Trip

2 Columbia River Gorge & Mt Hood

From The Dalles, it's only about 30 miles east along Hwy 84 and the Columbia River Gorge to Maryhill.

19 Hells Canyon Scenic Byway

The Hells Canyon Scenic Byway begins in Baker City, right where this trip ends, so they link up perfectly.

01 STONEHENGE

Although not part of the official byway, the perfect place to kick off your time travel is at the full-scale replica of **Stonehenge**. Built by eccentric businessman Sam Hill as a memorial to the 13 men in Klickitat County killed in WWI, the site is a completed version of the Salisbury Plain monument, although its detractors argue that the keystone is incorrectly aligned with the stars. It's just east of Hwy 97, on the Washington side of the Columbia River.

THE DRIVE

Turn left on Hwy 14 and drive about 4 miles to the Maryhill Museum of Art.

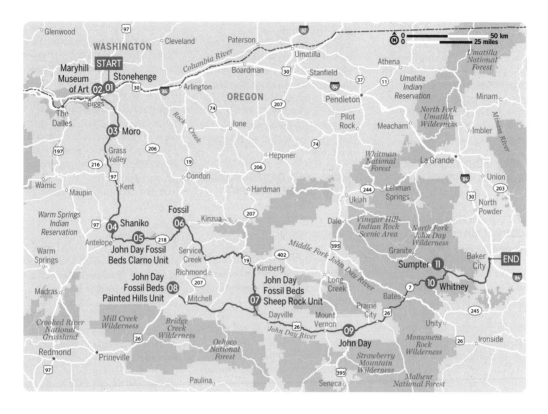

02 MARYHILL MUSEUM OF ART

The spectacular **Mary-hill Museum of Art** (maryhill museum.org), set in a mansion on a bluff above the Columbia River, was another Sam Hill project. Among its eclectic exhibits is a noteworthy collection of Rodin sculptures, a room full of decadent objects once belonging to Queen Marie of Romania and Native American artifacts.

THE DRIVE

Make a right on Hwy 14 then another right 2 miles later onto Hwy 97, which takes you over the Columbia River via the Sam Hill Memorial Bridge. Fill up on gas at Biggs Junction, where the scenic by-way officially begins. From here it's about 20 miles to the next stop, past hills, wind farms and homesteads.

03 MORO

In Moro you'll find **Sherman County Historical Museum** (sherman museum.org). For a small-town museum it has some surprisingly interesting exhibits, including on the history of wheat production, Native Americans and rural living in the days of old. The town is also home to a handful of antique shops that are worth a browse.

THE DRIVE

South on Hwy 97 you'll be treated to breathtaking views of several volcanoes in the distance, including Mt Hood, Mt Jefferson and Mt Adams. Continue for 35 miles through the near-deserted towns of Grass Valley and Kent.

04 SHANIKO

This wee ghost town (population 37) was once the wool-shipping center of the US. Its decrepit old buildings make for good photo ops, and its architectural grand dame, the **Shaniko Hotel**, is one of the finer historic buildings in eastern Oregon. (It's been mid-refurbishment but closed for years.) A few shops and a tiny museum are open through summer.

THE DRIVE

Continue south on Hwy 218. About a mile out, the road narrows and winds as it descends through sagebrush-covered hills to the minuscule settlement of Antelope. Turn east here onto Hwy 218 and drive about 16 miles to the next stop.

05 JOHN DAY FOSSIL BEDS CLARNO UNIT

Dramatically eroded palisade cliffs mark your arrival at the **John Day Fossil Beds Clarno Unit** (www.nps.gov/joda), your first stop in the John Day Fossil Beds National Monument trilogy. The short trails and fossil remains plunge you into a time more than 40 million years ago, when the region was subtropical forest. From the base of the palisades, wander the half-mile Geologic Time Trail to the Trail of Fossils, and you'll see boulder-sized fossils of logs, seeds and other remains from the ancient forest. The quarter-mile Arch Trail leads to a natural arch in the striking palisade cliffs.

THE DRIVE

Continue 18 miles northeast to Fossil.

06 FOSSIL

The town of Fossil (population 447) is aptly named given that it's in the middle of paleontology heaven. It's a good stop for lunch and you can browse the town's very small **Fossil Museum** or dig for fossils in the public **digging area**. You're pretty much guaranteed to find something and there's usually someone around to help explain what you've dug up.

THE DRIVE

Head 20 miles southeast on Hwy 19 to tiny Service Creek (population 2), an old stagecoach stop that consists of a recommended inn and a rafting-put-in-cum-campground on the John Day River. It's exceptionally scenic along the river valley for the next 40 miles to the next stop.

07 JOHN DAY FOSSIL BEDS SHEEP ROCK UNIT

The rust-colored walls of the river canyon narrow and then open up again before reaching the spectacular John Day Fossil Beds Sheep Rock Unit. Continue 3 miles south to the **Thomas Condon Paleontology Center** (nps.gov/joda). This is where everything comes together. With giant murals and exhibits of fossilized skulls, skeletons, leaves, nuts and branches, the center brings the region's history to life. After filling your head with paleontology, drive across the highway to the historic **Cant Ranch House** (nps.gov/joda) for

TOP TIP:

Short Cut to Mitchell

Taking Hwy 207 from Service Creek 30 miles to Mitchell will shave about 50 miles off your route. It also saves you from having to backtrack east along Hwy 26, although you'll miss some exceptional scenery along the John Day River.

a picnic or snack on the wooden tables overlooking the John Day River. Then backtrack the 3 miles (north) to the **Blue Basin Area** parking lot at the Sheep Rock Unit. Hike the 0.6-mile Island in Time Trail and the 3-mile Blue Basin Overlook Trail. The former passes replicas of large mammal fossils and ends in a massive amphitheater of towering greenish pinnacles, while the latter leads around and above the amphitheater.

THE DRIVE

From Hwy 19 turn west onto Hwy 26, from where it's 36 miles to Mitchell. At 25 miles check out the tree on the north side of the road covered with shoes. It's been there as long as anyone can remember – string a pair up for good luck. From Mitchell it's another 10 miles to the Painted Hills Unit.

08 JOHN DAY FOSSIL BEDS PAINTED HILLS UNIT

This is a detour off the official byway but it's arguably the most striking unit of the John Day Fossil Beds, so you won't want to miss it. The goal is to see the low-slung, colorfully banded **Painted Hills** (nps.gov/joda) at sunset, when the evening light emphasizes the ochres, blacks, beiges and yellows of the eroded hillsides; an honorable reason to stay overnight in Mitchell. At the site, choose from four trails including the 0.5-mile Painted Hills Overlook and Trail (the most picturesque of the area) and the Painted Cove Trail, which takes you via boardwalk around a hill (five to 10 minutes) to see the area's popcorn-textured clay stone up close.

THE DRIVE

Backtrack east along Hwy 26 and pass the Hwy 19 junction to Picture Gorge, a canyon hemmed in by stone pillars known as Picture Gorge Basalts. Two miles along is the Mascall Formation Overlook, where you'll get spectacular views of the John Day River, Strawberry Mountains, Picture Gorge and Mascall and Rattlesnake Formations. It's another 36 miles to John Day.

09 JOHN DAY

After so many small towns, the one-stoplight town of John Day (population 1821) feels like a metropolis. Make your way to the outstanding **Kam Wah Chung State Heritage Site** (oregonstateparks.org), which served as an apothecary, community center, temple and general store for Chinese gold miners and settlers from the late 19th century until the 1940s. Today it's a widely acclaimed museum, featuring the history of the building and the region's Chinese past.

THE DRIVE

Drive east past stop-for-the-night-worthy Prairie City into the lush, conifer-clad Blue Mountains. Up the first grade, pull off at the Strawberry Mountain Overlook for views of the John Day River valley and the Strawberry Mountains. Continue northeast over Dixie Pass (elevation 5280ft), swing left onto Hwy 7, cross Tipton Summit (elevation 5124ft) and you'll drop into a lovely valley.

10 WHITNEY

This isolated and unsign-posted prairie settlement, a ghost town in the best sense of the description, was once a busy logging town and the primary stop on the Sumpter Valley Railroad. Its sagging wooden buildings, which lie on either side of a short dirt road that branches south from Hwy 7, are certainly worth a stop. Find it between mile markers 15 and 16.

THE DRIVE

About 9 miles east turn left on Sumpter Valley Hwy, then drive another 3 miles or so to Sumpter.

11 SUMPTER

Once home to 3500 people, the town today is a sleepy cluster of Old West buildings huddled along a dusty main drag. The official attraction is the **Sumpter Valley Dredge**, a massive relic of gold-mining engineering sitting beside the river. The dredge's 72-bucket 'digging ladder' extracted some 9 tons of gold.

THE DRIVE

Once you return from here to Hwy 7, it's 26 miles to the Eastern Oregon hub of Baker City.

Painted Hills

18

OREGON

Blue Mountains Loop

Oregon Trail Interpretive Park

DURATION	DISTANCE	GREAT FOR
3 days	386km / 240 miles	History, Outdoors

BEST TIME TO GO	June to September, the only time all the roads are open!

Historic Morrow County Courthouse

This trip takes you way off the beaten path through country that feels as if the pioneer days never ended. Start in the grain kingdoms of Morrow County before heading up and up into deep, remote, wildlife-filled forests. Just as you start craving a real cup of coffee, you'll descend back to civilization via the good ole cow-poking towns of Union and La Grande to lively, Western-chic Pendleton.

Link Your Trip

2 Columbia River Gorge & Mt Hood

It's about 60 miles east along Hwy 84 from The Dalles to the turnoff for Hwy 74.

17 Journey Through Time Scenic Byway

From Baker City, take the mountainous half of this route via Ukiah or I-84 to Pendleton to create a loop.

01 CECIL

Turning onto Hwy 74 from the Columbia River Gorge, stratified river country is quickly replaced by grassy fields and hillside tracts of space-age windmills. The first town you come to is the sheep- and grain-farming hamlet of Cecil, which was founded in the late 1800s, when William Cecil stopped here on the Oregon Trail to fix his wagon and ended up opening a wagon repair shop. Take Cecil's one road to the left off Hwy 74 to check out the ancient **Cecil Store**, a photogenic Old West–style building with a ghost town feel to it.

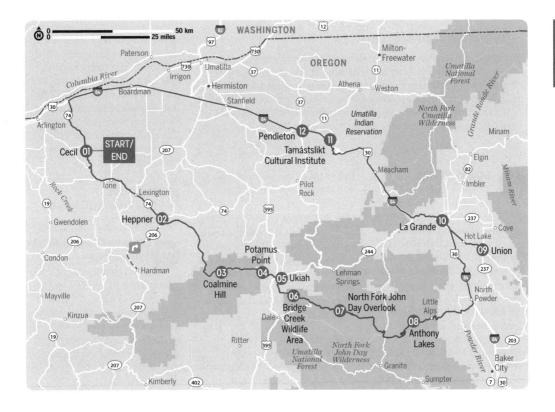

THE DRIVE

Continue 32 miles down Hwy 74 through the grain-elevator-dominated towns of Morgan (a ghost town), Ione and Lexington. The scenery here is the highlight: picture-perfect homesteads and grazing horses along a meandering creek bed.

02 HEPPNER

Welcome to the big smoke (although 'spoke' may be more fitting) of Morrow County. Heppner has a massive grain elevator, a small grid of wide streets and a few stately brick buildings. The town's pride and joy is the majestic **Historic Morrow County Courthouse**, built in 1903 and still in use,

making it one of the oldest continuously used courthouses in the state. It's also said to be haunted, perhaps by the 275 people who lost their lives in the 1903 Heppner Flood. Call ahead if you want a tour. Another worthwhile stop is the **Morrow County Museum** (morrow countymuseum.com), where you'll find a collection of pioneer and rural artifacts. Then, before you hit the road again, check in at the **US Forest Service Ranger Station** for maps, trail and road information.

THE DRIVE

Main St leads into Hwy 206/207. After about a mile, turn left toward

Willow Creek Reservoir on Hwy 53. From here it's 24 miles to Cutsforth Park, where the Umatilla National Forest officially starts. It's another 2 miles from here to Coalmine Hill.

DETOUR

Hardman
Start: 02 Heppner

Once a stagecoach stop named 'Rawdog,' Hardman's demise began in the late 1880s, when Heppner was chosen as the location for the train stop. The town's last business closed in 1968 and today it's one of the region's most scenic ghost towns. The most attractive building is the renovated dance hall. It's a 40-mile round-trip drive south from Heppner along Hwy 207.

NAVIGATING FOREST ROADS

It's easy to get lost in this tangle of forest roads, so make sure you fill up your tank in Heppner, bring plenty of water, snacks and emergency supplies, and let the ranger station know where you're going. Keep meticulous track of the route you've taken so that in a worst case scenario you can at least backtrack. Cell-phone reception and GPS coverage are iffy at best so don't expect to rely on anything besides your wits.

03 COALMINE HILL

The best way to explore the pine- and fir-tree loveliness of the 1.4-million-acre **Umatilla National Forest** is on foot. Stop at the **Coalmine Hill Trailhead** to tackle the 2.5-mile one-way **Bald Mountain Trail**, where you'll be rewarded with a view over Butter Creek. At about 1.25 miles you'll pass **Gibson Cave**, which provided shelter to Native American families long ago. During the 1930s Great Depression, a man named Gibson lived here and became known as a modern caveman.

THE DRIVE
Head south on NF-270 a little over a mile then turn right on NF-021/Western Raite Lane/Western Rt Rd. Continue 6 miles before hanging a right on Arbuckle Mt Rd/NF-180. Follow Arbuckle Mt Rd for about 2.5 miles, before turning right on NF-030 then right onto NF-5316 5 miles on, and finally right 1.5 miles later on NF-360.

04 POTAMUS POINT

This is the best viewpoint of the trip, looking over North Fork John Day River. In winter herds of elk can be seen from here, but unfortunately the road is closed at this time. In the summer months, enjoy the vistas of mountain ponds and unusual rock formations.

THE DRIVE
Backtrack to NF-030 then take a quick right onto NF-5316. After around 6 miles, turn right on NF-053. After 10 miles this turns into OR-244 E/Ukiah-Hilgard Hwy and, a little over a mile later, you'll be back to civilization in Ukiah.

05 UKIAH

Nestled within the Camas Prairie, this tiny town is surrounded by rolling grasslands and cut by clear Camas Creek. It's the low, flat heart of the Blue Mountains and a pleasant place for a leg stretch, but there's not much on offer besides the small supply shop.

THE DRIVE
Travel west on OR-244 W/Main St/Ukiah-Hilgard Hwy for a little over a mile, then turn right at Granite-Ukiah Rd 52 and travel 4 miles. The entrance to the wildlife area is on the right side of the road.

06 BRIDGE CREEK WILDLIFE AREA

This protected area is known mostly as a wintering ground for elk, but in summer (the only time of year it's accessible without specialty equipment – plus you need a permit to enter between December 1 and April 30) you'll see plenty of birdlife, including mountain bluebirds and horned larks. For a bit of exercise, take the 0.2-mile-long Ron Bridges Memorial Trail for views over Bridge Creek Flats. The trailhead is on the right, 1 mile after the wilderness area on Granite-Ukiah Rd 52.

THE DRIVE
Drive 9 miles east on Granite-Ukiah Rd 52.

07 NORTH FORK JOHN DAY OVERLOOK

Pull over for spectacular views (when it's clear) over the patchwork of color of the John Day Wilderness to the north, the majestic Strawberry Mountains to the south and the river-filled Bridge Creek Flats to the southeast. If it's early or late in season you may be able to spot elk.

THE DRIVE
Continue east on Granite-Ukiah Rd 52 then turn left on NF-73. Drive around 16 miles, then turn right toward NF-300/172 and follow the signs to Anthony Lakes.

08 ANTHONY LAKES

Known for its powdery winter skiing, Anthony Lakes is also a trove of excellent hiking in summer, with alpine landscapes, five lakes and craggy granite peaks. **Anthony Lake**, the only lake accessible by car, is the biggest and most crowded. Better, take the 1-mile hike to **Black Lake**, which is just as beautiful, to find serious tranquility. Find the trailhead at the Anthony Lakes Campground.

THE DRIVE

Head back to NF-73 and turn right into Anthony Lake Rd, which eventually turns into Anthony Lakes Hwy. After about 9 miles of winding downhill through pines, turn left on Ellis Rd/Ermey Davis Rd and take the first right on River Lane. This will lead you onto OR-237 N/La Grande-Baker Hwy toward Union. The total distance is 36 miles.

09 UNION

One of eastern Oregon's most likeable and unpretentious towns, Victorian-era, brick-solid Union is like a smaller, cuter version of La Grande and is a quieter place to spend the night if you're ready for a stop. While you're here,

Photo opportunity

Potamus Point, for a panorama of a Wild West quilt of color.

learn more about cowboys then and now at the **Union County Museum** (ucmuseumoregon. com).

THE DRIVE

Get back on the La Grande-Baker Hwy. In about 13 miles you'll see the first exit for La Grande.

10 LA GRANDE

Apart from its pleasant historic area downtown, La Grande is really just a stop for food, gas and lodging. Some 13 miles west of town, however, is the **Oregon Trail Interpretive Park**, a great place for a visceral feeling of what it was like for Oregon pioneers crossing the Blue Mountains. Paths wind through the forest to ruts left by pioneer wagons – still visible after 150 years. Find the park on well-marked roads from freeway exit 248.

THE DRIVE

Continue on I-84 towards Pendleton. About 25 miles along you'll find yourself descending Emigrant Hill on

MICHAEL BARAJAS/SHUTTERSTOCK ©

La Grande

Pendleton Woolen Mills

a 6% downgrade. Stop at the Cabbage Hill Viewpoint to experience something akin to looking down from the heavens. Just before Pendleton, take exit 216 to the Tamástslikt Cultural Institute. Total distance: 50 miles.

11 TAMÁSTSLIKT CULTURAL INSTITUTE

You've learned all about the pioneers so now it's time to delve into the cultures that were here long before covered wagons. State-of-the-art exhibits weave voices, memories and artifacts through an evolving history of the region at this grand **cultural center** (tamastslikt.org).

THE DRIVE

Get back onto I-84 W. In about 2.5 miles you'll see the first exit for Pendleton.

12 PENDLETON

Eastern Oregon's largest city, 'wild and woolly' Pendleton is a handsome old town famous for its wool shirts and rowdy, big-name rodeo. The town has managed to retain a glint of its cow-poking past, though in the last few years at least one small boutique winery has popped up, not to mention art galleries and antique shops. Take a free tour of **Pendleton Woolen Mills** (pendleton-usa. com), which has been weaving blankets for more than 100 years, and is especially known for its Native American designs.

THE DRIVE

From here it's about 70 miles to the Hwy 74 turnoff to Cecil, where the loop began.

19

OREGON

Hells Canyon Scenic Byway

BEST DAY

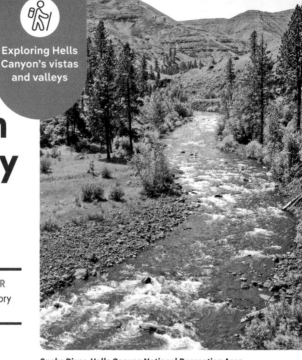

Exploring Hells Canyon's vistas and valleys

DURATION	DISTANCE	GREAT FOR
4 days	450km / 280 miles	Nature, History
BEST TIME TO GO	June to September, when the Imnaha–Halfway road is open	

Snake River, Hells Canyon National Recreation Area

In this remote corner of Oregon, at the foot of the Seven Devils Mountains, lies one of the Pacific Northwest's most spectacular sights: Hells Canyon, measuring 8043ft deep from peak to river. The few roads that access the canyon are open much of the year, but the mountains above that offer spectacular vistas are only open in summer, once the snows have melted and temperatures soar.

Link Your Trip

17 Journey Through Time Scenic Byway

It's a seamless link: start in Baker City, where the Journey Through Time Scenic Byway ends.

18 Blue Mountains Loop

From La Grande, drive south 25 miles on Hwy 84 to North Powder, or northwest toward Pendleton to hook up with this varied circuit.

01 **LA GRANDE**
The Oregon Trail crossed this valley, and pioneers rested here before traversing the challenging Blue Mountains. La Grande is the best place in the region to stock up on provisions (trail mix? sunscreen? water?) before driving into the boondocks. Despite the number of services and the few blocks of historical brick architecture, the city isn't that memorable.

THE DRIVE
Take I-82 east and you'll soon be in farmlands hemmed in by mountains. After the tiny town of Minam,

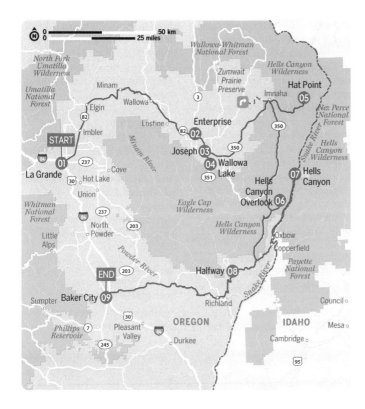

TOP TIP:
Ollokot Campground

One of our favorite spots to go is Ollokot Campground, not just for camping, but because it's so beautiful in there with the river and the trees. It's just off the Wallowa Mountain Loop Rd (USFS Rd 39), an hour or so drive from Imnaha.

the road veers right to run along the Minam River through a beautiful, slim valley with pine-covered hillsides. You'll eventually drive through the small settlements of Wallowa and Lostine.

02 ENTERPRISE

Unlike nearby Joseph (which has arguably become *too* cute), Enterprise maintains its good old small-town atmosphere. In fact, its downtown – two blocks of handsome buildings – feels quite lonesome at times. It's a good, economical place to rest for the night and get any gear you may realize you need after all (fish hooks? bug spray?).

THE DRIVE

Joseph is only 6 miles down I-62.

03 JOSEPH

If ever there was a trendy eastern Oregon town, it's Joseph. You can see its wealth right on the brick sidewalks, where well-groomed planter boxes and huge bronze statues sit proudly on every downtown corner. In fact, Joseph is noted for its cast-bronze sculptures, thanks in part to **Valley Bronze** (valleybronze.com). You can also visit the **Wallowa County Museum** (co.wallowa.or.us), housed in an 1888 bank building and notable for its displays on pioneer and

Nez Percé histories. Stock up on maps and information about Hells Canyon and surrounding areas at the **Wallowa Mountains Forest Service Office** (fs.usda.gov).

THE DRIVE

Drive 6 miles south on Wallowa Lake Rd (Hwy 351).

04 WALLOWA LAKE

Over 5 miles long and glacially formed, Wallowa Lake sits at the foot of the Wallowa Mountains, dominated at its southern end by 9617ft Chief Joseph Mountain. Giant old-growth conifers tower over a grassy beach area here, and families lounge in the sun, fish and otherwise frolic away the summer afternoons. A major trailhead starts at the southern end of Wallowa Lake Rd. One popular trail from here is the 6-mile (one-way) jaunt to the gorgeous **Aneroid Lake**. Otherwise ascend 8255ft-high Mt Howard the easy way, on the **Wallowa Lake Tramway** (wallowalaketramway.com), for stunning views over the lake and surrounding area.

THE DRIVE
Backtrack to Joseph then take Hwy 350 east. After leaving Joseph, the road passes a highway sign that tellingly reads 'Open Range Next 23 Miles,' before meeting up with Little Sheep Creek, which it follows all the way to Imnaha. It's 30 miles to Imnaha, then another 24 miles to Hat Point.

05 HAT POINT
Now it's time to leave civilization behind. Get an early start for the 30-mile drive to

Imnaha, one of the most isolated towns in the US. You may want to stay the night here (if you didn't in Joseph or Enterprise) before tackling the route ahead. The area around Imnaha has some of the most dramatic scenery of the trip. A 24-mile gravel road leads to Hat Point (elevation 6982ft) from Imnaha. Good news: only the first 5 or 6 miles are steep. The road follows a forested ridge, offering stunning views along the way. Be sure to stop at the **Granny View Vista** pullout. By the time you get to Hat Point, you'll wonder if the views could get any better. They do. Atop Hat Point stands the 82ft **Hat Point lookout tower**, a fire lookout offering dizzying 360-degree views of the Seven Devils, the Wallowas and Hells Canyon itself. And, yes, you can

climb to the top. Without a doubt, this is one of the grandest views in the Pacific Northwest. From around July through September, the road is usually passable for all passenger cars.

THE DRIVE
Head 24 miles back to Imnaha and follow the gravel Upper Imnaha Rd south for 30 miles to USFS Rd 39 (also called Wallowa Mountain Loop Rd). This is a dusty, scenic drive along the Imnaha River valley. If you wish to avoid the dust, backtrack along Little Sheep Creek Hwy to USFS Rd 39 and swing left.

DETOUR
Umwait Prairie Reserve
Start: **Hat Point**

If you have a high-clearance vehicle and three to five hours to spare,

Aneroid Lake

detour up to Zumwait Prairie Preserve. Owned by the Nature Conservancy, this 51-sq-mile preserve is the largest remaining grassland of its kind in the US. Several trails meander through the prairie, which is home to a vast number of hawks and eagles. To get there, take the dirt Camp Creek Rd, which departs Little Sheep Creek Hwy about 1 mile south of Imnaha.

06 HELLS CANYON OVERLOOK

Whichever route you take, after joining USFS Rd 39, continue southeast until the turnoff for the Hells Canyon Overlook. This is the *only* overlook into Hells Canyon that's accessible by paved road, so take advantage of it. Although you don't get the same 360-degree views as from Hat Point, it's a marvelous vista nonetheless.

THE DRIVE
This southern end of USFS Rd 39 is bucolic, with meadows and old farmhouses flanking the river. When you reach Hwy 86, turn left toward Copperfield and Oxbow.

07 HELLS CANYON

At Copperfield, you'll reach Snake River and officially be at the very bottom of Hells Canyon. Down here, it's hot, hot, hot, and the canyon has no problem living up to its name. Cross Snake River into Idaho and turn onto Idaho's Forest Rd 454 (also called Hells Canyon Dam Rd), which eventually dead-ends at Hells Canyon Dam. Here you will find the **Hells Canyon Visitors Center** (fs.usda.gov), which is a must if you need hiking trail information. The **Stud**

Photo opportunity
Capture the majesty of an 8000ft rise from river to peak at Hat Point.

Creek Trail begins immediately below the visitor center and passes some great spots to relax above the river and ponder the immensity of your surroundings. North of Hells Canyon Dam and the visitor center, Snake River returns to its natural flowing self, descending through epic scenery and roaring rapids. You can float those rapids by signing on with **Hells Canyon Adventures** (hellscanyon.biz), which offers rafting and jet-boat trips into an otherwise inaccessible area. If there's time for a hike, tackle the 4.5-mile (out and back) **Allison Creek Trail**, which you'll pass about 12 miles north of Oxbow (10 miles before the dam); it has a total elevation gain of about 1200ft up Allison Creek Canyon.

THE DRIVE
From Hells Canyon, return by way of Hwy 86 to Halfway.

08 HALFWAY

Halfway is an idyllic little town lying on the southern edge of the Wallowa Mountains, surrounded by beautiful meadows dotted with old barns and hay fields. It's also a friendly spot with just enough tourist services to make it a decent base to explore the Hells

Canyon Dam area. The **Pine Ranger Station**, 1 mile south of Halfway, acts as the region's tourist information office. The **Pine Valley Museum** is located right in the middle of town and displays a few of the region's old photos and relics. It's open on weekdays and by request for a $5 suggested donation.

THE DRIVE
You're way more than halfway there! It's 54 miles through pastoral countryside to the end of the trail at Baker City.

09 BAKER CITY

In the gold-rush days, Baker City was the largest metropolis between Salt Lake City and Portland, and a heady mix of miners, cowboys, shopkeepers and loggers kept the city's many saloons, brothels and gaming halls boisterously alive. Today the city's wide downtown streets and historical architecture recall its rich bygone days, while a little gentrification is filling shops with gourmet goodies. To remind yourself how easy your modern road trip is, stop in at the evocative **National Historic Oregon Trail Interpretive Center** (blm.gov), one of the best museums in the state. Lying atop a hill 7 miles east of town along Hwy 86, the center contains interactive displays, artifacts and films that brilliantly illustrate the day-to-day realities of the pioneers who crossed this region in the 1800s. Outside, you can stroll on the 4-mile interpretive path and spot the actual Oregon Trail.

20

OREGON

To Bend
& Back

BEST MUSEUM

Bend's High
Desert Museum

South Falls, Silver Falls State Park

DURATION	DISTANCE	GREAT FOR
5 days	450km / 280 miles	Families, Nature

BEST TIME TO GO	April to October, though there's always something to do

Pack your snowshoes, swimsuit, hiking boots, day pack and kayak: you'll need them all in Bend. This high desert town enjoys glorious weather and blue skies 250 days a year – not to mention microbreweries and a quirky character for when you're ready to have fun. Along the drive to Bend, you'll experience waterfalls, hot springs and miles and miles of forest, making this an ideal trip for the outdoor adventurer.

Link Your Trip

21 Oregon Cascades Scenic Byways

This trip also takes you to Bend via different routes; mix and match to build your dream itinerary.

22 Essential I-5

Your trip starts and ends along this major thoroughfare, and you can pick it up going in either direction.

01 **SALEM**
Your trip begins in the state capital, just an hour south of Portland. Before setting off on your journey, stop for a little pioneer history at the **Willamette Heritage Center** (willametteheritage. org), which includes two homes, a parsonage, a Presbyterian church and a mill, all looking much like they did in the 1840s and '50s. If you've got kids in tow, stop in the **Enchanted Forest** (enchantedforest.com), 7 miles south of Salem. This theme park is a fun fantasyland offering rides, a haunted house, a European village and a Western town, among other things. Opening hours vary, so check the website.

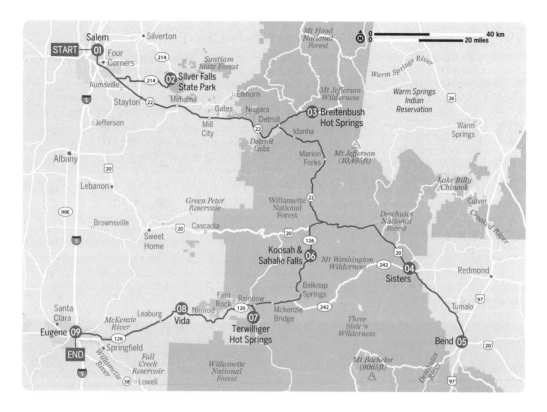

THE DRIVE
Head 10 miles southeast on Hwy 22, then take Hwy 214 10 miles west to Silver Falls.

02 SILVER FALLS STATE PARK
Hoping to glimpse a waterfall or two on your trip? How about 10? Oregon's largest state park packs in 10 waterfalls ranging in height from 27ft to 177ft, and you can see each and every one of them by hiking an 8-mile loop trail known as the **Trail of Ten Falls**. The best place to start is the South Falls parking lot, where you can kick off your hike with a bang by walking behind **South Falls**, the park's highest.

It's not just waterfalls that contribute to the park's beauty: within the 9000 acres stand cool forests of Douglas fir, western hemlock, big-leaf maples and cedars, with ferns, Oregon grape and salmonberry cover the forest floor.

THE DRIVE
Head back to Santiam Hwy/ Hwy 22 and continue west for 40 miles, then strike north for 10 miles on Breitenbush Rd, just past Detroit Lake.

03 BREITENBUSH HOT SPRINGS
Set above the Breitenbush River on a 154-acre reserve inside Willamette National Forest, Breitenbush Hot Springs is as Oregon as it gets. Along with a fantastically relaxing soak, you'll get a solid dose of earthy Oregonian mellowness. Hot mineral water burbles out of several springs at a scorching 180°F to 200°F (82°C to 93°C) and is cooled to prime soaking temperatures with water from the river. There are seven pools in all. Three overlook a pretty meadow and one of these is a silent pool. Another four pools are arranged in order of temperature, from 100°F to 107°F (37°C to 41°C). Elsewhere, a sauna sits over an open spring and is entirely heated by the steam.

🚗 THE DRIVE
Head back to Hwy 22 and drive south for 31 miles. This scenic stretch of road will meet up with Hwy 20, and then it's 26 more miles to Sisters.

04 SISTERS
Looking like a movie set for a spaghetti Western, Sisters was once a stagecoach stop and trade town for loggers and ranchers. Today, it's a bustling tourist destination whose main street is lined with boutiques, art galleries and eateries housed in Western-facade buildings. There's nothing specific here that you have to see – unless you're in town for the **Outdoor Quilt Show** (sisters

FIRE ON MT WASHINGTON
About a mile after you join Hwy 20, the lush greenery dwindles and the trees start to look like a weird art project involving charred toothpicks. This is the handiwork of a pair of wildfires – the Bear Butte Fire and the Booth Fire – that joined together in the summer of 2003 to become the B&B Complex Fire, burning over 90,000 acres of the Cascades.

It's hard not to want to stare at the devastation. But keep your eyes on the road for now, because you can pull over at the Mt Washington Viewpoint, between Miles 84 and 85. Here you'll find dramatic views of the mountains and seven interpretive signs that give you the full picture.

outdoorquiltshow.org) – but it's still a cute town to mosey around in for a while.

🚗 THE DRIVE
From Sister it's a quick 20-minute hop down to Bend.

05 BEND
Hip, outdoorsy, and enjoying ridiculously good weather, Bend is the darling of the high desert. You could spend a week here, hiking, paddling, climbing, mountain biking – the list goes on. Stop by the **Bend**

AG'S PHOTOS/SHUTTERSTOCK ©

Kayaking, Deschutes River

Visitor Center (visitbend.com) to explore your options. With the lovely Deschutes River carving its way through the heart of the city, Bend also offers an attractive downtown: explore its boutiques, galleries, breweries and dining options on foot. To learn more about the area, don't miss the superb – and rather extensive – **High Desert Museum** (highdesertmuseum.org), which covers everything from Native American culture to live animal displays on 135 acres of pine forest.

THE DRIVE
Take Hwy 20 north, curving back through Sisters, then go south where Hwy 126/McKenzie Hwy splits off. Look for the turnoff to the Koosah and Sahalie Falls about 5 miles later. Total distance: 57 miles.

06 **KOOSAH & SAHALIE FALLS**
Right off McKenzie Hwy are two of Oregon's most impressive waterfalls. The McKenzie River plunges 120ft over Sahalie Falls, the more dramatic of the two: after a good snowmelt, it drenches everything around it in mist as it roars into the frothy pool below. Only 0.3 miles downstream, Koosah Falls measures 90ft and is wider and easier going than its upstream neighbor. The stretch of the McKenzie River between the falls is utterly spectacular, with roaring

Photo opportunity

South Falls in Silver Falls State Park.

cascades that tumble over basalt boulders, through massive logjams and into deep, dark pools.

THE DRIVE
Keep following Hwy 126 another 24 miles and turn left on Aufderheide Rd. Continue on for 8 miles more.

07 **TERWILLIGER HOT SPRINGS**
Also known as Cougar Hot Springs for its proximity to Cougar Reservoir, this wildly popular hot springs near Terwilliger Reservoir has a beautiful setting among the trees in the Willamette National Forest.

THE DRIVE
Keep following Hwy 126 another 19 miles to the town of Vida.

08 **VIDA**
Oregon is known for its wooden bridges, and Vida has the state's second-longest, **Goodpasture Bridge**. A wooden truss bridge, it's painted white and looks almost like a small-

town church – albeit a 237ft-long church that straddles a river. It's right on the highway, so you can stop for a picture (it is a rather good-looking bridge) or just point and say, 'Oooooh,' as you whiz past. Look for it on the left after Mile 26.

THE DRIVE
You're on the home stretch: it's just under 30 miles to Eugene.

09 **EUGENE**
It's back to civilization in dynamic and liberal Eugene, full of energetic college students, pretty riverside parks and a plethora of restaurant choices. Where to start? For great fun and a quintessential introduction to Eugene's peculiar vitality, try to time your visit to catch the **Saturday Market** (eugenesaturdaymarket.org). Otherwise, wander the **5th Street Public Market** (5stmarket.com), an old mill that now anchors several dozen restaurants, cafes and boutique stores. To wrap up your trip with a bit of culture, stop by the **Jordan Schnitzer Museum of Art** (jsma.uoregon.edu). This renowned museum offers a 13,000-piece rotating permanent collection with an Asian art specialty. Highlights include a 10-panel Korean folding screen and a standing Thai Buddha in gold leaf.

21

OREGON

Oregon Cascades Scenic Byways

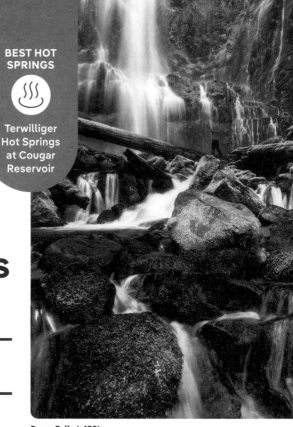

BEST HOT SPRINGS

Terwilliger Hot Springs at Cougar Reservoir

Proxy Falls (p138)

DURATION	DISTANCE	GREAT FOR
4 days	386km / 240 miles	Outdoors, Families

BEST TIME TO GO	June through September to avoid seasonal road closures.

The region around Oregon's Central Cascades is, without a doubt, some of the most spectacular terrain in the entire state. But one scenic byway just isn't enough to see it all. Here you have our version of an Oregon sampler platter: a loop that brings together several of the best roads to create a majestic route full of the state's best features.

Link Your Trip

20 To Bend & Back

One trip isn't enough to cover the Cascades; this complementary route offers alternate paths through the same countryside.

23 Crater Lake Circuit

Crater Lake is a must-see, and it's just south of the Cascades. Take Hwy 97 south from Bend to join this route.

01 WESTFIR

Before you spend several days enjoying abundant natural wonders, start with a quick photo op of an entirely fabricated one: Oregon's longest covered bridge, the 180ft Office Bridge. Built in 1944, the bridge features a covered walkway to enable pedestrians to share the way with logging trucks crossing the Willamette River.

If you plan to do some exploring or mountain biking in the area, pick up a map of the Willamette National Forest at **Middle Fork Ranger Station** (fs.usda.gov).

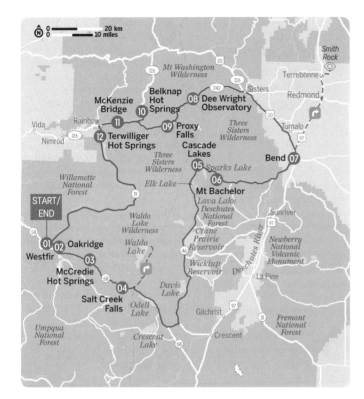

can hit it early in the morning or late in the evening midweek, you could have the place to yourself.

There are five pools in all: two upper pools that are often dangerously hot (as in don't-even-dip-your-foot-in hot), two warm riverside pools and one smaller, murkier, but usually perfectly heated pool, tucked back into the trees. Salt Creek rushes past only steps from the springs and is ideal for splashing down with icy water.

 THE DRIVE
Keep heading east another 12 miles and pull off the highway at the signed parking lot.

04 SALT CREEK FALLS
At 286ft, this monster of a waterfall is Oregon's second-highest. After a good snowmelt, this aqueous behemoth really roars, making for one of the most spectacular sights on the trip. Walk from the parking lot to the viewpoint and there below, in a massive basalt amphitheater hidden by the towering trees, 50,000 gallons of water pour every minute over a cliff into a giant, dark, tumultuous pool. Be sure to hike the short trail downhill toward the bottom of the falls. It's lined with rhododendrons that put on a colorful show in springtime, and the views of the falls on the way down are stunning. Salt Creek Falls is also the starting point for some excellent short hikes, including a 1.5-mile jaunt to Diamond Creek Falls and a 4.75-mile walk to Vivian Lake.

THE DRIVE
Continue 19 miles along Hwy 58 until you reach the Cascade Lakes

THE DRIVE
Oakridge is just a few miles to the east on either Hwy 58 or Westfir–Oakridge Rd.

02 OAKRIDGE
Oakridge is one of Oregon's mountain-biking hot spots. Hundreds of miles of trails around town range from short, easy loops to challenging singletrack routes. For novice riders, the **Warrior Fitness Trail** is a mostly flat 12-mile loop. The **Larison Creek Trail** is a challenging ride through old-growth forests, and the 16-mile **Alpine Trail** is considered the 'crown jewel' of the local trails for its 7-mile downhill stretch.

THE DRIVE
From Oakridge, Hwy 58 climbs steadily up the Cascade Range's densely forested western slope. Your next stop is about 10 miles east of Oakridge; park on the right just past mile marker 45.

03 MCCREDIE HOT SPRINGS
Because **McCredie Hot Springs** (fs.usda.gov) lies just off the highway, it's a very popular spot for everyone from mountain bikers fresh off the trails near Oakridge to truckers plying Hwy 58. Despite this, it's worth a stop, if only because it's the site of one of the largest – and hottest – thermal pools in Oregon. If you

Scenic Byway (Hwy 46), which winds its way north through numerous tiny lakes and up to Mt Bachelor. This road is closed from November to May; as an alternative, follow Hwy 97 to Bend.

DETOUR
Waldo Lake
Start: 04 **Salt Creek Falls**

There's no shortage of lakes in the area, but lovely Waldo Lake stands out for its amazing clarity. Because it's at the crest of the Cascades, water doesn't flow into it from other sources; the only water that enters it is rainfall and snowfall, making it one of the purest bodies of water in the world. In fact, it's so clear that objects in the water are visible 100ft below the surface. You can swim in the summer months (it's too cold in the winter), and if you're feeling ambitious after playing 'I Spy' on the lakebed, you can hike the Waldo Lake Trail, a 22-mile loop that circumnavigates the lake.

To get there, head 2 miles east of Salt Creek Falls on Hwy 58, and turn left at the Waldo Lake Sno-Park; follow the signs for 8 more miles to the lake.

05 CASCADE LAKES

We could get all scientific and explain how lava from nearby volcanoes created the lakes around this area, or we could just tell you that Hwy 46 isn't called the Cascade Lakes Scenic Byway for nothing. The road winds past lake after beautiful lake – Davis Lake, Crane Prairie Reservoir, Lava Lake, Elk Lake – all worth a stop. Most have outstanding camping, trout fishing, boating and invigorating swimming ('invigorating' being a euphemism for cold).

We love **Sparks Lake** for its scenic beauty set against the backdrop of Mt Bachelor, and it's

Photo Opportunity
Salt Creek Falls, the second-highest waterfall in Oregon.

perfect for peaceful paddling. If you find yourself without a boat, **Wanderlust Tours** (wanderlusttours.com) can hook you up with a guided canoe or kayak tour.

THE DRIVE
Mt Bachelor is just a few miles past Sparks Lake. If Hwy 46 is closed for the season, you can backtrack from Bend to reach Mt Bachelor.

06 MT BACHELOR

Glorious Mt Bachelor (9065ft) provides Oregon's best skiing. Here, Central Oregon's cold, continental air meets up with the warm, wet Pacific air. The result is tons of fairly dry snow and plenty of sunshine, and with 370in of snow a year, the season begins in November and can last until May.

At **Mount Bachelor Ski Resort** (mtbachelor.com), rentals are available at the base of the lifts. Mt Bachelor grooms about 35 miles of cross-country trails, though the day pass cost may prompt skiers to check out the free trails at **Dutchman Flat Sno-Park**, just past the turnoff for Mt Bachelor on Hwy 46.

THE DRIVE
Ready to add a little civilization to your rugged outdoor adventure? Head east to Bend, which is just 22 miles away.

07 BEND

Sporting gear is de rigueur in a town where you can go rock climbing in the morning, hike through lava caves in the afternoon, and stand-up paddleboard yourself into the sunset. Plus, you'll probably be enjoying all that activity in great weather, as the area gets more than 250 days of sunshine each year (don't forget the sunscreen!).

Explore downtown on foot, and be sure to check out the excellent **High Desert Museum** (highdesertmuseum.org). It charts the exploration and settlement of the Pacific Northwest, but it's no slog through history. The fascinating Native American exhibit shows off several wigwams' worth of impressive artifacts, and live animal exhibits and living history are sure to be hits with the kids.

THE DRIVE
Head 22 miles north to Sisters, then drive northwest along Hwy 242. This is part of the McKenzie Pass–Santiam Pass Scenic Byway – closed during the winter months. Your next stop is 15 miles from Sisters.

DETOUR
Smith Rock
Start: 07 **Bend**

Best known for its glorious rock climbing, Smith Rock State Park (stateparks.oregon.gov) boasts rust-colored 800ft cliffs that tower over the pretty Crooked River, just 25 miles north of Bend. Non-climbers can enjoy miles of hiking trails, some of which involve a little rock scrambling.

08 DEE WRIGHT OBSERVATORY

Perched on a giant mound of lava rock, built entirely of lava rock, in the middle of

McKenzie Bridge (p139)

VOLCANO SIGHTS IN THE CASCADES

The Cascades are a region of immense volcanic importance. Lava fields can be seen from McKenzie Pass and along Hwy 46, and road cuts expose gray ash flows. Stratovolcanoes such as South Sister and Mt Bachelor, and shield volcanoes like Mt Washington, tower over the landscape. Although it's not instantly obvious when you drive to the center of Newberry National Volcanic Monument (13 miles south of Bend), you're actually inside the caldera of a 500-sq-mile volcano. What could be stranger than that? It's still active.

a field of lava rock, stands the historic **Dee Wright Observatory** (fs.usda.go). The structure, built in 1935 by Franklin D Roosevelt's Civilian Conservation Corps, offers spectacular views in all directions. The observatory windows, called 'lava tubes,' were placed to highlight all the prominent Cascade peaks that can be seen from the summit, including Mt Washington, Mt Jefferson, North Sister, Middle Sister and a host of others.

THE DRIVE
Head west on Hwy 242 for 13 miles to mile marker 64 and look for the well-signed Proxy Falls trailhead.

PROXY FALLS
09 With all the waterfalls around the Central Cascades – hundreds of them in Oregon alone – it's easy to feel like 'You've seen one, you've seen 'em all.' Not so fast. Grab your camera and see if you're not at least a little impressed by photogenic Proxy Falls. If there were a beauty contest for waterfalls, Proxy would certainly be in the running, scattering into sheer veils down a mossy wall of columnar basalt. It's not even like the falls make you work for it: it's an easy 1.3-mile loop from the parking area. If you want to save the best for last, take the path in the opposite direction from what the sign suggests, so you hit

Sparks Lake and Mt Bachelor (p136)

Upper Proxy Falls first and you can build up to the even better Lower Proxy Falls.

THE DRIVE
Nine miles from the falls, turn right on Hwy 126 (McKenzie Hwy); Belknap is just 1.4 miles away.

10 BELKNAP HOT SPRINGS
Although nudity is the norm at most hot springs, Belknap is the sort of hot spring resort you can take your grandmother to and neither of you will feel out of place. Two giant swimming pools filled with 103°F (40°C) mineral water provide optimum soaking conditions in a family environment. The McKenzie River rushes by below, trees tower over everything, and everyone has a good time. An excellent alternative to camping, the resort has rooms for nearly all budgets.

THE DRIVE
Head southwest on Hwy 126 for 6 miles to reach your next stop.

11 MCKENZIE BRIDGE
Although from the road it looks like there is nothing but trees, there's actually plenty to do around here, including fishing on the McKenzie River and hiking on the nearby McKenzie River National Recreation Trail. To learn more about all your recreational options, stop at the **McKenzie Ranger Station** (fs. usda.gov), about 2 miles east of town. The rangers are fonts of information, plus you can find

Terwilliger Hot Springs

everything you ever wanted to know about the McKenzie River trail, including maps and books.

THE DRIVE
About 6 miles west of McKenzie Bridge, turn left on Hwy 19 (aka Aufderheide Memorial Drive) just past Rainbow. After almost 8 miles, you'll come to the parking lot from which you'll take a 0.25-mile trail through old-growth forest.

12 TERWILLIGER HOT SPRINGS
In a picturesque canyon in the Willamette National Forest is one of the state's most stunning (and clothing-optional) hot springs, Terwilliger Hot Springs

(also known as Cougar Hot Springs). From a fern-shrouded hole, scorching water spills into a pool that maintains a steady minimum temperature of 108°F (42°C). The water then cascades into three successive pools, each one cooler than the one above it. Sitting there staring up at the trees is an utterly sublime experience. After hiking back to the car, you can even jump into Cougar Reservoir from the rocky shore below the parking lot.

THE DRIVE
From Terwilliger Hot Springs, take Aufderheide/Hwy 19 south 41 miles to return to Westfir.

22

OREGON

Essential I-5

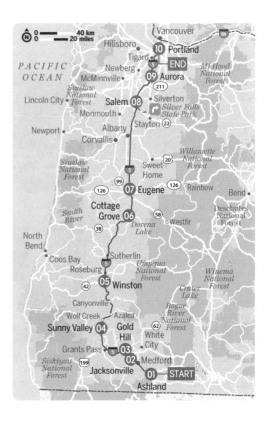

DURATION	DISTANCE	GREAT FOR
1–2 days	483km / 300 miles	Families, Nature, History

BEST TIME TO GO	March through October, when everything is open.

The word 'interstate' seldom evokes a road-tripper's dream itinerary, but I-5 will dash those preconceived notions. Oregon's major thoroughfare takes you through mountains, farmland and forests, and there's plenty to see and do along the way – provided you know which exits to take. Just off the highway, you'll find historical sites, roadside attractions and more. It's also the jumping-off place for many of Oregon's back-road gems.

Link Your Trip

21 Oregon Cascades Scenic Byways

From Eugene, drive 42 miles east to Westfir to kick off a tour of some of the state's most beautiful scenery.

23 Crater Lake Circuit

Hop off at Medford for an inland loop that includes the serene and mysterious Crater Lake.

01 ASHLAND

Prithee, fair traveler, get thee to the box office, for the players of the **Oregon Shakespeare Festival** (osfashland.or) do strut and fret upon three stages each year from February through October. Back in the Victorian era, Ashland was known for its sulfurous mineral springs that smell not unlike rotten eggs. But now the festival's 10 productions are Ashland's primary claim to fame, drawing visitors from all over. The whole town gets in on the act, with nods to the bard found at every turn. Explore the town's historic heart on foot.

BEST FOR CULTURE

Theater at Ashland's Shakespeare Festival

Ashland

🚗 **THE DRIVE**
From Ashland, head 11 miles north on I-5 and take exit 30, then go west on OR-238 for 6 miles.

02 JACKSONVILLE
This former gold-prospecting town is the oldest settlement in southern Oregon and a National Historic Landmark. Small but endearing, the town's main drag, California St, is lined with well-preserved brick-and-wood buildings dating from the 1880s. But the way to get in touch with local history is to wander the 32-acre **Jacksonville Cemetery**, at the top of Cemetery Rd, which you access at East E St and N Oregon St.

Its historic pioneer grave sites chronicle wars, epidemics and other causes of untimely deaths.

🚗 **THE DRIVE**
Take Oregon St north and it will meet up with I-5 in Gold Hill. The well-signed Vortex is a bit over 4 miles north of Gold Hill on Sardine Creek Rd.

03 GOLD HILL
Some attractions will suck you in more than others, but Gold Hill's **Oregon Vortex** (oregonvortex.com) has gravitational pull on its side, luring visitors with its unexplained phenomena: how did that broom stand up on its own? What made

that water run uphill? Detractors will try to explain the mysterious events that have drawn crowds since the 1930s, but it just sounds like, 'Blah, blah, physics, blah.' Isn't it more fun to just believe?

🚗 **THE DRIVE**
Backtrack to I-5 and go north 27 miles to exit 71. Sunny Valley is right off the highway.

04 SUNNY VALLEY
Sunny Valley serves as a quick, convenient stop for a little Oregon pioneer history. Visible from the highway, you could mistake it for a Western-themed rest stop, thanks mostly to the **Applegate Trail**

Interpretive Center (rogueweb. com/interpretive), a little museum gussied up like a movie Western storefront. If the museum's closed, you can still check out the **covered bridge** that crosses **Grave Creek** and the namesake grave itself, belonging to one Martha Crowley, a pioneer girl who died of typhoid fever on the Applegate wagon train.

 THE DRIVE
Get back on I-5 and travel 71 miles to exit 112. Take Hwy 99 N for just under 9 miles.

05 WINSTON
Tiny Winston itself isn't much of a drawcard, but 10 miles southwest is the **Wildlife Safari** (wildlifesafari. net) – an animal attraction you don't even have to get out of your car for. You can drive around the 600-acre park dotted with inquisitive ostriches, camels, giraffes, lions, tigers and bears (oh, my!) among other exotic animals, then hop right back on the highway and keep driving.

THE DRIVE
Follow OR-42 north to I-5, then travel 48 miles north to get to Cottage Grove. To get to the Mosby Creek bridges, go east on Main St, pass under I-5, then continue 2.5 miles on Mosby Creek Rd and turn left on Layng Rd to access trailhead parking.

06 COTTAGE GROVE
With seven covered bridges around town, Cottage Grove has rightfully earned its nickname of the Covered Bridge Capital of Oregon. The most famous bridge here is a small, open-top railroad trestle that had a cameo at the

Photo opportunity
Any of the covered bridges of Cottage Grove.

beginning of the movie *Stand By Me,* when the four preteen boys set off on their journey into the woods. The rails have been paved over, and the **Mosby Creek Trestle Bridge** is now part of the **Row River Trail**, easily accessible for hikers, bikers and film buffs. It's also kind of a twofer, as it crosses the creek just a couple hundred feet from Lane County's oldest covered bridge, the photogenic **Mosby Creek Bridge** built in 1920.

THE DRIVE
Take Mosby Creek Rd back to I-5, then travel north 17.5 miles and take exit 192 for Eugene.

07 EUGENE
Fun-loving Eugene is full of youthful energy, liberal politics and alternative lifestylers, making it a vibrant stop along your I-5 travels. Here you'll find a great art scene, exceptionally fine restaurants, boisterous festivals, miles of riverside paths and several lovely parks. A hike up wooded **Skinner Butte**, directly north of downtown, provides good orientation and a bit of exercise (though you can drive up if you're feeling lazy). If you want to get a dose of history while you're at it, stop at the **Museum of Natural and Cultural History** (natural-his tory.uoregon.edu). Housed in a replica of a Native American

longhouse, this museum contains good displays on Native American artifacts and fossils.

THE DRIVE
Get back on I-5 and travel north 66 miles to the capital of Oregon.

08 SALEM
Given that you're driving across the Beaver State, be sure to stop by and pay homage – perhaps even sing a few bars of 'Oregon, My Oregon' – at the **Oregon State Capitol** (oregonlegislature.gov). The third Oregon capitol building (the first two burned down) is a sleek, deco-style structure faced with gray marble. The most notable features of the capitol are four Works Progress Administration–era murals lining the rotunda. Check the schedule – you might be able to catch a free tour.

THE DRIVE
Take I-5 north another 20 miles, then take exit 278 toward Aurora.

DETOUR
Silver Falls State Park
Start: **08** Salem

Sure, most of Oregon's 100-plus waterfalls are tucked away in the mountains, but that doesn't mean you have to take a whole separate trip. You can see 10 of them just 22 miles east of Salem at spectacular **Silver Falls State Park** (oregonstateparks.org). Take an 8-mile loop to see them all, or skip straight to the tallest, 177ft **South Falls**.

09 AURORA
Originally built as a religious commune, the town of Aurora still has a common purpose, but now it's antique shops galore (rather

than the Golden Rule–based teachings of founder Wilhelm Keil). Dozens of shops line the main streets with offerings that range from rustic to quirky to garage-sale-esque. If you like your antiques big and chunky, then make your way immediately to the awesome **Aurora Mills Agricultural Salvage Yard** (auroramills.com). An enormous, two-story building houses a cornucopia of vintage signs, architectural elements and dazzling miscellany that has the ability to both inspire and overwhelm.

THE DRIVE
Aurora is practically a suburb of Portland, so hop back on I-5 and drive 25 miles to reach downtown and your final destination.

10 PORTLAND
Stay for more than 10 minutes and you're bound to feel like you're in an episode of *Portlandia* at some point. Quirky, friendly and laid-back – but with a slightly disproportionate number of hipsters sporting bushy beards – Portland is a must-do on any I-5 itinerary. Stop a while to experience some of the best food, art, beer and music the Pacific Northwest has to offer. If you didn't book a room at the McMenamin brothers' **Kennedy School** (mcmenamins.com), you should at least pop into this former elementary school that's now a hotel, brewpub and movie theater. Wander the halls to check out its colorful collection of mosaics, collages and other cool artworks. Be sure to poke around the hip boutiques, cafes, bars, bike shops and bookstores along three east-side streets: N Mississippi Ave, NE Alberta St and SE Hawthorne Blvd. Then head downtown and explore some of its best stop-offs.

Mosby Creek Trestle Bridge

23

OREGON

Crater Lake Circuit

BEST WATERFALL

Two-tiered Toketee Falls is our favorite

Lithia Park

DURATION	DISTANCE	GREAT FOR
2–3 days	587km / 365 miles	Nature, Families

BEST TIME TO GO	Late May to mid-October, when all the roads are open.

The star attraction of this trip is Crater Lake, considered by many to be the most beautiful spot in all of Oregon. The sight of the still, clear and ridiculously blue water that fills an ancient volcanic caldera is worth the trip alone, but the drive there is lined with beautiful hikes, dramatic waterfalls and natural hot springs, all right off the highway.

Link Your Trip

24 Caves of Highway 199

Go from forest to caves to beach with this trip that starts in Grants Pass, between Medford and Roseburg.

22 Essential I-5

Join up with this tour of Oregon's major thoroughfare at Ashland, Medford or Roseburg.

01 ASHLAND

A favorite base for day trips to Crater Lake, Ashland is bursting at the seams with lovely places to sleep and eat (though you'll want to book your hotel room far in advance during the busy summer months). Home of the **Oregon Shakespeare Festival** (osfashland.org), it has more culture than most towns its size, and is just far enough off the highway to resist becoming a chain-motel mecca.

It's not just Shakespeare that makes Ashland the cultural heart of southern Oregon. If you like contemporary art, check out the **Schneider Museum**

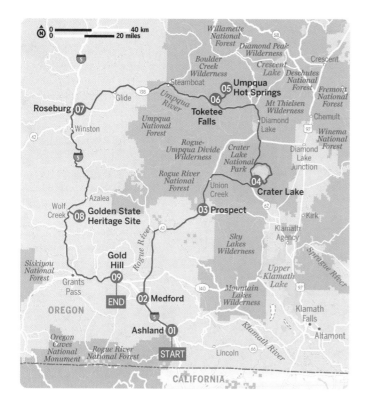

begins. Your next stop is 45 miles northeast in Prospect.

03 PROSPECT

No wonder they changed the name of Mill Creek Falls Scenic Area – that implies you're just going to see another waterfall (not that there's anything wrong with that). But the real treat at Prospect State Scenic Viewpoint is hiking down to the **Avenue of Giant Boulders**, where the Rogue River crashes dramatically through huge chunks of rock and a little bit of scrambling offers the most rewarding views.

Take the trail from the southernmost of two parking lots on Mill Creek Dr. Keep left to get to the boulders or right for a short hike to two viewpoints for Mill Creek Falls and Barr Creek Falls. If you've got one more falls-sighting left in you, take the short hike from the upper parking lot to the lovely **Pearsony Falls**.

THE DRIVE

Follow Hwy 62 for another 28 miles to reach the Crater Lake National Park turnoff at Munson Valley Rd.

04 CRATER LAKE

This is it: the main highlight and reason for this entire trip is Oregon's most beautiful body of fresh water, **Crater Lake** (nps.gov/crla). This amazingly blue lake is filled with some of the clearest, purest water you can imagine – you can easily peer 100ft down – and sits inside a 6-mile-wide caldera, created when Mt Mazama erupted nearly 8000 years ago. Protruding from the water and

---

of Art (sma.sou.edu). Ashland's historic downtown and lovely **Lithia Park** (59 Winburn Way) make it a dandy place to go for a walk before or after your journey to Crater Lake.

THE DRIVE

Medford is 13 miles north of Ashland on I-5.

02 MEDFORD

Southern Oregon's largest metropolis is where you hop off I-5 for your trek out to Crater Lake, and it can also serve as a suitable base of operations if you want a cheap, convenient place to bunk down for the night.

On your way out, check out the **Table Rocks**, impressive 800ft mesas that speak of the area's volcanic past and are home to unique plant and animal species. Flowery spring is the best time for hiking to the flat tops, which were revered Native American sites. After **TouVelle State Park** (stateparks.oregon. gov), fork either left to reach the trailhead to Lower Table Rock (3.5-mile round-trip hike) or right for Upper Table Rock (2.5-mile round-trip hike).

THE DRIVE

The drive along Hwy 62 isn't much until after Shady Cove, when urban sprawl stops and forest

STAS MOROZ/SHUTTERSTOCK ©

Crater Lake (p145)

adding to the drama of the landscape is **Wizard Island**, a volcanic cinder cone topped by its own mini crater called Witches Cauldron.

Get the overview with the 33-mile Rim Drive, which offers over 30 viewpoints as it winds around the edge of Crater Lake. The gloriously still waters reflect surrounding mountain peaks like a giant dark-blue mirror, making for spectacular photographs and breathtaking panoramas.

You can also camp, ski or hike in the surrounding old-growth forests. The popular and steep

TOP TIP:

Visiting Crater Lake

Crater Lake's popular south entrance is open year-round. In winter you can only go up to the lake's rim and back down the same way; no other roads are plowed. The north entrance is only open from early June to late October, depending on snowfall.

mile-long Cleetwood Cove Trail, at the northern end of the crater, provides the only water access at the cove. Alternatively, get up close on a two-hour **boat tour** (travelcraterlake.com/things-to-do/boat-tours).

THE DRIVE
Head north on Hwy 138 for 41 miles and turn right on Rd 34.

05 UMPQUA HOT SPRINGS
Set on a mountainside overlooking the North Umpqua River, Umpqua is one of Oregon's

most splendid hot springs, with a little bit of height-induced adrenaline thanks to its position atop a rocky bluff.

Springs are known for soothing weary muscles, so earn your soak at Umpqua by starting with a hike – it is in a national forest, after all – where you'll be treated to lush, old-growth forest and waterfalls punctuating the landscape. Half a mile from the parking lot is the spectacularly scenic **North Umpqua Trail** (fs. usda.gov).

THE DRIVE
The turnout for Toketee Falls is right on Hwy 138, 2 miles past the Umpqua turnoff.

06 TOKETEE FALLS
More than half a dozen waterfalls line this section of the Rogue-Umpqua Scenic Byway, but the one that truly demands a stop is the stunning, two-tiered **Toketee Falls** (USFS Rd 34). The falls' first tier drops 40ft into an upper pool behind a cliff of columnar basalt, from where the water crashes another 80ft down the rock columns into

yet another gorgeous, green-blue pool below.

One tiny disclaimer: although the hike is just 0.4 miles, there's a staircase of 200 steps down to the viewpoint, so climbing back up to your car is a bit of a workout.

THE DRIVE
From here, the scenery tapers back down to only moderately spectacular as you leave the Umpqua National Forest. It's just one hour to Roseburg.

07 ROSEBURG

Sprawling Roseburg lies in a valley near the confluence of the South and North Umpqua Rivers. The city is mostly a cheap, modern sleepover for travelers headed for other places (such as Crater Lake), but it does have a cute, historic downtown area and is surrounded by award-winning wineries.

Don't miss the excellent Douglas **County Museum** (umpqua valleymuseums.org), which displays the area's cultural and natural histories. Especially interesting are the railroad derailment photos and History of Wine exhibit. Kids have an interactive area and live snakes to look at.

🚗 THE DRIVE

Go south on I-5 for 47 miles and take the Wolf Creek exit. Follow Old State Hwy 99 to curve back under the interstate. Golden is 3.2 miles east on Coyote Creek Rd.

Photo Opportunity

No surprise here: Crater Lake.

08 GOLDEN STATE HERITAGE SITE

Not ready to return to civilization quite yet? Stop off in the ghost town of Golden, population zero. A former mining town that had over 100 residents in the mid-1800s, Golden was built on the banks of Coyote Creek when gold was discovered there.

A handful of structures remain, as well as some newfangled interpretive signs that tell the tale of a curiously devout community that eschewed drinking and dancing, all giving a fascinating glimpse of what life was like back then. The weathered wooden buildings include a residence, the general store/post office, and a classic country church. Fun fact: the town was once used as a location for the long-running American Western TV series *Gunsmoke*.

🚗 THE DRIVE

Go south another 45 miles on I-5 and take exit 43. The Oregon Vortex is 4.2 miles north of the access road.

09 GOLD HILL

Just outside the town of Gold Hill lies the **Oregon Vortex** (oregonvortex.com), where the laws of physics don't seem to apply – or is it all just an optical illusion created by skewed buildings on steep hillsides? However you see it, the place is definitely bizarre: objects roll uphill, a person's height changes depending on where they stand, and brooms stand up on their own...or so it seems.

Toketee Falls (p147)

24

OREGON

Caves of Highway 199

BEST BOTANY LESSON

The *Darlingtonia* plant on the Eight Dollar Mountain Boardwalk Trail

Darlingtonia californica (Pitcher Plant)

DURATION	DISTANCE	GREAT FOR
2 days	248km / 154 miles	Families, Nature

BEST TIME TO GO	April through October, when the caves are open

Think Hwy 199 is just a convenient connector from the interstate to the coast and Hwy 101? Well, you could buzz through it in a couple of hours and think, 'My, what pretty trees we passed.' But take your time and you'll discover an amazing amount of natural diversity, all conveniently packaged into one compact area. Prepare to picnic, hike, climb, swim and explore all along the Redwood Hwy.

Link Your Trip

14 Highway 101 Oregon Coast

From Crescent City, drive 26 miles north to Brookings to kick off your Oregon coastal adventure.

22 Essential I-5

Grants Pass is right on this major thoroughfare that gets you where you're going and has some fun along the way.

01 **GRANTS PASS**

As a modern and not particularly scenic city, Grants Pass isn't a huge tourist destination, but its location on the banks of the Rogue River makes it a portal to adventure. White-water rafting, fine fishing and jet-boat excursions are the biggest attractions, and there's good camping and hiking in the area. If you're here on a Saturday between mid-March and Thanksgiving, be sure to check out the **Outdoors Growers' Market** (growersmarket. org), a farmers and craft market that draws the city together. Since the theme of this trip is caves, be

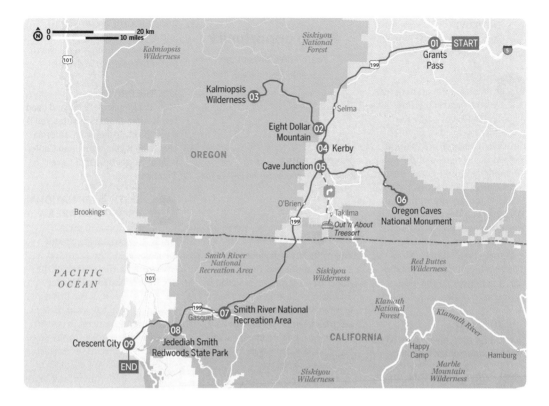

sure to stop by the **visitor center** and snap a picture with the local caveman statue for posterity.

🚗 THE DRIVE
Take Hwy 199 24 miles southwest and turn right on Eight Dollar Rd, just 3.5 miles past Selma. The trailheads mentioned in the next stop are less than a mile from the turnout.

02 EIGHT DOLLAR MOUNTAIN
If seeing some rare, carnivorous plants would just about make your trip, you've come to the right place. This area is one of the only places on earth where you'll find the *Darlingtonia californica* (also called the Pitcher

Plant, the Cobra Lily and 'that little plant that eats bugs'). Beautiful and deadly (but not to humans), this lily-like plant gobbles up insects and digests them. The **Eight Dollar Mountain Boardwalk Trail** offers easy viewing of the *Darlingtonia* with a gentle stroll on a boardwalk trail – or if you refuse to be coddled, opt for the still-not-that-strenuous 1-mile hike that overlooks the Illinois River.

🚗 THE DRIVE
Continue west on USFS Rd 4201 (Eight Dollar Rd). The next stop is 16 long, winding miles from the boardwalk, taking a little over an hour to navigate.

03 KALMIOPSIS WILDERNESS
One of Oregon's largest wilderness areas, the remote Kalmiopsis Wilderness is famous for its rare plant life. About 150 million years ago, the area was separated from North America by a wide gulf and vegetation evolved on its own, so by the time the mountains fused to the continent, the plant life was very different from that of the mainland. These unique plant species are showcased on the steep, 0.75-mile hike to **Babyfoot Lake**. In addition to the carnivorous *Darlingtonia,* the pink-flowered *Kalmiopsis leachiana* and rare Port Orford cedar are found almost nowhere else on earth.

THE DRIVE
Backtrack to US 199. Turn right and go 2.7 miles south to Kerby.

04 KERBY
With a population of just 400 – and sometimes listed as a ghost town – tiny Kerby has a surprising amount going for it.The **Kerbyville Museum**, located in an 1880s pioneer home, offers insight into pioneer life and Native American history. For real roadside fun, try the whimsical **It's a Burl Gallery**, which looks like a hobbit home on the highway. Part gallery, part attraction, it features fantastical carvings, driftwood sculptures and elaborate tree houses. At the least, stop by and admire the garden gallery.

THE DRIVE
Go 2.4 short miles south on US 199 to the town of Cave Junction.

05 CAVE JUNCTION
Relatively bustling among the towns along US 199, Cave Junction is the jumping-off point for the Oregon Caves National Monument. The local terroir – taking advantage of coastal and inland climates – lends itself nicely to pinot noir and chardonnay, which you can sample at several local wineries. While you're out here, stop in to **Taylor's Country Store** (taylorsausage.com). It looks like a hole in the wall from outside, but opens up to a bustling store and restaurant surrounding a meat counter. Meals are amazingly cheap, it's a very local scene and it even has live music on Friday nights. The family has been making sausages with recipes from their European ancestors since the 1930s.

Photo opportunity
You, on the banks of the scenic Smith River.

THE DRIVE
Drive southeast on OR-46 for 19 miles.

DETOUR
Treetop Trek
Start: 05 Cave Junction

Why settle for a motel when you can sleep in a tree house? The **Out 'n' About Treesort** (treehouses.com) in Takilma, near Cave Junction, offers 16 different kinds of tree houses that sleep between two and six guests. If it's booked up (reservations are crucial), consider stopping by for a zipline or a horseback trail ride.

06 OREGON CAVES NATIONAL MONUMENT
The 'Marble Halls of Oregon' are the highlight of any US 199 trip. During your spelunking adventure at **Oregon Caves National Monument** (nps.gov/orca), expect to climb, twist and wiggle your way through 3 miles of passages and stairs on the 90-minute tour. Your reward is myriad cave formations, such as cave popcorn, pearls, moon milk, classic pipe organs, columns and stalactites. Guided tours run at least hourly – half-hourly in July and August. Dress warmly, wear good shoes and be prepared to get dripped on. For safety reasons, children less than 42in tall are not allowed on tours. A handful of short nature trails surround the area, such as the

0.75-mile **Cliff Nature Trail** and the 3.3-mile **Big Tree Trail**, which loops through old-growth forest to a huge Douglas fir.

THE DRIVE
Backtrack to US 199 and head south. After about 15 minutes you'll cross the state line into California. The Smith River Information Center is 34 miles southwest of Cave Junction.

07 SMITH RIVER NATIONAL RECREATION AREA
For about 16 miles, Smith River weaves back and forth alongside the Redwood Hwy, making this stretch of the **Six Rivers National Forest** the prettiest part of the drive. In summer you can swim in the clear, emerald waters; in winter you can try to land a trophy-sized salmon or steelhead (or at least something modest for dinner). Short, easy and right off the highway, the 2-mile **Myrtle Creek Trail** (redwoodparksconservancy. org) is a popular hike that's lush and green. As you traipse through wildflowers, ferns and red alder, look for unusual species that will bring out the botany enthusiast in you. To learn more about the area, stop by the **Smith River Information Center** (fs.usda.gov).

THE DRIVE
Drive 9.2 miles west on US 199 to get to the Jedediah Smith Redwoods State Park visitor center.

08 JEDEDIAH SMITH REDWOODS STATE PARK
Tree-huggers can find plenty to hug in this forest filled with centuries-old redwoods, spruce, hemlock and Douglas firs – and

with 20 miles of hiking and nature trails, there's a lot to explore, even if you choose not to canoodle. **Jedediah Smith Redwoods State Park** (parks.ca.gov) is a blissfully undeveloped spot full of old-growth redwoods, which can grow up to 300ft tall. The park's best scenery can be found at **Stout Grove**. To get there, go south on South Fork Rd. After half a mile, turn right on Douglas Park Rd then continue onto the narrow, unpaved Howland Hill Rd for one of the best redwood routes anywhere.

 THE DRIVE

Go 4.5 miles west to the junction of Hwy 101, then take 101 south 4.5 more miles into Crescent City.

09 CRESCENT CITY

You've made it! After nonstop trees, mountains and rivers, you get a change of pace when US 199 dead-ends at the Pacific Ocean. Slightly scruffy Crescent City is hardly the crown jewel of the Pacific Coast, but its **Beachfront Park** is a great harborside beach for families, with picnic tables, a bicycle

trail and no waves. The **Battery Point Lighthouse** (delnortehistory.org) offers tours, but only at low tide, and only April through September. But if you luck out (call first) you'll see the keeper's quarters and over 150 years of artifacts, plus a spectacular ocean view from the top.

Nearby, you can hike through the wetlands at the 5000-acre **Tolowa Dunes State Park** to find sand dunes, beaches strewn with driftwood, two lakes and more than 250 species of birds.

FDASTUDILLO/ISTOCK/GETTY IMAGES ©

Oregon Caves National Monument

LINDA C MACLEAN/SHUTTERSTOCK ©

Lake Cowichan (p182)

British Columbia

Explore

British Columbia

Canada's westernmost province wows visitors with its mighty mountains, deep forests and dramatic coastlines. But there's much more to British Columbia than its larger-than-life natural beauty – take for example cosmopolitan Vancouver, a film-friendly city that fuses cuisines and cultures from Asia and beyond. The jewel-like capital city, Victoria, has an outsized impact, with its picturesque harbor and plentiful gardens. And don't forget the legendary ski haven and outdoor adventure headquarters of Whistler.

The Okanagan wine country is increasingly renowned beyond Canadian borders, and the remote islands of Haida Gwaii beckon adventurers looking to explore the very edges of the region.

Vancouver

Vancouver is a sparkling, cosmopolitan city set against a backdrop of rugged natural beauty. Its welcoming downtown is flanked by the forested seawall of Stanley Park, which makes a perfect 9km cycling or walking route, and the neighborhoods contain easily walkable shopping streets. Wander historic Gastown, artsy Granville Island and the colorful West End.

You won't really need a car for in-town exploring: it's easy to get around on foot, by bus or by cab. The TransLink network includes buses, SkyTrain and SeaBus and offers all-day, all-zone passes.

The best streets for food include downtown's Robson St for Japanese izakaya, Yaletown's Hamilton and Mainland Sts for upscale dining, Gastown for bars, Commercial Dr for ethnic food, and the West End's Denman and Davie Sts for midrange options. Swanky sleepovers abound downtown, as do midrange hotels. To split the geographical difference between downtown and the great outdoors, head to the North Shore. Hostels are scattered across the city; there are several good ones near the University of British Columbia (UBC).

Victoria

British Columbia's beautiful capital, at the tip of Vancouver Island, has plenty of hotels and restaurants as well as museums, galleries and gardens to explore. Check out the Royal BC Museum for the area's history,

WHEN TO GO

As with the rest of the Pacific Northwest, BC is hottest in August and coldest in December. The winter months (November to April) get the most rain, but this brings an explosion of wildflowers in April/May. At higher elevations, roads may be treacherous (or closed) October to May. Hotel prices increase in July and August but that's the best time for driving.

or wander around in the 55-acre Butchart Gardens to immerse yourself in botanical wonders.

Visitors are most likely to arrive here by ferry from either Seattle (passenger ferry, about 2½ hours one-way) or Port Angeles (cars and passengers, 90 minutes), Washington. Hotels on either side may include or offer shuttle services to and from the ferry if you don't have your own wheels. The adventurous can also take a seaplane from Seattle, or a regional airline to Victoria International Airport north of town, where there are car rental offices, gas stations, supermarkets and other amenities.

Whistler

The quintessential mountain town of Whistler draws outdoorsy visitors in winter for its world-class ski slopes and in summer for everything from hiking to ziplining. The town took its name from the distinctive noise made by furry marmots

TRANSPORT

Visitors to BC often fly into Vancouver International Airport or arrive by ferry from Washington State to Victoria. You can also drive north on Interstate 5/BC 99. Vancouver is about a two-hour drive from Bellingham. Amtrak trains also run between Vancouver, BC, and Portland, OR, with multiple stops. To reach Haida Gwaii, take BC Ferries from Prince Rupert in northern BC.

who inhabit the surrounding area. Whistler Village, site of the 2010 Winter Olympics and Paralympics, is a walkable place full of shops, upscale lodgings, cafes and restaurants. The HI hostel here was built to house Olympic athletes; it's a few miles south of the village but easily reached by bus.

WHERE TO STAY

If you're a fan of remote wilderness lodges where you can fish or kayak from the front deck, this is the region for you. Just know that the more special and remote a wilderness lodge is, the further in advance you'll need to book. There are also lodgings full of character in the hub cities, from renovated historic landmark hotels to boutique inns to gleaming high-design luxury digs. You'll find good hostels in Victoria and Whistler, eco-lodges in Vancouver's remote north, and beach camping and B&Bs in Haida Gwaii.

 WHAT'S ON

Vancouver International Jazz Festival

Big-name entertainers perform at various venues around the city. (June/July)

Nanaimo Dragon Boat Festival

Dragon-boat races and a family-friendly festival start off the summer season. (July)

Revelstoke Wildflower Festival

The alpine landscape is washed in color for a few weeks each year. (August)

BC Culture Days

A three-week celebration of arts and culture from all across Canada. (September/October)

Resources

Tourism British Columbia (hellobc.com) Official tourism site for the province.

BC Wildfire Service (wildfire situation.nrs.gov.bc.ca) Alerts and information about fires.

City of Vancouver (vancouver. ca) Resource-packed official city site.

Inside Vancouver (inside vancouver.ca) What to do in and around the city.

Tourism Victoria (tourism victoria.com) Travel tips, links to ferry schedules and maps.

25

BRITISH COLUMBIA

Vancouver & the Fraser Valley

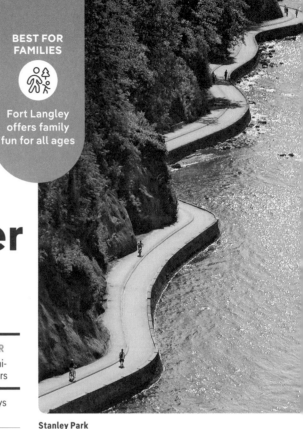

BEST FOR FAMILIES

Fort Langley offers family fun for all ages

Stanley Park

DURATION	DISTANCE	GREAT FOR
2 days	186km / 116 miles	History, Families, Outdoors

BEST TIME TO GO	June to September for warm days and ripened fruit

As you step onto the swinging Capilano Suspension Bridge, get eyed up by a grizzly bear atop Grouse Mountain or watch your children hone their bartering skills over wolverine skins at Fort Langley, you might wonder what happened to the promised pretty valley drive. But don't worry; it's here. With dramatic mountains rising on either side, a tour along the Fraser River is as action-packed as it is scenic.

Link Your Trip

26 Sea to Sky Highway

Head northwest from Vancouver, rather than east, and wind your way up into the mountains.

27 A Strait Hop

Drive onto the ferry at Horseshoe Bay in West Vancouver.

01 **STANLEY PARK**

Just steps from downtown Vancouver (also worth a walk around), but seemingly worlds away, **Stanley Park** (vancouver.ca/parks) is a spectacular urban oasis, covered in a quarter of a million trees that tower up to 80m (260ft). Rivaling New York's Central Park, this peninsula is a favorite hangout for locals, who walk, run or cycle around the 9km (5.5-mile) super-scenic seawall that circles the outer edge of the park.

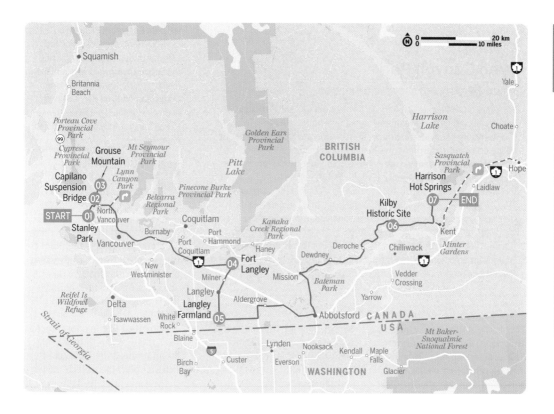

The pathway offers shimmering views of Burrard Inlet and passes impressive totem poles, squat **Brockton Point Lighthouse** and log-strewn Third Beach, where you can also take a dip. Watch for the dramatic **Siwash Rock**, standing sentry off the western shoreline. Meaning 'he is standing up,' it was named after a traditional First Nations legend that indicates it is a man transformed into stone; the hole in the rock is where he kept his fishing tackle.

Looking out across tree-fringed English Bay, Second Beach has a heated outdoor **swimming pool** (open May to September) that's wildly popular with families. From here, a long sandy beach stretches south along Beach Ave. Looking for some kid-friendly action? The park's eastern shoreline is home to a fantastic **water park** that will keep your youngsters happily squealing for hours.

Also in the park is the ever-popular **Vancouver Aquarium** (vanaqua.or). One of the city's biggest attractions, it's home to penguins, otters and a plethora of BC marine critters.

 THE DRIVE
Head north on Stanley Park Causeway and cross the beautiful Lions Gate Bridge to North Vancouver.

Head east on Marine Dr for a block and turn left onto Capilano Rd, heading north for 2.4km (1.5 miles).

02 **CAPILANO SUSPENSION BRIDGE**
Not for the faint of heart, **Capilano Suspension Bridge Park** (capbridge.com) is home to one of the world's longest (140m/460ft) and highest (70m/230ft) pedestrian suspension bridges, swaying gently over the roiling waters of Capilano Canyon. As you gingerly cross, try to remember that the steel cables you are gripping are embedded in huge concrete blocks on either side.

DETOUR:

Lynn Canyon Park

START: 02 CAPILANO SUSPENSION BRIDGE

For a free alternative to Capilano, divert to **Lynn Canyon Park** (lynn-canyon.ca), a temperate rainforest area that's home to its own lofty but slightly smaller suspension bridge. There are also plenty of excellent hiking trails and some great tree-hugging picnic spots here. Check out the park's **Ecology Centre** (lynncanyonecologycentre.ca) for displays on the region's rich biodiversity. If you're really keen on local flora, drop into a bookstore on your travels and pick up a copy of the *Vancouver Tree Book* (David Tracey, 2016). It details many of the region's leafy wonders and shows you how to spot them while you're here. While you're weaving around the trails at Lynn Canyon or any other tree-hugging hot spot you discover during your drive, look out for cedars, hemlocks, Douglas fir and more. To find the park, head east on Hwy 1 from Capilano Rd and turn left on Lynn Valley Rd.

This is the region's most popular attraction, hence the summertime crowds. The grounds here include rainforest walks, totem poles and some smaller bridges strung between the trees that offer a lovely squirrel's-eye forest walk. You can also test your bravery on the **Cliffwalk**, a glass-and-steel walkway secured with horizontal bars to a granite cliff face and suspended 90m (295ft)over the canyon floor. Deep breath...

THE DRIVE
Continue north on Capilano Rd. This turns into Nancy Greene Way, which ends at the next stop.

03 GROUSE MOUNTAIN
One of the region's most popular outdoor hangouts, **Grouse Mountain** (grousemountain.com) rises 1231m (4039ft) over North Vancouver's skyline. In summer,

Skyride gondola tickets to the top include access to lumberjack shows, bird of prey displays and alpine hiking trails plus a **nature reserve** that's home to orphaned grizzly bears and timber wolves. You can also brave the two-hour, five-line **zipline course** (C$89, excluding Skyride) or the 'Eye of the Wind' tour, which takes you to the top of a 20-story wind turbine tower for spectacular 360-degree views. In winter, Grouse is a very popular magnet for local and visiting skiers and snowboarders.

THE DRIVE
Return south down Nancy Greene Way and Capilano Rd, taking a

TRAFFIC REPORTS
Traffic over the Lions Gate Bridge and along Hwy 1 can be heavy enough to bring you to a standstill at times. Check the website of DriveBC (drivebc.ca) for traffic, construction and incident reports.

left onto Edgemont Blvd, which leads to Hwy 1. Head east, following the highway through Burnaby, crossing the Second Narrows Bridge and then the impressive 10-lane Port Mann Bridge. Continue on Hwy 1, exiting at 88 Ave East and following signs to Fort Langley. Trip takes around an hour.

04 FORT LANGLEY
Little Fort Langley's tree-lined streets and 19th-century storefronts make it one of the Lower Mainland's most picturesque historic villages. Its main heritage highlight is the evocative **Fort Langley National Historic Site** (parkscanada.gc.ca/fortlangley), perhaps the region's most important old-school landmark.

A fortified trading post since 1827, this is where James Douglas announced the creation of British Columbia in 1858, giving the site a legitimate claim to being the province's birthplace. Chat with costumed re-enactors knitting, working on beaver pelts or sweeping their pioneer homes. Also open to explore are re-created artisan workshops and a **gold-panning area** that's very popular with kids. And when you need a rest, sample baking and lunchtime meals from the 1800s in the **Lelem' Cafe**.

Be sure to check the fort's website before you arrive: there's a wide array of events that bring the past back to life, including a

summertime evening campfire program that will take you right back to the pioneer days of the 1800s.

THE DRIVE
Head south out of the village on Glover Rd, crossing Hwy 1 and then taking a slight left so that you're traveling south on 216th St. The next stop is just past 16th Ave.

05 **LANGLEY FARMLAND**
The vine-covered grounds of **Chaberton Estate Winery** (chabertonwin ery.com) are the setting for the Fraser Valley's oldest wine-making operation, here since

Photo opportunity
Wobbling over the Capilano Suspension Bridge.

1991. The French-influenced, 22-hectare (55-acre) vineyard specializes in cool-climate whites: its subtle, riesling-style Bacchus is dangerously easy to drink. There's also a handy bistro here.

Head south and right on 4th St to the charming **Vista D'oro** (vis tadoro.com), a working farm and

winery where you can load up on fresh pears, plums, apples and stripy heirloom tomatoes. Sample preserves such as piquant mango lime salsa and sweet rhubarb and vanilla jam. Also pick up a bottle of its utterly delicious, port-style walnut wine that's made from nuts grown just outside the shop. It's definitely small batch, so if you see it buy it.

The Fraser Valley is home to countless farms, producing everything from tulips to cheese. Many accept visitors, give tours and sell their wares in farm shops. If you're keen to visit some more, go to www.circle farmtour.com for details.

YVETTE CARDOZO/ALAMY ©

Vineyard, Vista D'oro

THE DRIVE
Return north up 216th St and turn right on North Bluff Rd. Continue east for four blocks and turn left onto 248th St, which takes you to the Fraser Hwy. Head east toward Abbotsford, and then north on the Abbotsford Mission Hwy over the Fraser River to Hwy 7. Turn right and follow the road along the river. Approximately 1½ hours.

06 KILBY HISTORIC SITE
To get to **Kilby Historic Site** (kilby.ca), turn right onto School Rd and then right again onto Kilby Rd. The clocks turn back to the 1920s when you enter this site, all that remains of the once thriving Harrison Mills community. Join a tour led by costumed interpreters as you explore the general store, hotel, post office and working farm, complete with friendly farm animals. Save time for treats made with traditional ice cream.

THE DRIVE
Return to Hwy 7 and carry on east, passing through farmland and hazelnut orchards. Turn left on Hwy 9, which takes you to Harrison Hot Springs, for a total drive of 21km (13 miles).

◇ **DETOUR:**
Hope

START: **HARRISON HOT SPRINGS**

Hope's nickname is the 'Chainsaw Capital' and this rather unusual moniker certainly draws attention. The name was earned by the wooden sculptures peppered throughout the town. Hope is a small community at the eastern edge of the Fraser Valley, set beneath the shadow of the Cascade Mountains. The 70-plus chainsaw sculptures are the products of both local and visiting artists. Most depict wildlife, including the Sasquatch who is believed to live in the nearby woods.

If Hope looks oddly familiar, you may be dating yourself. The original *Rambo* movie was filmed here in 1982. For a self-guided tour map of the sculptures and *Rambo* locations, drop into the visitor center on the edge of town. Hope is 40km (25 miles) east of Harrison Hot Springs on Hwy 7.

---

07 HARRISON HOT SPRINGS
Set on the edge of Harrison Lake with views to the forest-carpeted mountains, **Harrison Hot Springs** (tourismharrison.com) is a resort town that draws both locals and visitors to its sandy beach, warm lagoon and lakeside promenade. While the lake itself is glacier-fed, two hot springs bubble at the southern end of the lake and the warm water can be enjoyed year-round at the town's upscale resort and the indoor public pool. If you're smart, you'll time your Harrison visit for the area's biggest cultural festival. July's multiday Harrison Festival of the Arts (harrisonfestival.com) has been running for more than 30 years, bringing live music, gallery shows, creative workshops and more to the area's beachfront streets.

26

Sea to Sky Highway

DURATION	DISTANCE	GREAT FOR
1–2 days	82km / 132 miles	History, Nature, Families

BEST TIME TO GO!	November to March has the best snow; June to September offers sunny hiking, plus driving without chains.

Drive out of North Vancouver and straight onto the wild west coast. This short excursion reveals the essence of British Columbia's shoreline with majestic sea and mountain vistas, outdoor activity opportunities, wildlife-watching possibilities and a peek into the regional First Nations culture and pioneer history that's woven along the route. There's even freshly roasted, organic coffee along the way. How much more 'BC' can you get?

Link Your Trip

25 Vancouver & the Fraser Valley

Highway 99 begins in North Vancouver where you can divert onto this multifarious exploration of Vancouver and its fertile hinterland.

27 A Strait Hop

This shore-tracking tour of Vancouver Island and the Sunshine Coast goes through Horseshoe Bay (the first stop on this trip).

HORSESHOE BAY

01 Standing at the foot of Horseshoe Bay as clouds and mist drift in across the snow-capped mountains of Howe Sound may well make you feel like you've stepped into Middle Earth. Green-forested hills tumble down around the village, which has a small-town vibe that doesn't attest to its proximity to Vancouver. Grab a coffee and some fish-and-chips from one of the many waterfront cafes and watch the bobbling boats from the seaside park. This first stop is all about slowing down and taking it all in.

JOANNA SZYPULSKA/SHUTTERSTOCK ©

BEST FOR OUTDOORS

Ski Olympic-style down Whistler Mountain

Horseshoe Bay

Have a wander through the **Spirit Gallery** (spirit-gallery.com), which is filled with classic and contemporary First Nations art and design from the region. You'll find everything from eye glasses to animal hand-puppets, prints, pewter and carvings.

 THE DRIVE
Head north for 25km (15.5 miles) on Hwy 99, which curves around the coast and follows Howe Sound. You'll be traveling between steep mountainsides, down which waterfalls plummet, and the often misty ocean where islands are perched like sleeping giants. Watch out for Tunnel Point Lookout on the western side of the highway for a vantage point across the sound.

02 PORTEAU COVE PROVINCIAL PARK
Once popular with regional First Nations communities for sturgeon fishing, Porteau Cove is one of the oldest archaeological sites on the northwest coast. These days it's a haven for divers, with a sunken ship and reefs supporting countless species of marine life, such as octopus and wolf eels. The rocky beach is good for exploring, with plenty of logs to clamber on, and in summer the water is just about warm enough for a quick dip.

 THE DRIVE
From here, the sound narrows and as you continue 8km (5 miles) north on Hwy 99, mountains from the opposite shore begin to loom over you.

03 BRITANNIA BEACH
Don a hard hat and hop on a bone-shaking train that trundles you through a floodlit mine tunnel. With hands-on exhibits, gold panning, an engaging film and entry into the dizzying 20-story mill, the **Britannia Mine Museum** (britanniaminemuseum.ca) has plenty to keep you (and any kids in tow) busy. Factor in a couple of hours here.

WHY I LOVE THIS TRIP

Brendan Sainsbury, writer

If you live in BC (as I do), this is where you take any visiting friend or relative to instantly impress them. It's BC's greatest hits in one morning (or afternoon) – mountains, water, forests, wildlife, First Nations myths, and a rugged but well-maintained road that never strays far from the wilderness. A stop in Squamish for coffee and a quick 'run' up the Chief is de rigueur.

 THE DRIVE
Continue 7km (4.25 miles) north on Hwy 99, through the lush green Murrin Provincial Park.

04 **SHANNON FALLS**
Torpedoing 335m (1099ft) over the mountaintop, **Shannon Falls** (bcparks.ca) is the third-largest flume in the province. Historically, the medicine people of the Squamish First Nation trained alongside these falls. A short, picturesque walk through the woods leads to a viewing platform.

You can also hike from here to the peak of the **Stawamus Chief** (two to three hours round-trip) or hop back in your car and continue another minute or two along Hwy 99 to the Sea to Sky Gondola (seatoskygondola.com) where a cable-car zips you up to a summit lodge at 885m (2904ft). From here you can walk across a shaky suspension bridge to access a network of above-the-treeline trails.

 THE DRIVE
Continue north on Hwy 99, past the Stawamus Chief and through Squamish, where you can stop for gas or sample from a raft of craft breweries and distilleries. Carry on along the highway, taking a left on Depot Rd and then another left onto Government Rd. The next stop is a few minutes up the road on your right.

05 **BRACKENDALE**
Brackendale is home to one of the largest populations of wintering bald eagles in North America. Visit between November and February to see an almost overwhelming number of these massive, magnificent birds feasting on salmon in the Squamish River. A path running alongside the riverbank offers a short walk and plenty of easy eagle-spotting opportunities. Across the river are the tall trees of **Brackendale Eagles Provincial Park**, where the beady-eyed birds perch in the night.

TOP TIP:

Gas Station

There is nowhere to fill your tank between North Vancouver and Squamish, a distance of around 50km (31 miles). This is mountain driving so make sure you've got at least half a tank when you set out.

Also in this neighborhood is the historic **West Coast Railway Heritage Park** (wcra.org). This large, mostly outdoor museum is the final resting place of British Columbia's legendary *Royal Hudson* steam engine and has dozens of other historic railcars, including working engines and cabooses, sumptuous sleepers and a cool vintage mail car. Check out the handsome Roundhouse building, housing the park's most precious trains and artifacts.

 THE DRIVE
Hwy 99 leaves the Squamish River 5km (3 miles) north of Brackendale and heads into the trees. The next stop is on the right.

06 **ALICE LAKE**
Delve into an old-growth hemlock forest for hiking and biking trails as well as lakeside picnic opportunities. Surrounded by a ring of towering mountains and offering two sandy beaches fringed by relatively warm water in summer, **Alice Lake Provincial Park** (discovercamping.ca) is a popular spot for a dip, a walk and an alfresco lunch.

Next stretch your legs on the 6km (3.75-mile) **Four Lakes Trail**, an easy hike that does a loop around all four lakes in the park, passing through stands of Douglas fir and western red cedar. Keep your eyes (and your ears) peeled for warblers, Steller's jays and chickadees as well as for the box turtles that sometimes sun themselves on the logs at Stump Lake.

THE DRIVE
Continue north along Hwy 99 for around 6km (3.75 miles) to Brohm Lake.

07 **BROHM LAKE**
Less developed than Alice Lake Provincial Park, **Brohm Lake Interpretive Forest** has 10km (6.25 miles) of walking trails, many of them easy and flat. The lake is warm enough for summer swimming as the sun filters down onto the tree-studded shoreline.

Archaeological digs from this area have unearthed arrowheads and tools from early First Nations communities that date back 10,000 years. The area was later the scene of a logging mill and today is home to **Tenderfoot Fish Hatchery**, a facility aimed at replenishing depleted chum and Chinook salmon stocks, which fell from around 25,000 in the 1960s to around 1500 in the early 1980s. You can visit the hatchery and take a self-guided tour by following a 3km (2-mile) trail from Brohm Lake.

THE DRIVE
Continue up Hwy 99 just over 3km (2 miles) to the next stop.

08 **TANTALUS LOOKOUT**
This viewpoint looks out across the Tantalus Mountain Range. Tantalus was a character in Greek mythology who gave us the word 'tantalize'; apparently the mountains were named by an explorer who was tempted to climb the range's snowy peaks, but was stuck on the other side of the turbulent Squamish River. In addition to Mt Tantalus, the Greek hero's

entire family is here – his wife Mt Dione, his daughter Mt Niobe, his son Mt Pelops and his grandson Mt Thyestes.

The Squamish people once used this area to train in hunting and believe that long ago, hunters and their dogs were immortalized here, becoming the soaring mountain range. Those stone hunters must be

rather tantalized themselves; the forested slopes of the mountains are home to grizzly bears, elk, wolverines, wolves and cougars.

THE DRIVE
Follow Hwy 99 22km (13.7 miles) north through the woods, skirting the edge of Daisy Lake before reaching the next stop on your right.

CAVAN IMAGES/SHUTTERSTOCK ©

Stawamus Chief

THE STAWAMUS CHIEF
Towering 700m (2297ft) above the waters of Howe Sound like 'The Wall' in *Game of Thrones*, the Chief is the world's second-largest freestanding granite monolith. The three peaks have long been considered a sacred place to the Squamish people; they once came here seeking spiritual renewal. It's also the nesting grounds of peregrine falcons, who are increasingly returning to the area.

The views from the top are unbelievable. The sheer face of the monolith has become a magnet to rock climbers, while hikers can take a steep trail starting from the base station of the Sea to Sky Gondola to one or all of the three summits.

09 BRANDYWINE FALLS PROVINCIAL PARK

Surging powerfully over the edge of a volcanic escarpment, **Brandywine Falls** (bcparks.ca/brandywine-falls -park) plunge a dramatic 70m (230ft) – a straight shot into the pool below. Follow the easy 10-minute trail through the woods and step out onto the viewing platform, directly over the falls.

From here you can also see **Mt Garibaldi**, the most easily recognizable mountain in the Coast Range. Its distinctive jagged top and color has earned it the name Black Tusk. This mountain is of particular significance to local First Nations groups who believe the great Thunderbird landed here. With its supernatural ways, it shot bolts of lightning from its eyes, creating the color and shape of the mountaintop.

A 7km (4.25-mile) looped trail leads further through the park's dense forest and ancient lava beds to **Cal-Cheak Suspension Bridge**.

THE STORY BEGINS

As you enter the Squamish Lil'wat Cultural Centre (slcc.ca) in Whistler, take a look at the carved cedar doors you're passing through. According to the center's guide map, the door on the left shows a grizzly bear – protector of the Lil'wat – with a salmon in its mouth, representing sharing. The carving references a mother bear and cub that walked into the center during construction. The door on the right, depicting a human face and hands up, symbolizes the Squamish welcoming all visitors.

Photo opportunity

Get the ultimate snowy-peak picture from Tantalus Lookout.

THE DRIVE

Continue north for 17km (10.5 miles) along Hwy 99, passing Creek-side Village and carrying on to the main Whistler village entrance (it's well signposted and obvious once you see it).

10 WHISTLER

Nestled in the shade of the formidable Whistler and Blackcomb Mountains, Whistler has long been BC's golden child. Popular in winter for its world-class ski slopes and in summer for everything from hiking to one of North America's longest ziplines, it draws fans from around the world. It was named for the furry marmots that fill the area with their loud

whistle, but there are also plenty of berry-snuffling black bears about.

The site of many of the outdoor events at the 2010 Winter Olympic and Paralympic Games, Whistler village is well worth a stroll and is filled with an eclectic mix of stores, flash hotels and seemingly countless cafes and restaurants.

Crisscrossed with over 200 runs, the **Whistler-Blackcomb** (whistlerblackcomb.com) sister mountains are linked by a 4.4km (2.75-mile) gondola that includes the world's longest unsupported span. Ski season runs from late November to April on Whistler and to June on Blackcomb. **Ziptrek Ecotours** (ziptrek.com) offers year-round zip-line courses that will have you screaming with gut-quivering pleasure.

While you're here, be sure to take in the wood-beamed **Squamish Lil'wat Cultural Centre**, built to resemble a traditional longhouse. It's filled with art, images and displays that illuminate the traditional and contemporary cultures of the Squamish and Lil'wat Nations.

A short stroll away, **Audain Art Museum** (audainartmus eum.com) is home to an array of paintings from BC icons, including Emily Carr and EJ Hughes, plus a collection of historic and contemporary First Nations works. Allow at least an hour here.

Whistler

27

BRITISH COLUMBIA

A Strait Hop

BEST FOR FOODIES

Dive into regional flavors in Cowichan Bay

DURATION	DISTANCE	GREAT FOR
2–3 days	351km / 219 miles	Nature, Food & drink

BEST TIME TO GO	June to September offers the most sunshine and least rain

Victoria

Perhaps it's the way sunlight reflects across the ever-shifting ocean, or the forest walks and beachcombing that seem an essential part of coastal life. Whatever the reason, the towns and villages snuggled next to the Pacific draw artistic folk from around the world to settle here and create strong communities and beautiful art. Take this leisurely tour for a slice of life on both the mainland and Vancouver Island.

Link Your Trip

26 Sea to Sky Highway

Join this trip at Horseshoe Bay winding your way up Hwy 99 past the climbing hub of Squamish to the peerless ski-town of Whistler.

29 Vancouver Island's Remote North

From Nanaimo explore the more remote flavor of Vancouver Island by pitching north to Qualicum Beach or west to Tofino.

01 VICTORIA

British Columbia's lovely, walkable and increasingly bike-friendly capital is dripping with colonial architecture and has enough museums, attractions, hotels and restaurants to keep many visitors enthralled for an extra night or two.

Must-see attractions include the excellent **Royal BC Museum** (royalbcmuseum.bc.ca). Come eye to beady eye with a woolly mammoth and look out for cougars and grizzlies peeking from behind the trees. Step aboard Captain Vancouver's ship, enter a First Nations cedar longhouse, and explore a

Cougar!

Weighing in at up to 70kg (155lb), cougars are stealthy in the extreme and can, on their own, hunt and kill a 300kg (660lb) moose. While they're rarely seen, they can (and do) occasionally attack humans so it pays to be prepared – especially as the majority of the large cats in this region reside on the southern third of Vancouver Island.

Cougars are most active at dusk and dawn and most encounters take place in late spring and summer; however, cougars roam and hunt at any time of the day or night and in all seasons. Almost all human-based cougar attacks are on children, so keep your young ones close when you're outside and pick them up immediately if you see a cougar. Hike in groups of two or more and make enough noise to prevent surprising a cougar. If you come across a cougar, always give it an avenue of escape. Talk to the cougar in a confident voice, face it and remain upright. Do not turn your back on the cougar. Do not run. Try to back away from the cougar slowly. If the cougar appears aggressive, do all you can to enlarge your image. Don't crouch down or try to hide. Pick up sticks or branches and wave them about. Convince the cougar that you are a threat, not prey. And if a cougar does attack, fight back!

re-created early colonial street complete with shops, a movie house and an evocative replica Chinatown. A few minutes' stroll away, you'll also find the hidden gem **Miniature World** (miniatureworld.com), an immaculate, old-school attraction crammed with 80 diminutive dioramas themed on everything from Arthurian Britain to a futuristic sci-fi realm.

Also worth visiting is the **Art Gallery of Greater Victoria** (aggv.ca), home to one of Canada's best Emily Carr collections. Aside from Carr's swirling nature canvases, you'll find an ever-changing array of temporary exhibitions.

And save time to hop on a not-much-bigger-than-a-bathtub-sized **Victoria Harbour Ferry** (victoriaharbourferry.com). This colorful armada of tiny tugboats stop at numerous docks along the waterfront, including the Inner Harbour, Songhees Park and Fisherman's Wharf (where alfresco fish and chips is heartily recommended).

THE DRIVE
Follow Hwy 1 (which begins its cross-country journey in Victoria) 19km (12 miles) west onto the sometimes narrow, heavily forested Malahat Dr section, also known as the Malahat Hwy.

02 GOLDSTREAM PROVINCIAL PARK

Alongside the Malahat, the abundantly forested **Goldstream Provincial Park** (goldstreampark.com) drips with ancient, moss-covered cedar trees and a moist carpet of plant life. The short walk through the woods to the **Freeman King Visitors Centre** is beautiful; once you're there, take in the center's hands-on exhibits about natural history.

The park is known for its salmon spawning season (from late October to December), when the water literally bubbles with thousands of struggling fish. Hungry bald eagles also swoop in at this time to feast on the full-grown salmon.

A short 700m (half-mile) trail leads to **Niagara Falls**, which is a lot narrower but only 4m (13ft) shorter than its famous Ontario namesake. Hike beyond the falls and you'll reach an impressive railway trestle (which you're not supposed to walk on).

 THE DRIVE

From Goldstream, the Malahat climbs north for 8km (5 miles) to its summit with a number of gorgeous viewpoints over Brentwood Bay. Continue on Hwy 1 for another 28km (17.5 miles), following signs east off the highway for Cowichan Bay.

↪ DETOUR
Merridale Estate Cidery
Start: 02 **Goldstream**

After leaving Goldstream, head west off the highway onto Cobble Hill Rd. This weaves through bucolic farmland and wine-growing country. Watch for asparagus farms, beady-eyed llamas, blueberry stalls and verdant vineyards. Stop in at charming **Merridale Estate Cidery** (merridalecider.com), an inviting apple-cider producer offering many varieties, as well as artisan gin and vodka. Cobble Hill Rd crosses over the highway and loops east to Cowichan Bay.

03 COWICHAN BAY

With a colorful string of wooden buildings perched on stilts over a mountain-shadowed ocean inlet, Cowichan Bay – Cow Bay to

locals – is well worth a stop. Wander along the pier of the **Maritime Centre** (classicboats.org) to peruse some salty boat-building exhibits and intricate models and get your camera out to shoot the handsome panoramic views of the harbor. Duck into the galleries and studios lining the waterfront or stretch your legs on a five-minute stroll to the **Cowichan Estuary Nature Centre** (cowichanestuary.ca), where area birdlife and marine critters are profiled.

Drop into the **Mud Room** (cowbaymudroom.com) to see potters at work making usable objects like cups and plates. Look for seaside-themed mugs and the popular yellow-glazed dragonfly motif pieces.

The artisans are also at work in Cow Bay's kitchens. This is a great place to gather the makings of a great picnic at **True Grain Bread** (truegrain.ca).

 THE DRIVE

Return to Hwy 1 and head north a further 12km (7.5 miles).

04 BC FOREST DISCOVERY CENTRE

You won't find Winnie-the-Pooh in this 40-hectare (100-acre) wood, but if you want to know more about those giants swaying overhead, stop in at the **BC Forest Discovery Centre** (bcforestdiscoverycentre.com). Woodland paths lead you among western yews, Garry oaks and 400-year-old fir trees with nesting bald eagles in their branches. Visit a 1920s sawmill and a 1905 wooden schoolhouse, and climb to the top of a wildfire lookout tower. Hop on a historical train for a ride around the grounds

RULE OF THE ROAD

Bone-shaking automobiles began popping up on the roads of British Columbia in the early years of the 20th century, often the toys of rich playboys with too much time on their hands. But for many years BC had few regulations governing the trundling procession of cars around the region: vehicles could drive on either side of the road in some communities, although the left-hand side (echoing the country's British colonial overlords) gradually became the accepted practice.

Aiming to match driving rules in the US (and in much of the rest of the world) – yet managing to confuse the local issue still further – BC began legislating drivers over to the right-hand side of the road in the early 1920s. One of the last areas to make the switch official was Vancouver Island. During the transition period, some minor accidents were reported around the region as forgetful drivers tootled toward each other before veering across at the last minute.

Cowichan Bay

and check out some cool logging trucks from the early 1900s. Visit the indoor exhibits for the lowdown on contemporary forest management.

🚗 THE DRIVE
It's a 20km (12.5-mile) journey to the next stop. Continue north on Hwy 1, turning right onto Henry Rd and then left onto Chemainus Rd.

05 CHEMAINUS
The residents of this tree-ringed settlement – a former resource community that almost became a ghost town – began commissioning **murals**

on its walls in the 1980s, part of a forward-thinking revitalization project. The paintings – there are now almost 50 – soon became visitor attractions, stoking the town's rebirth. Among the best are the 17m-long (55ft-) pioneer-town painting of Chemainus c 1891 on Mill St, the 15m-long (50ft-) depiction of First Nations faces and totems on Chemainus Rd, and the evocative Maple St mural showing the waterfront community as it was in 1948.

Pick up a walking-tour map of the murals from the **visitor center** next to Waterwheel Park (where there's also a parking lot).

In the same building, the town's small **museum** is well stocked with yesteryear reminders of the old town. Be sure to chat with the friendly volunteers; they'll regale you with real-life stories of the area's colorful past.

The lower part of the town is rather quiet but the southern end of Willow St has many cafes, restaurants and boutique galleries to keep you and your wallet occupied.

The impressive **Chemainus Theatre Festival** (chemainus theatrefestival.ca) is also popular, staging shows for much of the year.

Waterwheel Park, Chemainus

THE DRIVE

Head north on Hwy 1 toward Nanaimo. Follow the signs to Departure Bay and catch a BC Ferries vessel to mainland Horseshoe Bay. From there, hop a second 40-minute ferry ride to Langdale on the Sunshine Coast (there are many restaurants in Horseshoe Bay if you're waiting between ferries). From Langdale, it's a short drive along Hwy 101 to Gibsons.

DETOUR

Gabriola Island

Start: 05 **Chemainus**

If you're tempted by those mysterious little islands peeking at you off the coast of Vancouver Island, take the 20-minute BC Ferries (www.bcferries.com) service from Nanaimo's Inner Harbour to Gabriola Island (hello gabriola.ca). Home to dozens of artists plus a healthy smattering of old hippies, there's a tangible air of quietude to this rustic realm. Pack a picnic and spend the afternoon communing with the natural world in a setting rewardingly divorced from big-city life.

DETOUR

Wild Play Element Parks

Start: 05 **Chemainus**

Fancy zipping, swinging or jumping from a giant tree? It's an easy 21km (13-mile) drive north on Hwy 1 from Chemainus to **Wild Play Element Parks** (wildplay.com) for some woodland thrills involving canopy obstacle courses and a daredevil bungee-jump zone.

06 GIBSONS

Gibsons feels cozy. If you didn't know better, you'd think you were on an island – such is the strong community and almost isolated

Gibsons Public Art Gallery (p177)

SUNSHINE COAST GALLERY CRAWL

Along Hwy 101, keep your eyes peeled for jaunty purple flags fluttering in the breeze. These indicate that an artist is at work on the adjoining property. If your eyesight isn't up to the task (or you're the designated driver), pick up the handy Sunshine Coast Purple Banner flyer from area visitor centers and galleries to find out exactly where these artists are located. Some are open for drop-in visits while others prefer that you call ahead. The region is studded with arts and crafts creators, working with wood, glass, clay and just about everything else. For further information, check www.suncoastarts.com.

feel this town exudes. Head straight for the waterfront area – known as Gibsons Landing – where you can take in the many bright-painted clapboard buildings that back on to the water's edge, as well as intriguing artisan stores.

A walk along the town's main wooden jetty leads you past a colorful array of houseboats and floating garden plots. You'll also come to the sun-dappled gallery of **Sa Boothroyd** (saboothroyd.com). The artist is typically on hand to illuminate her browse-worthy and often humorous works. Although her bigger canvases are suitably pricey, there are lots of tempting original trivets, coasters and tea cozies.

Need more culture? Head to the charming **Gibsons Public Art Gallery** (gpag.ca), which showcases the work of local artists and changes its displays every month. Check the website for show openings, always a good time to meet the arty locals.

 THE DRIVE
Continue along tree-lined Hwy 101; expect glimpses of sandy coves

Photo opportunity
Clouds draped across mountaintops from the deck of a Horseshoe Bay ferry.

in the forests on your left. The highway leads through Sechelt (handy for supplies) then on to Earls Cove. Hop the BC Ferries service across Jervis Inlet to Saltery Bay. This achingly beautiful 50-minute trip threads past islands and forested coastlines. From Saltery Bay, take Hwy 101 to Powell River.

07 **POWELL RIVER**
Powell River is one of the Sunshine Coast's most vibrant communities. It was founded in the early 1900s when three Minnesota businessmen dammed the river to create a massive hydroelectric power plant. Not long after, a pulp mill was built to take advantage of the surrounding forests and

handy deepwater harbor, with the first sheets of paper trundling off its steamy production line in 1912. Within a few years, the mill had become the world's largest producer of newsprint, churning out 275 tonnes daily.

Today there's an active and artsy vibe to this waterfront town, including its historic **Townsite** area, which is great for on-foot wandering. Many of Powell River's oldest streets are named after trees and some are still lined with the original mill workers' cottages that kickstarted the settlement. The steam-plumed mill is still here, too – although it's shrinking every year and its former grounds are being transformed into parkland. Dip into this history at the **Qathet Museum** (qathetmuseum.ca), which covers the area's First Nations heritage and its tough pioneer days.

If you spend the night in town, catch a film at the quaint **Patricia Theatre** (patriciatheatre.com), Canada's oldest continually operating cinema.

28

BRITISH COLUMBIA

Southern Vancouver Island Tour

BEST FOR OUTDOORS

BEST FOR OUTDOORS

Salt Spring Island for cycling, hiking and kayaking

Butchart Gardens

DURATION	DISTANCE	GREAT FOR
4–5 days	290km / 182 miles	Food & drink, Outdoors

BEST TIME TO GO	June to September for frequent ferries and warm weather

Whether you're standing on the deck of a Gulf Islands ferry or on the sandy expanse of China Beach, the untamed ocean is an essential part of life in this part of the world. It seems to foster pods of creativity – small islands where artisans practice crafts from pottery to cheese-making – and it salt-licks the dramatic coastline into shape, with sandy coves fringed by dense, wind-bent woodlands.

Link Your Trip

25 Vancouver & the Fraser Valley

From the Gulf Islands, catch a ferry to Tsawwassen to get a closer look at Vancouver and the farm-dotted Fraser River Valley.

29 Vancouver Island's Remote North

When you reach Hwy 1 after leaving Salt Spring Island, you can carry on north for a taste of off-the-beaten-track Vancouver Island.

01 **SIDNEY**

A short trip north of Victoria, the sunny seaside town of Sidney is ideal for wandering. Along the main street, an almost unseemly number of bookstores jostle for space with boutique shops and cafes. The best for serious bibliophiles is vaguely Dickensian **The Haunted Bookshop**. When you reach the water, you'll find the Seaside Sculpture Walk – showcasing a dozen or so locally created artworks – plus a picturesque pier with twinkling island vistas.

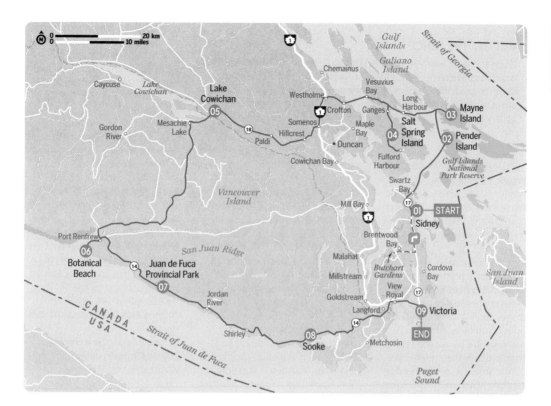

While you're at the waterfront, visit the compact but brilliant **Shaw Centre for the Salish Sea** (salishseacentre.org). It opens your eyes to the color and diversity in the neighboring Salish Sea with aquariums, touch tanks and plenty of hands-on exhibits. The staff are well versed and the gift shop is a treasure trove.

THE DRIVE

Follow Hwy 17 (Patricia Bay Hwy) north for 6km (3.75 miles) to its end at the BC Ferries terminal. Board a boat for a beautiful 40-minute crossing to Pender Island.

DETOUR
Butchart Gardens
Start: 01 Sidney

A 16km (10-mile) drive south of Sidney on Hwy 17, turning west on Keating Cross Rd, brings you to Benvenuto Ave and British Columbia's most famous botanical attraction. The century-old **Butchart Gardens** (butchartgardens. com), which originated from an attempt to beautify an old cement factory site, has been cleverly planned to ensure there's always something in bloom, no matter what the season. In summer, there are Saturday night fireworks displays and in winter the twinkling seasonal lights are magical. Whatever time of year you arrive, give yourself at least a couple of hours to enjoy the spectacle.

02 PENDER ISLAND

Arriving on this small island, you are quickly enveloped in a sense of tangible quietude. Narrow roads wind within deep forests where you'll see countless walking trails, quail crossings and confident deer.

Pender is actually two islands – North and South, joined by a small bridge. **Gowland** and **Tilly Point** on South Pender have beach access; head to Tilly Point for tidal pools and Mt Baker views. Sheltered, sandy **Medicine Beach** on the North Island has lots of clamber-worthy logs. While on the beaches, look out for bald eagles, seals and otters.

ART OFF THE FENCE

Going strong for nearly 25 years, Art Off the Fence started as just that – an artist exhibiting her work all over her fence. Each year in mid-July, a dozen or so additional artists hang their work on the fence and in the orchard of a Pender property, creating a weekend-long grassroots outdoor gallery. Look, shop, enjoy the live music and meet the island locals.

Pender is also home to many artists. Pick up a copy of the Pender Island Artists Guide on the ferry. A great place to start is at Talisman Books & Gallery (talismanbooks.ca) in the central Driftwood Centre where you'll also find great cakes and coffee.

For locally produced wine, head to **Sea Star Vineyards** (seastarvineyards.ca). Using grapes from its own vine-striped hills, it produces tasty small-batch tipples plus a wide array of fruit from kiwis to raspberries.

Also worth a look is **Pender Islands Museum** (penderislands museum.ca), housed in a 1908 farmhouse. Explore the history of the island through its re-created rooms, vintage photos and evocative exhibits.

THE DRIVE
Return to the ferry terminal on North Pender and board a ferry for the 25-minute voyage through the channel to Mayne Island.

03 MAYNE ISLAND
As the boat pulls into Mayne Island, you're greeted with colorful wooden houses, quaint communities and lots of deer. Head to **Georgina Point Lighthouse** for ocean and mountain-filled views across Active Pass. The water literally bubbles here with the strength of the current. This is a popular spot for eagles to fish and you're also likely to see (and hear) sea lions resting on nearby rocks.

For a quiet retreat, visit the **Japanese Garden**, dedicated to the many Japanese families who settled on the island from 1900 onward. Once constituting a third of the population, they contributed more than half of the island's farming, milling and fish-preservation work. During WWII the government saw them as a national threat and forced their removal. The garden contains traditional Japanese elements within a forest, including shrines and a peace bell.

THE DRIVE
Return to the ferry terminal and board a ferry to Long Harbour on Salt Spring Island. The trip takes around 45 minutes to an hour.

04 SALT SPRING ISLAND
When folks from Vancouver talk about quitting their jobs and making jam for a living, they're likely mulling a move to Salt Spring. Once a hippie haven and later a yuppie retreat, it's now home to anyone who craves a quieter life without sacrificing everyday conveniences. The main town of Ganges has it all, from grocery stores to galleries. It's a wonderful place to explore.

Salt Spring is also home to many an artisan, from bakers to carvers and winemakers. Stop in at **Waterfront Gallery** (waterfrontgallery.ca), which carries the work of many local artists with pottery, glassware, knitwear, candles and even birdhouses prominent. Also stop in at **Salt Spring Mercantile** (saltspringmer cantile.ca), which sells lots of local products, including Salish Sea Chocolates (try the cherry with hazelnut), jars of fresh chutney and flower-petal-packed soaps.

Save time for **Salt Spring Island Cheese** (saltspring cheese.com) on Weston Creek Farm. Meet the goats and sheep that produce milk for the cheese, see it being made, and be awed by the beautiful finale – taste cheeses adorned with lemon slices, flowers and chilies.

Head to Ruckle Park for ragged shorelines, gnarly arbutus forests and sun-kissed farmlands. There are trails here for all skill levels as well as great ocean views for a picnic. Mt Maxwell offers a steep but worthwhile hike and Cushion Lake and St Mary's Lake are summertime swimming haunts. Fancy

MARKET DAY

If you arrive on Salt Spring Island on a summer weekend, the best way to dive into the community is at the legendary Saturday Market where you can tuck into luscious island-grown fruit and piquant cheeses while perusing locally produced arts and crafts.

Local produce, Salt Spring Island

exploring sans car? Visit **Salt Spring Adventure Co** (saltspringadventures.com) to rent kayaks and join excursions.

THE DRIVE
Head 7km (4.25 miles) north of Ganges to Vesuvius Bay and take a 25-minute ferry ride to Crofton on Vancouver Island. From the east coast, curve inland for 38km (23.5 miles) along Hwy 18 and the glassy-calm waters of Lake Cowichan.

05 LAKE COWICHAN
Hop out of the car at Lake Cowichan for some deep breaths at the ultra-clear, tree-fringed lakefront. This is a perfect spot for swimming or setting out for a hike along the lakeside trails.

Photo opportunity

Botanical Beach's crashing waves.

THE DRIVE
From Lake Cowichan, follow South Shore Rd and then Pacific Marine Rd to Port Renfrew and on to Botanical Beach, 66km (41 miles) from Lake Cowichan.

06 BOTANICAL BEACH
It's worth the effort to get to **Botanical Beach**, which feels like the end of the earth. Follow the winding road from Port Renfrew and then the sometimes steep pathway down to the beach. The tidal pools here are rich in colorful marine life, including chitons, anemones, gooseneck barnacles, sea palms and purple sea urchins. Surrounded by windblown coastline and crashing waves, this is also a favorite springtime haunt of orcas and gray whales, plus a feeding ground for harbor seals.

The rocks here can be slippery and the waves huge; take care and watch the tide.

THE DRIVE
Head southeast on Hwy 14 for around 40km (25 miles) to nearby Juan de Fuca Provincial Park.

KARAMYSH/SHUTTERSTOCK ©

Lake Cowichan

WIRESTOCK CREATORS/SHUTTERSTOCK ©

Juan de Fuca Provincial Park

07 JUAN DE FUCA PROVINCIAL PARK

Welcome to the dramatic coastal wilderness of **Juan de Fuca Provincial Park** (bcparks. ca/juan-de-fuca-park). There are good stop-off points along this rugged stretch, providing memorable views of the rocky, ocean-carved seafront where trees cling for dear life and whales slide past just off the coast. Our favorite is **China Beach**, reached along a fairly gentle, well-maintained trail through dense forest. The prize is a long stretch of windswept sand. **French Beach** is also popular with day-trippers and requires less of a leg-stretch.

THE DRIVE

Continue southeast along Hwy 14, skirting the coastline to Sooke, 74km (46 miles) away.

08 SOOKE

Once considered the middle of nowhere, seaside Sooke is gaining popularity thanks in part to the thriving 55km (34 miles) Galloping Goose trail, a cycling and hiking path linking it with Victoria. For an introduction to the area, stop at **Sooke Region Museum** (sooke regionmuseum.com), which has intriguing exhibits on the district's pioneer past, including the tiny **Moss Cottage**, one of the island's oldest pioneer homes.

THE DRIVE

From Sooke, follow Hwy 14 (Sooke Rd) east, all the way to Hwy 1. Join the eastbound traffic, which will lead you on to nearby Victoria, 40km (25 miles) from Sooke.

09 VICTORIA

The provincial capital is vibrant, charming and highly walkable. The boat-filled Inner Harbour, magnetic boutique shopping and belly-thrilling cuisine make it understandably popular. Add an outgoing university crowd plus a strong arts community and you get an interesting, diverse population.

29

BRITISH COLUMBIA

Vancouver Island's Remote North

BEST FOR STORM WATCHERS

Watch massive, frothy waves crashing onto Long Beach

Surfing, Tofino

DURATION	DISTANCE	GREAT FOR
2–3 days	537km / 336 miles	Families, History

BEST TIME TO GO	May to September: the most sunshine and the least chance of relentless rain

Following this trip is like following Alice down the rabbit hole – you'll feel you've entered an enchanted land that's beyond the reach of day-to-day life. Ancient, moss-covered trees will leave you feeling tiny, as bald eagles swoop above and around you like pigeons. You'll see bears munching dandelions and watching you inscrutably. And totem poles, standing like forests, will seem to whisper secrets of the past. Go on. Jump in.

Link Your Trip

27 A Strait Hop

From Qualicum Beach, travel south on Hwy 19 to Nanaimo, where you can hook up with this water-hugging circuit of the Georgia Strait.

28 Southern Vancouver Island Tour

Drive east from Coombs on Hwy 4A, then south on Hwy 1 for a vision of the island's more cultivated side.

01 **TOFINO**

Packed with activities and blessed with stunning beaches, former fishing town Tofino sits on Clayoquot (clay-kwot) Sound, where forests rise from roiling waves that continually batter the coastline. Visitors come to surf, whale-watch, kayak, hike and hug trees. For the scoop on what to do, hit the **visitor center** (tourismtofino.com).

The area's biggest draw is Long Beach, part of Pacific Rim National Park. Accessible by car along the Pacific Rim Hwy, this wide sandy swath has untamed

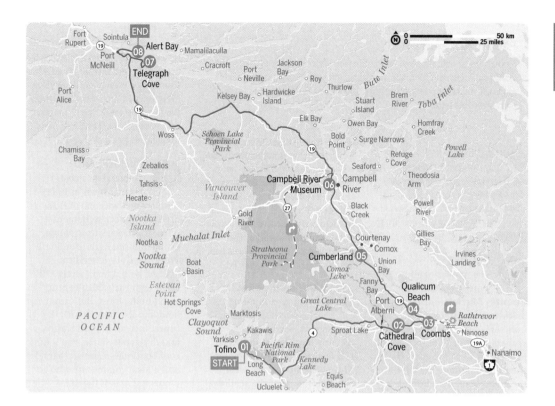

surf, beachcombing nooks and a living museum of old-growth trees. There are plenty of walking trails; look for swooping eagles and huge banana slugs. Tread carefully over slippery surfaces and never turn your back on the mischievous surf.

Kwisitis Visitor Centre houses exhibits on the region, including a First Nations canoe and a look at what's in the watery depths.

While you're in Tofino, don't miss **Roy Henry Vickers' Eagle Aerie Gallery** (royhenryvickers. com), housed in an atmospheric traditional longhouse. Vickers is one of Canada's most successful and prolific indigenous artists.

If you're freshly arrived in Tofino and want to know what makes this place so special, head down First St and join the undulating 1.2km (0.75-mile) gravel trail to **Tonquin Beach** where a magical parting of the trees reveals a rock-punctuated swath of sand well known for its life-affirming sunsets.

 THE DRIVE
Follow Pacific Rim Hwy 4 southeast, and then north as it turns into the Mackenzie Range. Mountains rise up on the right as you weave past the unfathomably deep Kennedy Lake. The road carries on along the racing Kennedy River. Continue to the next stop, just past Port Alberni. This long-

ish 140km (87-mile) leg should take a little over two hours.

02 **CATHEDRAL GROVE**
East of Port Alberni, **Cathedral Grove** (bc parks.ca /macmillan-park) is the spiritual home of tree huggers and the highlight of MacMillan Provincial Park. Look waaaaay up and the vertigo-inducing views of the swaying treetops will leave you swooning. Extremely popular in summer, its accessible forest trails wind through dense woodland, offering glimpses of some of British Columbia's oldest trees, including centuries-old Douglas firs more than 3m (10ft) in diameter. Try hugging that.

PACIFIC RIM PARK PASS

First-timers should drop by the **Pacific Rim Visitors Centre** (pacificrim visitor.ca) in Ucuelet for maps and advice on exploring this spectacular region. If you're stopping in the park, you'll need to pay and display a pass, available here.

 THE DRIVE
Continue east for 17km (10.5 miles) on Hwy 4, past Cameron Lake, with swimming beaches and supposedly a resident monster. From Hwy 4, follow Hwy 4A for 2km (1.25 miles) into Coombs.

 COOMBS
03 The mother of all pit stops, **Coombs Old Country Market** (oldcountry market.com) attracts huge numbers of visitors almost year-round. You'll get inquisitive looks from a herd of goats that spends the summer season on the grassy roof, a tradition here for decades. Nip inside for giant ice-cream cones, heaped pizzas and all the deli makings of a great picnic, then spend an hour or two wandering around the attendant stores, which are filled with unique crafts, clothes and antiques.

 THE DRIVE
Continue east for 9km (5.5 miles) on Hwy 4A, crossing Hwy 19 to Parksville on the coast. Turn left and follow the coastline west past pretty French Creek for 11km (6.75 miles) and on to Qualicum Beach.

DETOUR
Rathtrevor Beach
Start: 03 Coombs

It's only around 20 minutes from Coombs, but Rathtrevor Beach feels like it's a million miles away. Visit when the tide is out and you'll face a huge expanse of sand. Bring buckets, shovels and the kids, who'll spend hours digging, catching crabs and hunting for shells. The beach is in a provincial park just east of Parksville, and is backed by a forested picnic area. To get there from Coombs, drive east on Hwy 4A, connecting to Hwy 19 northwest and then turning off at Rathtrevor Rd.

 QUALICUM BEACH
04 A small community of classic seafront motels and a giant beachcomber-friendly bay, Qualicum Beach is a favorite family destination. This coastline is thick with shellfish; many of the scallops, oysters and mussels that restaurants serve up come from here. Wander the beach for shells, and look for sand dollars – they're readily found here.

TOP TIP:
Vancouver Island North

For maps, activities, tide charts and photos to inspire you, visit vancouverislandnorth.ca.

 THE DRIVE
While it's slower than Hwy 19, Hwy 19A is a scenic drive, following the coast north past the Fanny Bay Oyster Farm and Denman Island. After 55km (34 miles) turn left just north of Union Bay to connect with Hwy 19. Turn right, continue north for 5km (3 miles) and take the exit for Cumberland.

CUMBERLAND
05 Founded as a coal-mining town in 1888, Cumberland was one of BC's original pioneer settlements, home to workers from Japan, China and the American South. These days, it's officially a 'village' with a main street still lined with early 20th-century wood-built stores. But Cumberland has also moved with the times. Instead of blacksmiths and dry-goods shops, you'll find cool boutiques, espresso bars and a local community who've pioneered one of the finest mountain-biking networks in BC in an adjacent forest. You can get kitted out for two-wheeled action at **Dodge City Cycles** (dodgecitycycles.com). If you prefer something more sedentary, take time to peruse the very impressive **Cumberland Museum** (cumberlandmuseum. ca), which explores the area's coal-mining past.

 THE DRIVE
Carry on north on Hwy 19, with mountain and islan d views. Turn right onto Hamm Rd, heading east across farmland and passing a bison farm. Turn left onto Hwy 19A, which skirts Oyster Bay. The next stop is on your left, on the outskirts of Campbell River. Total distance: 55km (34 miles).

Qualicum Beach

06 CAMPBELL RIVER MUSEUM

Stretch your legs and your curiosity with a wander through the **Museum at Campbell River** (crmuseum.ca). Hop behind the wheel of an early logging truck, explore a settler's cabin, see First Nations masks and watch footage of the removal of the legendary, ship-destroying Ripple Rock, which was blasted with the largest non-nuclear explosion in history.

THE DRIVE
From Campbell River, head northwest on Hwy 19. As you inch into Vancouver Island's north, follow the signs and an increasingly narrow road for 16km (10 miles) to Telegraph Cove.

Photo opportunity

The forest of totem poles watching over the sea at Alert Bay.

En route, you'll pass Beaver Cove with its flotilla of logs waiting to be hauled away for milling. It's a beautiful drive, but isolated. Fuel up before you head out.

07 TELEGRAPH COVE

Built on stilts over the water in 1912, Telegraph Cove was originally a station for the northern terminus of

the island's telegraph. A salmon saltery and sawmill were later added. Extremely popular with summer day-trippers, the boardwalk and its many houses have been charmingly restored, with plaques illuminating their original residents. During the season, the waters off the cove are also home to orcas. See (and hear) them on a trip with **Prince of Whales** (princeofwhales.com). You might also encounter minke and humpback whales as well as dolphins and porpoises.

THE DRIVE
Return to Hwy 19 and carry on for 26km (16 miles) to Port McNeill, from where you can catch a BC Ferries vessel for the 45-minute journey to Alert Bay on Cormorant Island.

JEROEN MIKKERS/SHUTTERSTOCK ©

Orcas, Telegraph Cove

CAPITAN CRZELINI/SHUTTERSTOCK ©

Namgis Burial Grounds

08 **ALERT BAY**
This spread-out island village has an ancient and mythical appeal underpinned by its strong First Nations culture and community. In some respects, it feels like an open-air museum. On the southern side is an old pioneer fishing settlement and the traditional **Namgis Burial Grounds**, where dozens of gracefully weathering totem poles stand like a forest of ageless art.

Next to the site of the now-demolished St Michael's Residential School is a much more enduring symbol of First Nations community. The must-see **U'mista Cultural Centre** (umista.ca) houses ceremonial masks and other items confiscated by the Canadian government in the 1920s and now repatriated from museums around the world.

Continue over the hill to the Big House, where traditional **dance performances** are held for visitors. One of the world's tallest totem poles is also here. Alert Bay is home to many professional carvers and you'll see their work in galleries around the village.

Head to the bay's **visitor center** (alertbay.ca) for more information.

⟳ **DETOUR:**
Strathcona Provincial Park

START: 06 CAMPBELL RIVER MUSEUM

BC's oldest protected area and also Vancouver Island's largest park, **Strathcona** (bcparks.ca/strathcona-park) is a 40km (25-mile) drive west on Hwy 28 from Campbell River. Centered on Mt Golden Hinde, the island's highest point (2200m/7218ft), it's a pristine wilderness crisscrossed with trail systems that deliver you to waterfalls, alpine meadows, glacial lakes and looming crags.

On arrival at the main entrance, get your bearings at Strathcona Park Lodge & Outdoor Education Centre. It's a one-stop shop for park activities, including kayaking, guided treks and rock climbing for all ages.

30

BRITISH COLUMBIA

Okanagan Valley Wine Tour

BEST FOR FOODIES

Stop for fresh fruits in season

Mission Hill Family Estate

DURATION	DISTANCE	GREAT FOR
2 days	35km / 22 miles	Food & Wine

BEST TIME TO GO	July and September bring hot sunny days

Filling up on sun-ripened fruit at roadside stalls has long been a highlight of traveling through the Okanagan on a hot summer day. Since the 1980s, the region has widened its embrace of the culinary world by striping its hillsides with grapes. Over 180 vineyards take advantage of the Okanagan's cool winters and long summers. Ice wine, made from grapes frozen on the vine, is a unique take-home tipple. And when you're done soaking up the wine, you can soak up the scenery at the countless beaches along the way.

Link Your Trip

25 Vancouver & the Fraser Valley

Follow Hwys 3A and 3 from the southern end of Okanagan Lake to Hope and the pastoral Fraser Valley.

26 Sea to Sky Highway

Head northwest from Okanagan Lake on Hwy 97 through Kamloops to Hwy 99 for this spectacular melding of mountains and sea.

01 **MISSION HILL FAMILY ESTATE**
Begin your leisurely taste-tripping trawl on the western shore of the 100km-long Okanagan Lake, the region's centerpiece. Following Boucherie Rd north, between the lake and Hwy 97, will bring you to Westbank's **Mission Hill Family Estate** (missionhillwinery.com). The estate is a modernist reinterpretation of mission buildings, reached through imposing gates and dominated by a 26m (85ft) bell-tower. Several tours and tastings are available, with some that include lunch. Aside from checking out vineyards and cellars, you

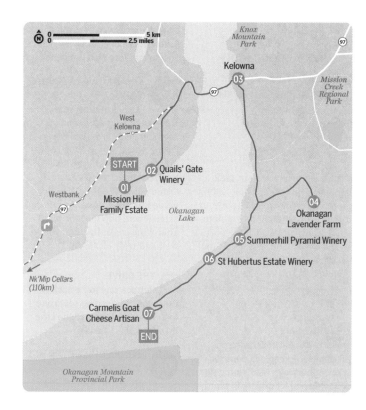

The Ogopogo

For centuries, traditional First Nations legends have told of a 15m (50ft) sea serpent living in Okanagan Lake. Called the N'ha-a-itk (Lake Demon), it was believed to live in a cave near Rattlesnake Island, just off-shore from Peachland. People would only enter the waters around the island with an offering, otherwise they believed the monster would raise a storm and claim lives.

Beginning in the mid-1800s, Europeans also began reporting sightings of a creature with a horse-shaped head and serpent-like body. Nicknamed Ogopogo, the serpent has been seen along the length of the 129km (80 mile) lake, but most commonly around Peachland. In 1926, 30 carloads of people all claimed to have seen the monster and film footage from 1968 has been analyzed, concluding that a solid, three-dimensional object was moving through the water.

Cryptozoologist Karl Shuker suggests that the Ogopogo may be a type of primitive whale like the basilosaurus. Keep your eyes peeled, but if you don't have any luck spotting it, you can visit a statue of the Ogopogo at Kelowna's City Park.

---

may be lucky enough to see an amazing (and rare) tapestry by French-Russian artist Marc Chagall in one of the rooms.

The winery's **Terrace** restaurant sits atop a glorious terrace overlooking vineyards and lake. Its spectacular food matches the setting. Nearby, a grassy amphitheater hosts summer concerts (accompanied by wine, of course). You can also visit the shop for souvenir bottles. Try Oculus, the winery's premium and unique Bordeaux blend.

🚗 **THE DRIVE**
Return to Boucherie Rd and continue 2km (1.25 miles) north, following the lakeshore.

 QUAILS' GATE WINERY
Charming stone and beam architecture reigns at **Quails' Gate Winery** (quailsgate.com). Tours run throughout spring and summer and begin in an on-site pioneer home built in 1873. Tastings are held throughout the day – the rhubarby chenin blanc and pleasantly peppery reserve pinot noir are recommended. The winery's Old Vines restaurant is a foodie favorite, with a menu showcasing seasonal BC ingredients and a commitment to sourcing sustainable seafood. Or you could just chill at vine-side picnic benches.

🚗 **THE DRIVE**
Head 9km (5.5 miles) northeast on Boucherie Rd before merging with Hwy 97. Cross the lake at the new William R Bennett Bridge and head for the 'east coast' town of Kelowna, the Okanagan capital.

03 KELOWNA

The wine industry has turned Kelowna into a bit of a boomtown. The population has almost doubled since the early 1990s and property prices have risen accordingly. A wander (especially along Ellis St) will unearth plenty of art galleries and lakeside parks, along with cafes and wine bars.

Continue your wine education at the **Okanagan Wine and Orchard Museum** (kelowna museums.ca). Housed in the historic Laurel Packinghouse, the museum offers a look at celebrated bottles, labels and equipment, along with an overview of wine-making in the region. There's a separate section on fruit packing.

With vineyards cozied up to Knox Mountain, **Sandhill Wines** (sandhillwines.ca), formerly Calona Vineyards, was the Okanagan's first winery,

Photo opportunity

View from the terrace at Mission Hill Family Estate winery.

kicking off production in 1932. Its architecturally striking tasting room is an atmospheric spot to try the ever-popular, melon-note pinot blanc, along with the port-style dessert wine. You'll find the winery north of Hwy 97.

Note that the Kelowna area is prone to wildfires, most recently and seriously in 2023.

THE DRIVE
Head south of Kelowna on Lakeshore Rd, keeping Okanagan Lake on your right. Take a left onto Dehart Rd and follow it to Bedford Rd. Turn right and then right again

so that you're heading south on Takla Rd. The 10km (6.25-mile) drive should take less than 15 minutes.

04 OKANAGAN LAVENDER FARM

Visiting **Okanagan Lavender Farm** (okanagan lavender.com) is a heady experience. Rows and rows of over 60 types of lavender waft in the breeze against the backdrop of Okanagan Lake. You can enjoy a guided or self-guided tour of the acreage and pop into the shop. Your wine-soaked palate will be well and truly cleansed.

THE DRIVE
Retrace your route back to Lakeshore Rd, heading south and then veering left onto Chute Lake Rd after 6.5km (4 miles).

05 SUMMERHILL PYRAMID WINERY

In the hills along the lake's eastern shore, you'll soon come to one of the Okanagan's most colorful wineries. **Summerhill Pyramid Winery** (sum merhill.bc.ca) combines a traditional tasting room with a huge pyramid where every Summerhill wine ages in barrels, owing to the belief that sacred geometry has a positive effect on liquids. The winery's vegan-friendly Sunset Organic Bistro is much loved and the Ehrenfelser ice wine is particularly delightful.

THE DRIVE
Return to Lakeside Rd and continue south for 2.5km (1.5 miles). The next stop is across from Cedar Creek Park.

DETOUR:

Nk'Mip

START: 02 **QUAILS' GATE**

Add a day to your visit and head for this multifarious **cultural center** (nkmipdesert.com) just east of Osoyoos, part of a First Nations empire that includes a desert golf course, the noted winery Nk'Mip Cellars, a resort and more. The architecturally slick cultural center celebrates the Syilx people of the Okanagan Nation and the delicate desert ecosystem where they traditionally live. Those with a little reptilian courage can also check out the on-site rattlesnake enclosure.

Save a bit more time to sample one of the region's most distinctive wineries at Nk'Mip Cellars, North America's first indigenous-owned and -operated winery when it opened in 2003. Tastings of five different wines cost C$5. The place is known for its ice wines and is open 10am to 6pm in the summer (to 5pm November to March). The two Nk'Mip sites are located about 112km (70 miles) south of Westbank along Hwy 97.

Lavendar farm, Okanagan Valley

06 ST HUBERTUS ESTATE WINERY

Lakeside **St Hubertus Estate Winery** (st-hubertus. bc.ca) is another twist on the winery approach. Visiting is like being at a traditional northern European vineyard, complete with Bavarian architectural flourishes.

Despite its emphasis on Germanic wines, including riesling, St Hubertus isn't conservative: try its floral, somewhat spicy casselas and the rich marechal foch. While there are no formal tours, you can stroll around the vineyard or head to the complimentary tasting room to try four different wines. There's also a shop selling artisan foods and, of course, wine.

 THE DRIVE
Continue south on Lakeside for 4km (2.5 miles) and then take the left turning onto Rimrock Rd. Follow it for 200m (220yd) to a T-junction and take a right onto Timberline Rd.

07 CARMELIS GOAT CHEESE ARTISAN

End your tour by treating your driver to something they can sample at **Carmelis Goat Cheese Artisan** (facebook. com/carmelisgoatcheese/). Call ahead to book a tour of the dairy, milking station and cellar. Even without the tour, you can sample the cheeses. For those who prefer something milder, try the super-soft unripened versions like feta and yogurt cheese. The showstopper is the goat's-milk gelato which comes in 24 different flavors.

ALEXEY SPEHALSKI/SHUTTERSTOCK ©

Apples, Okanagan Valley

FRUITS & FESTIVALS

Farms sell their ripened fruit at stalls along the road, and fresh fruit and veggie markets are plentiful. Harvest times bring lower prices and top nosh. Here's what to watch for when:

Strawberries June and July

Raspberries July

Cherries June to August

Apricots July and August

Peaches July to September

Pears August and September

Apples September to October

Table grapes September to October

The Okanagan stages four major multiday seasonal wine festivals (thewinefestivals.com) throughout the year. Time your visit right and dip into one of these:

Winter Festival January

Spring Wine Festival May

Summer Wine Festival August

Fall Wine Festival October

St Hubertus Estate Winery

31

BRITISH COLUMBIA

Haida Gwaii Adventure

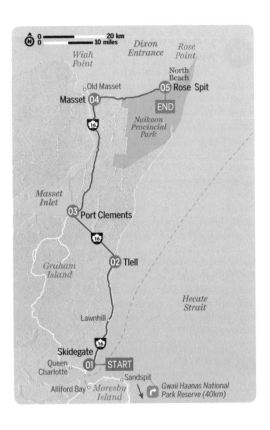

DURATION	DISTANCE	GREAT FOR
2 days	136km/85 miles	History, Nature

BEST TIME TO GO	July and August: more likely sunshine and less vicious wind

You'll be welcomed to what feels like the edge of the earth. Once known as the Queen Charlotte Islands, this rugged northwestern archipelago maintains its independent spirit, evident in its quirky museums, rustic cafes, down-to-earth art and nature-loving locals. You'll feel closer to the natural world than ever before, and some of the Northern Hemisphere's most extraordinary cultural artifacts are found here.

Link Your Trip

29 Vancouver Island's Remote North

After a seven-hour boat ride from Skidegate to Prince Rupert you travel along the inside passage on a 22-hour ferry to Port Hardy. From here drive 40 km (25 miles) along Hwy 9 to Port McNeill to pick up this trip.

01 SKIDEGATE

If you're not bringing your car, you can rent a car in advance of your BC Ferries arrival in Skidegate on Graham Island (or air arrival in Sandspit). Spend some time perusing the clapboard houses or fueling up at the home-style pub or cafes in nearby Queen Charlotte. Save an hour or two for the unmissable **Haida Heritage Centre** (haidaheritagecentre.com), a striking crescent of totem-fronted cedar longhouses that's arguably British

Sea lions, Gwaii Haanas National Park Reserve

Columbia's best First Nations attraction. Check out ancient carvings and artifacts recalling 10,000 years of Haida history and look for the exquisite artworks of the legendary Bill Reid, such as huge canoes and totem poles. Hitting Hwy 16, head north to explore the distinctive settlements that make latter-day Haida Gwaii tick. You'll wind along stretches of rustic waterfront and through shadowy woodland areas while a permanent detachment of beady-eyed eagles follows your progress.

 THE DRIVE
Follow Hwy 16 north along the shoreline. Take a few minutes to walk down to the beach when you see the pullout and signage for Balancing Rock just out of Skidegate. At 35.4km (22 miles) you'll enter the flat, arable land around Tlell River. Turn left at Wiggins Rd when you see signs for Crystal Cabin, then right on Richardson Rd.

DETOUR
Gwaii Haanas National Park Reserve
Start: 01 **Skidegate**

Famed for its mystical élan, **Gwaii Haanas National Park Reserve** (pc. gc.ca/en/pn-np/bc/gwaiihaanas) covers much of Haida Gwaii's southern section, a rugged region only accessible by boat or floatplane. The reserve is the ancient site of Haida homes, burial caves and the derelict village of Ninstints with its seafront totem poles (now a Unesco World Heritage site). Visitors often remark on the area's magical and spiritual qualities, but you should only consider an extended visit if you are well prepared. It is essential to contact **Parks Canada** (250-559-8818, reservations 877-559-8818) in advance, as access to the park is very limited and most visitors will find it best to work with officially sanctioned tour operators.

02 **TIELL**
Crystal Cabin (crystal cabingallery.com) features the works of 20 Haida artists at the jewelry workshop of April and Sarah Dutheil, second-generation artisans and sisters who were taught by their

RETURN OF THE HAIDA

The Haida are one of Canada's First Nations peoples, and had lived here for thousands of years before Europeans turned up in the 18th century. Centered on the islands, these fearsome warriors had no immunity to such diseases as smallpox, measles and tuberculosis that were brought by the newcomers, and their population of tens of thousands was quickly decimated. By the early 20th century, their numbers had fallen to around 600.

Since the 1970s, the Haida population – and its cultural pride – has grown anew, and the Haida now make up about half of the 5000 residents on the islands. In 2009, the Government of British Columbia officially changed the name of the islands from the Queen Charlottes to Haida Gwaii ('Islands of the People') as part of the province's reconciliation process with the Haida.

Historically one of the most vibrant of First Nations cultures, the Haida have very strong narratives and oral history. Legends, beliefs, skills and more are passed down from one generation to the next and great importance is placed on the knowledge of past generations. Today the Haida seek to live in harmony with their environment. Traditional laws recognize the stunning nature of the islands and embrace both the past and look to the future.

To learn more about the Haida, visit haidanation.ca.

father, local legend and authority on island geology, Dutes. April has written on Haida Gwaii agate collecting and is happy to explain Dutes' Tlell Stone Circle, which is just outside the cabin. There are many forms of art here, including carvings from argillite, a local rock that can only be carved by Haida artisans.

THE DRIVE
Continue 21.7km (13.5 miles) northwest along Hwy 16. This incredibly straight route was a walking trail until 1920 when a road was built by placing wooden planks end-to-end along the ground. Watch for deer by the road and shrub-like shore pines along the now-paved route.

PORT CLEMENTS
03 At Port Clements, head through town on Bayview Ave until it turns south and becomes a gravel road. Follow this for 3.5km (2 miles) to the **Golden Spruce Trail**. The easy 15-minute (one-way) walk through the forest leads to the banks of the Yakoun River and the site of the legendary Golden Spruce. Tragically cut down in 1997 by a deranged environmentalist, the tree – a 45m (150ft), 300-year-old genetic aberration with luminous yellow needles – was revered by local Haida as the transformed spirit of a little boy. The tree's death was traumatic for many island residents. You can see a seedling taken from a cutting from the felled tree in Millennium Park in Port Clem-

ents. For a gripping read, pick up *The Golden Spruce: A True Story of Myth, Madness and Greed* by John Vaillant (2006).

Head back to the village and nip into **Port Clements Museum** (portclementsmuseum. ca), where you're welcomed by a forest of rusty logging machinery. Learn about early logging practices and check out toys and tools from pioneering days. You'll also encounter a stuffed albino raven, another genetic aberration that was also revered until it electrocuted itself on local power lines.

THE DRIVE
Head north along Hwy 16, which hugs Masset Inlet to the northern coast. Continue north to Masset and Old Masset, 43.5km (27 miles) from Port Clements. Hwy 16 is officially the Yellowhead Hwy and Mile 0 is at Masset. From here Yellowhead Hwy runs to Winnipeg, Manitoba, although you'll have to take the ferry between Haida Gwaii and Prince Rupert.

MASSET
04 Masset primarily occupies the rather stark, institutional buildings of a disused military base and the adjoining Old Masset is a First Nations village where wood-fired homes are fronted by broad, brooding totem poles. There are several stores here where visitors can peruse and buy Haida carvings and paintings.

Also in Masset is the **Dixon Entrance Maritime Museum** (massetbc.com/visitors/maritime-museum). Housed in what was once the local hospital, the museum features exhibits on the history of this seafaring community, with displays on shipbuilding, medical pioneers, military history, and nearby clam and crab canneries. Local artists also exhibit their work here.

THE DRIVE
Head east off Hwy 16 along a well-marked road signposted for North Beach and Naikoon Provincial Park. The next stop is 27.4km (17 miles) from Masset.

05 ROSE SPIT
The region's wild northern tip is home to **Naikoon Provincial Park** (bcparks.ca/naikoon-park). This dense, treed park has more than

GETTING THERE
From mainland Prince Rupert in northern BC, take the **BC Ferries** (bcferries.com) service to Skidegate on Graham Island. The crossing usually takes seven to eight hours.

96km (60 miles) of white-sand beach and is the area's most popular destination for summertime nature fans.

Continue along the tree-lined dirt road until you reach **Tow Hill**, a steep, dense and easily enjoyed short forest walk (1km/0.6 miles each way). Look out for trees where strips of bark have been carefully removed for Haida basket-making over the decades, then catch your breath at the summit while you gaze over the impenetrable coastal forest stretching into the mist.

Finally, head for the park's extreme coastal tip and **North Beach**. Leave the car here and tramp along the wave-smacked sandy expanse, where locals walk in the surf plucking Dungeness crabs for dinner. With the wind watering your eyes, you'll feel closer to nature than you've ever felt before.

CHASE CLAUSEN/SHUTTERSTOCK ©

Tow Hill

32

BEST FOR
OUTDOORS

Biking, hiking
and – best of
all – white-
water rafting

Around the Kootenays

DURATION	DISTANCE	GREAT FOR
5–6 days	835km / 519 miles	Nature, Families

BEST TIME TO GO	June to September when roads and trails are snow-free and accessible

Whitewater rafting, Kicking Horse River

The commanding ranges of the Monashee, Selkirk and Purcell Mountains striate the Kootenays, with the Arrow and Kootenay Lakes adding texture in the middle. This drive allows you to admire their placid alpine meadows and rugged sawtooth ridges while popping into appealing towns such as Revelstoke, Golden, Nelson and Radium Hot Springs in between. Herein lie plenty of launchpads for year-round outdoor adventures.

Link Your Trip

13 International Selkirk Loop

In Nelson, branch south on Hwy 6 toward the US border to join this designated Scenic Drive through BC and Washington State.

01 GOLDEN

Golden sits at the confluence of two rivers, three mountain ranges and five national parks – all of them less than 90 minutes drive away. The town is the center for white-water rafting trips on the turbulent and chilly Kicking Horse River. Along with the powerful grade III and IV rapids, the rugged scenery that guards the sheer walls of the Kicking Horse Valley makes this rafting experience one of North America's best.

Indelibly linked to Golden is the **Kicking Horse Mountain Resort** (kickinghorseresort.com), 6km (3.75 miles) to the west – a ski resort that opened in 2000 and is known for its abundance of expert runs. In the summer, the resort and its gondola are handed over to mountain

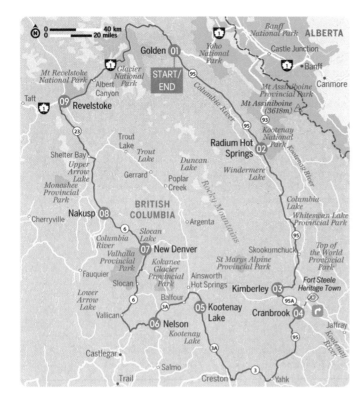

03 KIMBERLEY
Welcome to Kimberley, a town famous for its erstwhile lead mine, contemporary alpine skiing resort and Canada's largest cuckoo clock.

For well over half a century, Kimberley was home to the world's largest lead-zinc mine, the Sullivan mine, which was finally decommissioned in 2001. Since 2015, the local economy has switched track somewhat and now hosts Canada's largest solar farm.

In the 1970s, Kimberley experimented with a Bavarian theme in the hope of attracting more tourists. Remnants of the Teutonic makeover remain. The central pedestrian zone is named the Platzl and you can still bag plenty of tasty schnitzel and sausages in its restaurants, but these days the town is better known for the **Kimberley Alpine Resort** (skikimberley.com) with 700 hectares (1730 acres) of skiable terrain.

For a historical detour, take a 15km (9.25-mile) ride on **Kimberley's Underground Mining Railway** (kimberleysunder groundminingrailway.ca), where a tiny train putters through the steep-walled Mark Creek Valley toward some sweeping mountain vistas.

bikers and, more recently, climbers keen to tackle several newly installed via ferrata routes.

THE DRIVE
Head south on Hwy 95 through the Columbia River Wetlands, a hugely important ecological area that's home to 260 species of bird and numerous animals, including grizzly bears. In just over an hour, you will arrive in Radium Hot Springs.

02 RADIUM HOT SPRINGS
Lying just outside the southwest corner of Kootenay National Park, Radium Hot Springs is a major gateway to the entire Rocky Mountains national park area.

The town itself isn't much more than a gas and coffee pit stop. The main attraction is the namesake **hot springs** (pc.gc.ca/hotsprings) north of town at the jaws of Kootenay National Park (you can hike in via the Sinclair Canyon). One of three hot springs in the Rockies region, Radium is the only one that is odorless. Keeping its water between 37°C (100°F) and 40°C (103°F), the facility is more public baths than fancy spa, although the exposed rock and overhanging trees make for a pleasant setting.

THE DRIVE
It's a short 30-minute drive southeast out of Kimberley on Hwy 95A to Cranbrook where you'll merge with Hwy 95 just east of the town.

04 CRANBROOK
The region's main commercial center with a population of just under 20,000, Cranbrook is a modest crossroads. Hwy 3/95 bisects the town, which is a charmless array of strip malls.

The main reason for stopping here is to visit the multifarious **Cranbrook History Centre** (cranbrookhistorycentre.com). Dedicated primarily (though not exclusively) to train and rail travel, the center displays some fine examples of classic Canadian trains, including the luxurious 1929 edition of the Trans-Canada Limited, a legendary train that ran from Montréal to Vancouver. Also on-site is a fabulous model railway, the town museum (with plenty of First Nations and pre-human artifacts) and the elegant Alexandra Hall, part of a grand railway hotel that once stood in Winnipeg but was reconstructed in Cranbrook in 2004. The center has recently been undergoing major renovations to rehouse some of its prized locomotives, but remains open with minimal disruption.

THE DRIVE
Take Hwy 3 (Crowsnest Hwy) out of Cranbrook. The road is shared with Hwy 95 as far as Yahk, beyond which you pass through the Purcell Mountains to Creston. North of Creston, turn onto Hwy 3A and track alongside the east shore of Kootenay Lake. This leg takes around 2½ hours.

DETOUR
Fort Steele Heritage Town
Start: 04 Cranbrook

Fort Steele is an erstwhile gold rush town that fell into decline in the early 1900s when it was bypassed by the railway which went to Cranbrook instead. In the early 1960s, local authorities elected to save the place from total oblivion by turning it into a **heritage site** (fortsteele.ca) of pioneering mining culture. Buildings were subsequently rescued or completely rebuilt in vintage 19th-century style to lure in tourists. The site today consists of old shops, stores and a blacksmith, plus opportunities to partake in gold-panning, go on train rides or see a performance in a working theater. In summer there are all manner of activities and re-creations, which taper off to nothing in winter, although the site stays open.

TOP TIP:
Time Zones

Take note if you've got an urgent appointment. This drive straddles two different time zones. Golden and the Eastern Kootenays, including Radium Hot Springs and Cranbrook, are on Mountain Time, while Revelstoke and the Western Kootenays, including Nelson, are one hour behind on Pacific Time.

---

05 KOOTENAY LAKE
Lodged in the middle of the Kootenays between the Selkirk and Purcell Mountains, Kootenay Lake is one of the largest bodies of freshwater in BC. It's crossed by a year-round toll-free **ferry** (gov.bc.ca/gov/content/transportation/passenger-travel) that runs between the two small communities of Kootenay Bay on the east bank, and Balfour on the west. The ferry's a worthwhile side trip if traveling between Creston and Nelson for its long lake vistas of blue mountains rising sharply from the water. Ferries run every 50 minutes throughout the day and the crossing takes 35 minutes. On busy summer weekends, you may have to wait in a long line for a sailing or two before you get passage.

THE DRIVE
From where the ferry disembarks in Balfour on the western shore of Kootenay Lake, take Hwy 3A along the north shore of the West Arm for 32km (20 miles) before crossing the bridge into the town of Nelson.

06 NELSON
Nelson is an excellent reason to visit the Kootenays and should feature on any itinerary in the region. Tidy brick buildings climb the side of a hill overlooking the west arm of deep-blue Kootenay Lake, and the waterfront is lined with parks and beaches. The thriving cafe, culture and nightlife scene is a bonus. But what really propels Nelson is its personality: a funky mix of hippies, creative types and rugged individualists

Kootenay Lake

(many locals will tell you it's the coolest small town in BC). You can find all these along Baker St, the pedestrian-friendly main drag where wafts of patchouli mingle with hints of freshly roasted coffee.

Founded as a mining town in the late 1800s, Nelson embarked on a decades-long heritage-preservation project in 1977. Almost a third of Nelson's historic buildings have been restored to their original architectural splendor. Pick up the superb *Heritage Walking Tour* from the visitor center, which gives details on more than 30 buildings and offers a good lesson in Victorian architecture.

The town is also an excellent base for hiking, skiing, kayaking the nearby lakes, and – in recent

📷 Photo opportunity

The summit of
Mt Revelstoke.

years in particular – mountain-biking. Free-riding pedal-heads have plenty of favorite spots in British Columbia and the Rockies, but many particularly enjoy Nelson's unique juxtaposition of top-notch single-track and cool bikey ambiance. The surrounding area is striped with great trails, from the epic downhill of **Mountain Station** to the winding **Svoboda Road Trails** in West Arm Provincial Park.

THE DRIVE

Heading north from Nelson to Revelstoke, Hwy 6 threads west for 16km (10 miles) before turning north at South Slocan. The road eventually runs alongside pretty Slocan Lake for about 30km (18.5 miles) before reaching New Denver, 97km (60 miles) from Nelson.

07 NEW DENVER

With only around 500 residents, New Denver is a historic little gem that slumbers away peacefully right on the clear waters of Slocan Lake. Chapters in its not-so-sleepy history have included silver mining and a stint as a WWII Japanese internment camp. Details of the former can be found at the **Silvery Slocan Museum** (newdenver.ca/silvery-slocan-museum), which

Nelson

is located in an 1897 Bank of Montreal building.

⊙ **THE DRIVE**
It is an attractive but relatively straightforward 46km (28.5-mile) drive from New Denver to Nakusp on Hwy 6 via Summit Lake Provincial Park. Look out for mountain goats on the rocky outcrops.

08 NAKUSP

Situated right on Upper Arrow Lake, Nakusp was forever changed by BC's orgy of dam building in the 1950s and 1960s. The water level here was raised and the town was relocated to its current spot, which is why it has a 1960s-era look. It has some attractive cafes and a tiny museum. If you missed Radium Hot Springs or just can't get enough of the Rocky Mountains' thermal pleasures, divert to **Nakusp Hot Springs** (nakusphotsprings.com), 12km (7.5 miles) northeast of town.

⊙ **THE DRIVE**
Head north on Hwy 23 along the east shore of Arrow Lake for 48km (30 miles). You'll need to cross this lake, too, on a ferry between Galena and Shelter Bay. Hwy 23 continues on the west shore and will take you all the way to Revelstoke, 52km (32 miles) north of Shelter Bay.

09 REVELSTOKE

Gateway to serious mountains, Revelstoke doesn't need to blow its own trumpet – the ceaseless procession of freight trains through the town center makes more than enough noise. Built as an important point on the Canadian Pacific transcontinental railroad

RICHARD CAVALLERI/SHUTTERSTOCK ©

Mt Revelstoke

that first linked Eastern and Western Canada, Revelstoke echoes not just with whistles but with history. If you haven't yet been satiated with Canadian railway memorabilia, you can sample a bit more at the **Revelstoke Railway Museum** (railwaymuseum.com).

Revelstoke's compact center is lined with heritage buildings, yet it's more than a museum piece. **Grizzly Plaza**, between Mackenzie and Orton Aves, is a pedestrian precinct and the heart of downtown, where free live-music performances take place every evening in July and August.

Notwithstanding, this place is mainly about the adjacent wilderness and its boundless opportunities for hiking, kayaking and, most of all, skiing. North America's first ski jump was built here in 1915. One year before, Mt Revelstoke became Canada's

seventh national park. From the 2223m (7293ft) summit of **Mt Revelstoke**, the views of the mountains and the Columbia River valley are excellent. To ascend, take the 26km (16-mile) Meadows in the Sky Parkway, 1.6km (1-mile) east of Revelstoke off the Trans-Canada Hwy. Open after the thaw, from mid-May to mid-October, this paved road winds through lush cedar forests and alpine meadows and ends at Balsam Lake, within 2km (1.25 miles) of the peak. From here, walk to the top or take the free shuttle.

⊙ **THE DRIVE**
Keep your eyes on the road or, better yet, let someone else drive as you traverse the Trans-Canada Hwy (Hwy 1) for 148km (92 miles) between Revelstoke and Golden. Stunning mountain peaks follow one after another as you go.

TOOLKIT

The chapters in this section cover the most important topics you'll need to know about in the Pacific Northwest. They're full of nuts-and-bolts information and valuable insights to help you understand and navigate the Pacific Northwest and get the most out of your trip.

Arriving
p208

Getting Around
p209

Accomodations
p210

Cars
p211

Health & Safe Travel
p212

Responsible Travel
p213

Nuts & Bolts
p214

Oregon Coast (p96)
OWAKI · KULLA/GETTY IMAGES ©

Arriving

At all of the major arrival points in this region, taking public transport from the port of entry into town is fairly straightforward. There are also car rental facilities at all the airports. Note that you will need to show a passport and go through customs if you're traveling between the US and Canada, or into either country from abroad.

Car Rentals at Airport

All the major international rental agencies have offices throughout the Pacific Northwest, including at airports and in city centers. Smaller rental companies usually also have offices in or near the airport, which you can reach by free shuttle. Note that airport locations typically charge an extra fee to drop off rentals when compared to non-airport locations. There's also usually a fee if you drop your car at a different location from where you picked it up, airport or not.

To rent a car, you must have a valid driver's license, (usually) be at least 21 years of age and present a major credit card. For foreign visitors, your valid driver's license from your home country does the trick for renting and driving a car throughout the region; you won't need a separate international driving license to drive in Oregon, Washington or British Columbia.

Airport Transport

Seattle-Tacoma International Airport Light Link train to downtown Seattle; 38 minutes; from US$2.25

Portland International Airport MAX light-rail to downtown Portland; 30 minutes; from US$2.50

Vancouver International Airport Canada Line rail to downtown Vancouver; 30 minutes; from C$10

Vancouver International Airport BCFerries bus to Victoria; 3 hours 40 minutes; C$80

CUSTOMS

Entering Canada, you can claim goods up to C$800 duty-free; volume limits on alcohol and tobacco products. Entering the US, you must declare purchases made abroad; US$800 exemption for personal articles, including 1L of alcohol (over 21s).

ENTERING THE US

Visitors and US citizens must complete a Customs and Border Protection Declarations Form. You'll need a passport and (depending on citizenship) possibly a visa. Check travel.state.gov and cbp.gov/travel/international-visitors/esta for the latest.

ENTERING CANADA

All international travelers must carry acceptable identification, ideally a passport, and a valid visa (if traveling from a country where it's required) when entering Canada.

CASH & CREDIT

ATMs are widely available. Credit cards are routinely accepted at hotels, restaurants, shops and even food carts.

Getting Around

BEST WAYS TO GET AROUND

Public transportation is an excellent option for travel within the major cities of the Pacific Northwest. Buses and light-rail trains are frequent, affordable, and easy to use. Cars are best for getting between cities.

BORDER CROSSING

When driving between the US and Canada, Blaine/Douglas (aka Peace Arch; pictured below right) is the main border crossing, along I-5/Hwy 99 between Washington State and Vancouver, BC. Be prepared for long lines.

Police

If you're pulled over by police, stay in your car, keep your hands visible and be polite. They'll want to see your driver's license and proof of liability insurance. You may get a ticket or a warning if you've broken a rule.

Traffic Accidents

If there are no serious injuries and your car is operational, move over to the side of the road. If there are serious injuries, call 911 for an ambulance. Exchange information with the other driver, then file an accident report with the police.

Accommodations

It's tempting on a road trip to go the easy route with accommodations, pulling up to the nearest chain hotel with a big parking lot and free breakfast. After all, you're only sleeping there, right? But this region offers some truly special places to stay, and it's worth making the effort to find them.

Consider booking a night in one of the 'parkitecture'-style national park lodges, such as Crater Lake Lodge or Timberline Lodge in Oregon, or Mt Rainier's Paradise Inn and National Park Inn. Vancouver Island's remote north boasts equally impressive lodges.

HOW MUCH FOR A NIGHT IN...

Double room in a historic National Park lodge
US$295

Dorm bed in a hostel in Whistler
C$48–60

Double room in a motor inn
US$90–150

Hotels

Most hotels now have only nonsmoking rooms, but you can usually smoke outdoors. Air-conditioning is common in inland places but nearly nonexistent along the coast, which is much cooler. Many hotels take pets, but always ask beforehand (there's usually a fee). Wi-fi access is commonplace and usually free. Breakfast is usually included in hotel prices, but quality varies.

Hostels

Many hostels in the Pacific Northwest are members of HI-USA (hiusa.org), which is affiliated with Hostelling International. You don't need a HI-USA card to stay in one, but membership saves you a few bucks per night. You can buy one at the hostel when checking in.

Yurts

You'll find dome-shaped 'glamping' tents at many campgrounds across the region. Amenities vary, but they usually have wooden floors, wood stoves, beds and bedding. Some are pet-friendly. They cost from US$50 per night. Reserve months ahead, as they book up quickly.

Eco-Lodges

In some wilder areas, such as parts of the San Juan Islands, luxurious resorts are designed to mesh with their surroundings rather than detract from them. The idea is to combine spa-like accommodations with a reverence for the natural world and local community. Look for sustainability policies on websites – and book well in advance.

WILDERNESS RESORTS

The Pacific Northwest has an affinity for grand lodges in wilderness settings. Think oversize stone fireplaces, rough-hewn wooden beams, giant furniture, picture windows, Pendleton wool blankets, kayak rentals, local food and wine on the menu, wooden chairs on a patio with postcard views. Timberline Lodge on Mt Hood is one famous example. As with any high-end accommodation, book in advance.

Cars

HOW MUCH FOR A CAR?

Compact, economy
US$63/day

SUV
US$130/day

Tesla
From
US$150/day

Car Rental

Big international rental companies have desks at airports, major cities and some smaller towns. Check online for rates and to make reservations.

To rent a car, you must have a valid driver's license, (usually) be at least 21 years of age and present a major credit card.

The best deals are for pre-booking weekend or weeklong rentals. At busy times, you might not get the exact car you requested.

Basic liability insurance covers damage you may cause to another vehicle. A legal minimum level is set by each state, but you'll need more in a serious accident. Insurance against damage or loss to the car itself costs extra. Some credit cards provide coverage if you charge the entire cost of the rental to the card.

Electric Vehicles

Oregon and Washington are second only to California in embracing the EV future. Washington State has more than 8000 public charging stations and relatively cheap electricity. Oregon's electricity is also cheap, and the state has more than 4000 public charging stations. Thanks to the 'electric highway' along I-5, it's possible to make an all-electric trip from Canada to Mexico.

In British Columbia, nearly 18% of new vehicles purchased in 2022 were electric – the highest rate in North America. And BC has more than 3000 public charging stations. EV charging stations have also been added to increasingly remote areas, such as national parks, throughout the region. Apps like ABetterRouteplanner can tell you where the nearest charging stations are.

OTHER GEAR

Rental car companies no longer include things like a spare tire or tire jack in the rental car. Any extra safety equipment, such as child safety seats, will need to be rented or bought separately. Rental companies also have different policies about using tire chains for winter driving, so be sure to ask.

Health & Safe Travel

INSURANCE

Don't put the key into the ignition if you don't have insurance, which is legally required. You risk financial ruin and legal consequences if there's an accident. If you already have auto insurance, or if you buy travel insurance that covers car rentals, make sure your policy has adequate liability coverage for where you will be driving, as different states specify different minimum levels of coverage.

Crime

The Pacific Northwest is generally a friendly and safe place to travel, though crime does exist – mostly in bigger cities. Take the usual precautions. For example, don't leave valuables visible in your vehicle, whether you're in a busy downtown street or at a remote hiking trailhead, as break-ins are frequent.

Ice & Fire

Pacific Northwest drivers are notoriously terrible at handling snow and ice. When the infrequent snows hit Portland or Seattle, consider staying off the roads.

Conversely, climate change means more frequent forest fires. Obey posted fire-management signs. If there's smoke pollution from fire, use an N95 mask.

Bears

When camping in bear country, use bear containers or bear boxes provided by the campground, or hang food correctly.

While hiking in bear country, wear bear bells or talk loudly to avoid surprising them. Bears will generally avoid people when they can.

Never feed bears or other wildlife!

Rattlesnakes

Rattlesnakes live in dry desert country, and hikers can sometimes encounter them basking on trails. Give them a wide berth and they'll leave you alone. Wearing thick hiking boots or tall gaiters offers some protection, as does staying out of thick underbrush.

IN CASE OF EMERGENCY
Call 911

CAR BREAKDOWN

If your rental car breaks down, call the rental company. If it's your own car, membership in an automobile association will offer 24-hour roadside assistance, and you can join instantly if you aren't a member. For accidents, pull to the side of the road, share insurance information with other drivers involved, and call police to file a report.

Responsible Travel

Climate Change

It's impossible to ignore the impact we have when traveling, and the importance of making changes where we can. Lonely Planet urges all travelers to engage with their travel carbon footprint. There are many carbon calculators online that allow travelers to estimate the carbon emissions generated by their journey; try resurgence.org/resources/carbon-calculator.html. Many airlines and booking sites offer travelers the option of offsetting the impact of greenhouse gas emissions by contributing to climate-friendly initiatives around the world. We continue to offset the carbon footprint of all Lonely Planet staff travel, while recognizing this is a mitigation more than a solution.

Salmon Safe
salmonsafe.com
Salmon-safe wineries around the region.

Hello BC
hellobc.com
Searchable travel ideas.

Pacific Coast Parks
nps.gov/subjects/oceans/pacific-coast.htm
Get in touch with nature.

EAT LOCAL
Choosing restaurants with locally sourced ingredients – like Local Ocean (localocean.net) in Newport, or Watershed Cafe (watershedpnw.com) in Leavenworth – not only reduces the environmental impact of dining out, but also means fresher, tastier food.

SLEEP GREEN
When you book your stay, look for sustainability ratings from a reliable source, such as Green Key Global, or LEED certification. Or lower your impact by camping or choosing a Hostelling International hostel.

VEGGIE VACATION
The Pacific Northwest has abundant and delicious vegan and vegetarian eateries – use your road trip as an excuse to explore meat-free options, prepared by experts.

Nuts & Bolts

GOOD TO KNOW

Time Zone
GMT minus seven hours in summer, minus eight in winter

Country Code
+1

Emergency number
911

CURRENCY: US DOLLAR (US$), CANADIAN DOLLAR (C$)

Opening Hours

Businesses 9am–5pm

Restaurants and food carts 11:30am–9pm, often closed Monday and Tuesday

Coffeeshops 6:30am–3pm

Retail shops 10am–6pm Monday to Saturday, some noon–5pm Sunday

ELECTRICITY 120V/60HZ

Type A
120V/60Hz

Type B
120V/60Hz

Cash & Cards

Major credit cards are accepted nearly everywhere, even in many food carts thanks to portable credit-card apps like Square. If you do need cash – for example, at gas stations in very remote areas – ATMs are everywhere. Note that Canadian dollars and US dollars are not interchangeable.

Tipping

In restaurants, a standard tip is 20% of the total bill (excluding any taxes). At bars, use the same calculation or tip a dollar a drink for longer sessions. Leave $2–5 a day for hotel housekeeping staff in either country. For taxis, tip 10–15%.

Discounts

People over the age of 65 (or sometimes younger) often qualify for discounts; any identification showing your date of birth should suffice. Folks 62 or older visiting national parks can get a Senior Pass (store. usgs.gov/pass/senior.html). A recreation pass offers discounts on national or state parks or national forests – check nps.gov/planyour visit/passes.htm.

Water

Tap water is safe to drink throughout the region; carry a water bottle to refill.

HOW MUCH FOR A...

Coffee
US$4

Pint of IPA
US$7

Food cart item
US$10–16

museum entry
US$25

Index

THE WRITERS

This is the 6th edition of Lonely Planet's *Best Road Trips Pacific Northwest* guidebook, updated with new material by Becky Ohlsen. Writers on previous editions whose work also appears in this book are included below.

Becky Ohlsen

Becky writes about travel and outdoor adventures in the Pacific Northwest and elsewhere. She's written guidebooks about backpacking, tent camping and neighborhood walks, but long road trips are her current favorite travel mode. Hot tip: never skip a chance to get more ice. Instagram @fasterbecky

Contributing writers

Robert Balkovich, Celeste Brash, John Lee, Craig McLachlan, MaSovaida Morgan, Brendan Sainsbury

SEND US YOUR FEEDBACK

We love to hear from travelers – your comments keep us on our toes and help make our books better. Our well-travelled team reads every word on what you loved or loathed about this book. Although we cannot reply individually to your submissions, we always guarantee that your feedback goes straight to the appropriate writers, in time for the next edition. Each person who sends us information is thanked in the next edition.

Visit **lonelyplanet.com/contact** to submit your updates and suggestions or to ask for help. Our award-winning website also features inspirational travel stories and news.

Note: We may edit, reproduce and incorporate your comments in Lonely Planet products such as guidebooks, websites and digital products, so let us know if you are happy to have your name acknowledged. For a copy of our privacy policy visit **lonelyplanet.com/legal**.

BEHIND THE SCENES

This book was produced by the following:

Commissioning Editor
Darren O'Connell

Production Editor
Kate James

Book Designer
Clara Monitto

Cartographer
Corey Hutchison

Assisting Editors
Monique Choy, Melanie Dankel, Soo Hamilton, Graham O'Neill

Cover Researcher
Norma Brewer

Product Development
Marc Backwell, Ania Bartoszek, Fergal Condon, Amy Lynch, Katerina Pavkova

ACKNOWLEDGMENTS

Cover photograph
Glacier lake, Kootenays, British Columbia; EB Adventure Photography/Shutterstock ©